805

HARRISON FORD:

A Biography

Also by Minty Clinch:

CAGNEY
BURT LANCASTER
CLEAN BREAK

HARRISON FORD:

A Biography

Minty Clinch

NEW ENGLISH LIBRARY

First published in Great Britain in 1987 by
New English Library, Mill Road, Dunton Green, Sevenoaks, Kent.
Editorial office: 47 Bedford Square, London WC1B 3DP.

Typeset by Rowland Phototypesetting Ltd
Bury St Edmunds, Suffolk

Printed in Great Britain by
St Edmundsbury Press Ltd, Bury St Edmunds, Suffolk

British Library Cataloguing in Publication Data
Clinch, Minty
   Harrison Ford: a biography.
   1. Ford, Harrison   2. Moving-picture actors
   and actresses – United States – Biography
   I. Title
   791.43'028'0924   PN2287.F59

ISBN 0-450-39940-0

For my husband,
David Braham

Contents

List of Illustrations

Acknowledgments
1 British Film Institute (BFI) Film Archive. Columbia Pictures
2 BFI Film Archive. Universal Pictures (Lucasfilm)
3 BFI Film Archive. Universal Pictures
4 BFI Film Archive. Twentieth Century Fox (Lucasfilm)
5 TV Times Picture Library. Twentieth Century Fox (Lucasfilm)
6 TV Times Picture Library. Columbia Pictures
7 BFI Film Archive. American International Pictures
8 London Features International Ltd
9 Rex Features
10 Frank Spooner Pictures
11 Transworld Feature Syndicate (UK) Ltd. Copyright Yoram Kahana

1 The Genuine Gilt-edged Article

I WELL remember when *The Empire Strikes Back* opened in May, 1980 and its leading actors arrived in London to talk to the press. 'Which do you want?' I was asked, 'Mark Hamill, Carrie Fisher, Harrison Ford?' The Golden Boy, the Spoiled Princess, the Dashing Quipping Pilot? At the time, 'None of them' would probably have been the most accurate answer. But surely there was something a bit special about Harrison Ford?

The intervening years have proved what it was: star quality, the genuine, gilt-edged article, the kind they weren't supposed to make any more. The Harrison Ford I met on that and other days was the sort of man you would be proud to introduce to your mother. Tall, dark blond and handsome, modest, polite and neat, you could imagine him addressing her as 'Ma'am' with the courtesy of the southern gentleman he is not and smiling his shy, unassuming smile.

It is typical of Hollywood that it was initially unimpressed by such self-evident sterling worth. Harrison Ford, never an aggressive go-getter, who wore his ambition on his sleeve, was summarily rejected by the rump of the studio system in the 1960s; so much so that when he made *Star Wars* in the mid '70s, he was working more often as a carpenter than an actor. Earlier in the decade, his closest brushes with the aristocracy of the cinema came when he built bookcases for more successful peers, people with fat film fees to spend on home improvements. They were very good bookcases, and they're now collector's items, but their solid, self-taught craftsmanship gave no clue to the fact that their creator would be the idol of the 1980s, the only star to come out of the George Lucas–Steven Spielberg school of film making.

The premier 'Movie Brats' have a way with actors, a way of

picking them up, using them and casting them back into the obscurity whence they came. Can you remember who played the adult lead in *Poltergeist* or even *E.T.*? Probably not, because the effects, whether special or electronic, are designed to bury the performers. Essentially, Lucas and Spielberg are puppet-masters, manipulating the child in all of us, their tremendous box office successes built on old-style carnival showmanship in which glittering form obscures trivial content. So how did Harrison Ford, the ultimate boy next door, slip through their net into the limelight?

The competition for centre screen was particularly fierce in *Star Wars*. Lucas's time, energy and money were lavished on creations like Darth Vader, Chewbacca and the jolly robotic assemblies. C3PO and R2D2. Worse still, there was a legendary actor, Sir Alec Guinness, to provide a yardstick for his art, so it is hardly surprising that the three newcomers were upstaged, comprehensively at times and with Lucas's blessing. Fisher's Princess Leia and Hamill's Luke Skywalker emerged at the end of it as pretty faces, condemned to react rather than act. But Harrison Ford managed to give Han Solo a distinctive zaniness that made him a character rather than a cypher.

This fact was noted, in characteristically flowery style, in the French specialist magazine, *L'Ecran Fantastique*: 'Harrison Ford is the first seductive anti-hero of space opera. In this genre, he has given Han Solo an aura of cynicism and a deeply original irresistible mixture of gaucheness and humour which makes him more adult, more real than his colleagues. Han Solo, the mercenary, protects his friends like an older brother; his reticence distances him, giving him an immediate complicity with adult spectators.'

Fair enough. *Star Wars* is primarily a children's movie, but its appeal turned out to be universal as it leapt to the top of the list of box office best sellers of all time. Clearly the man who could corner the adult emotions in such a high flyer could do himself a good turn. Up to this moment, Ford's career owed a little to luck and a lot to persistence, but everyone deserves a break and his came shortly after *Star Wars* when Dr Indiana Jones, the quirky snake-fearing archaeologist who is so much more winning even than Han Solo, came up for grabs.

Spielberg, the director-to-be of *Raiders of the Lost Ark*, and

Lucas, the film's producer, wanted Tom Selleck for Indy, but his employers on the television series *Magnum* refused to release him, leaving Indy's battered hat to fall on Harrison's head. Again the part was two dimensional, the film farther removed in time, though less so in place, than *Star Wars*, the conflict between good and evil as basic as ever. But make no mistake, Indiana Jones is as vibrant and compelling as James Bond, a shabby bullwhip-wielding adventurer who hints at intellect as well as humour. The 'Movie Brats' and their scriptwriter, Lawrence Kasdan, who had spent their childhood Saturdays watching rollicking good yarns in their local cinemas in the 1950s, made Indy into a synthesis of yesterday's heroes, the many faces of Errol Flynn, Humphrey Bogart, Clark Gable and John Wayne.

The man who played him would be likened to all of them, and would end up as big a matinée idol as they were. And so it came to pass. Han Solo made Harrison Ford rich, but Indiana Jones made him immortal.

Not that Harrison the man has any belief in Harrison the star, a four letter word he uses rather less freely than other seemingly less polite ones. 'I want to be recognised for the job I do, which is acting. That's what I get paid for, not for touting myself around as a fascinating personality. I'm really quite incapable of doing that. I don't consider myself unique. I just work in the movie business.'

He speaks slowly and quietly, his grey-green eyes full of sardonic humour as if he finds some private amusement in his unsought status. His clothes make no concessions to fashion, but a lot to time and place; on this occasion, mid-morning in his suite in the Savoy. Unlike Indy's, they are impeccably pressed. On this our second meeting, he'd just turned forty, but appeared no more than twenty-eight, even as he faced directly into the light reflected off the Thames, glittering gun-metal grey in the rain outside.

His perennial youthfulness is the basis of his fortune for it is a fair bet that George Lucas did not have a thirty-five-year-old Solo in mind and that given an average ageing rate, Harrison would have missed it. However, his face has kept in step with his personality, both developing late, so that it is the mature but boyish man who is the success the raw boy was unable to be.

Of course there are advantages to late development, especially when it is linked to present achievement combined with solid disdain for the people and the system which rejected you in the first place. The 'Movie Brats' took over Hollywood in the nick of time for Harrison Ford, but there is a detachment about him which suggests that if they'd been too late he'd have gone on being a pretty contented carpenter. Not only does he still make furniture as a hobby, but he deliberately keeps a low profile when he's not working. One source of pride is his chameleon quality, his ability to mingle with the clean-cut White Anglo-Saxon Protestant element in America so well that the owner of the face that has launched at least a billion dollars can walk down the street unmolested, even unrecognised.

'If people aren't expecting me to be in a certain place at a certain time, it takes them a few seconds to realise it's me,' he said, with the self-satisfaction that comes from a trick well played. 'Often I'm gone before that happens. The secret of anonymity is to keep your head down, look at the pavement and avoid eye contact. I try to side-step circumstances in which I'd be recognised because it's to no one's advantage. It destroys the natural order of things. The lack of privacy is hard, but I don't resent it. I'm practical enough to realise it's the by-product of great good fortune in other areas. I don't take it personally. It's not who I am, but what I am.'

He shares this talent for camouflage with Robert de Niro, another actor who is able to merge into his surroundings, though they have little else in common. Ford's skill is based partly on a 'very plastic face', partly on behaving as differently from the characters he plays as possible, which is not exactly a problem because he doesn't 'leap and bound and display a caustic sense of humour' when he's being himself. Recognition, when it comes, may be intrusive but so far it's always been benign. Sylvester Stallone never goes out unescorted by two body-guards, the result of punters wanting to take a slug at Rocky with disastrous consequences for his creator. Happily, Ford claims, Han Solo and Indiana Jones generate a more benevolent interest among cinema regulars.

They also generate a great deal of cash. One certainty is that if Harrison Ford had remained a carpenter, God-given profession though it is, he'd not have been nearly as rich. Initially his *Star*

Wars deal gave him less than he was making with hammer and chisel. One of the advantages of hiring unknowns, as George Lucas was quick to appreciate, is that they aren't in a position to drive hard bargains. However the mogul has never been mean and he gave Harrison Ford, Carrie Fisher and Mark Hamill two-thirds of 1 per cent each. That may sound paltry until you translate it into cash terms: $53,000 apiece after the film had been on release for three months.

Today, with percentages in five of the nine biggest grossers in history, Ford must be among America's highest earners, a thought that excites him not at all. 'Money is only important when you don't have it,' he comments, with the authority of one who has known poverty and in the certainty that he will never know it again. 'It used to be a constant problem because I had a family to support, so I was relieved when I was able to stop worrying about it. I never had any ambition for the level of success I've reached. I never fantasised about anything more than making a living as an actor. Regular television: that was my ultimate goal.'

The money is invested by his business manager, and there is a distinct impression that the self-styled 'modest family man' might find it hard to unload even a fraction of the income. Certainly he is not in the spend, spend, spend mould. He hates parties, especially Hollywood ones. He has no taste for exotic holidays, reckoning that his job takes him anywhere he could conceivably wish to go and provides him with something to do when he gets there. Although he is the most unathletic man in California, a sworn enemy of jogging and all forms of organised sport, he likes to go to the beach from time to time, to which end he may be spotted on occasion at Hawaii's Kahala Hilton, a millionaire's watering hole separated from the surf and squalor of downtown Honolulu by the natural barrier of Diamond Head.

Otherwise he likes being at home, either a luxury house in a cul-de-sac above Beverly Hills or, better still, in the remote rural fastness of his bolt-hole in Wyoming. He keeps up the Los Angeles connection for his two sons, Ben and Willard, who live with his first wife, Mary, five miles down the road. His second wife is Melissa Mathison, she who gave the world *E.T.*

The couple met in the Philippines in 1978 when Ford played

a small part in *Apocalypse Now*, a film on which Melissa worked as Francis Ford Coppola's assistant. Two years later she visited her lover on the set of *Raiders of the Lost Ark* in Tunisia, only to be asked by Steven Spielberg if she would write the screenplay for his next project. She agreed and the rest is the kind of history that gives a basis for equality in a marriage.

Her face may not be as famous as Harrison's, but she certainly has enough clout to make him share the washing up. Not equally, he insists, but yes, he does put his hands into the suds. 'She does more than me because she's a better person,' he said, tongue in cheek, then confessed to hoovering as well. Are these the occupations of a matinée idol? Of course not but, as he keeps reminding you, his celebrity is not of his own devising.

'It beats me what I do when I'm not working. I do the ordinary things, get up in the morning, drink coffee and read newspapers. I run the usual errands of idle people. Am I basically lazy? I think that's probably not too inaccurate, but I have periods of quite enjoying being lazy. However, I do consider myself to be a very hard worker on the job.'

This opinion receives enthusiastic support from the 'Movie Brats' who made him, but it was only recently, with Peter Weir's first American film, *Witness*, that he found the kind of new horizons he's been looking for for some time. His previous attempts to break the heroic mould have ranged from disastrous, as in *Hanover Street* and *The Frisco Kid*, to mediocre, as in *Blade Runner*, but John Book, the Philadelphia detective who stumbles on romance in the Amish boondocks, has earned him comparisons with Bogart and his like from critics who previously ignored Ford the actor in favour of Ford the star.

'Of course it's nice to be praised rather than pilloried, but the real satisfaction comes from being seen for what I am. I've always been acting, but it's taken a long time for it to be noticed. It's not always been my ambition to portray fully rounded characters, you couldn't describe Han Solo in that way, but I was very happy to serve the *Star Wars* films in any way I could.

'You have to accept the circumstances you find in the script,' he elaborated on his theme. 'I disagree that a two-dimensional character is less successful than a three-dimensional character. By three-dimensional I take it you mean when the guy sits down with a cup of coffee and discusses his relationship with his mother. I don't do that. I create behaviour that tells the story and if it doesn't tell the story, it's not appropriate so it's out.'

The rise and rise of Harrison Ford has been marked by on-going differences with journalists and critics who want to pigeon-hole him for what he sees as their own convenience. Because he is essentially so decent and loyal to his employers, whoever they may be, he still meets the press whenever a film requires it, although his personal need for promotion has long gone. Once he's face to face, however, he has a reputation for being a difficult customer, a private man who makes no effort to keep a conversation going. Aware that you can't be phenomenally rich and phenomenally famous without people wanting to know what you eat for breakfast, he nevertheless wonders why scribes can't understand what he's about, why they can't accept that acting, like carpentry, is a craft rather than an art.

For Harrison, roles are like pieces of furniture: some are more complicated than others, but each requires understanding and precision if it's to fulfil its function. It comes naturally, as he sits in the Savoy, to look at its antiques and wonder how they're made, to analyse the joints and speculate as to how he'd create that particular effect at his carpenter's bench back home.

Developing a character, he insists, is not so very different. 'I'm interested in the technical side of it to the degree that I think of myself as a craftsman. I never expect to be completely pleased by anything I do because by nature I'm a perfectionist. An actor is basically an assistant story-teller. Your first responsibility is to understand the idea, what the picture is about, then help to convey it to the audience.'

Yes, Harrison Ford is a modest man, likeable, informal, contemporary, but with hidden depths he doesn't want investigated too closely. At times, he defends himself by talking like a letter from a local government office. 'I can anticipate no further involvement in the *Star Wars* series,' he told me once, meaning merely that if Lucas makes the next trilogy in his nine-part saga, it won't include Solo, Leia or Skywalker. At others, he becomes a pack leader in playing pranks on film sets, but he isn't much of a participant in Hollywood's grosser forms of razzamatazz. As he puts it, with characteristic hard-nosed objectivity, actors who rub shoulders with Lucas and Spielberg have no need to dress up and go out to tout for work.

There is remarkably little smugness in this statement. Any European who wants to get to the bottom of Harrison Ford must go back to his roots. He is American, a man for whom success and money are the ultimate cultural accolades, so much so that he can afford to be dismissive about their material benefits. He is a mid-westerner, not brash or ignorant or stupid, as our own stereotyping might have it, but middle class, ethical, capable of perceptiveness and guilt.

He is aware that his fame and fortune are based on violent fantasies, on encouraging teenagers to wallow in warfare and death, and that this may not be entirely a good thing. Unlike the puppet-masters Lucas and Spielberg, who have carried their childhood dreams into middle age, Harrison Ford is more sophisticated than his material. He wouldn't go to see his own films, indeed he wouldn't go to see any film, not even *Casablanca*, as he has frequently said. He'd rather read a good book or visit a museum. It's a habit he's had from childhood, a childhood spent in and around Chicago, which is where the mythology must begin.

2   A Carpenter for the Canyons

As FAR as guarding his privacy goes, Harrison Ford's greatest triumph has been in concealing the details of his early years, but there is no secret about his birth date, 13 July 1942, nor its place, Chicago, nor the suburban affluence in which his parents lived. His father comes from an Irish Catholic family, his mother from a Russian Jewish one: the kind of diverse combination that is typical of Chicago's melting pot. Harrison's grandfather had been in vaudeville and his father had done a stint as a radio actor, so there was an element of show business in the family.

However, it was on hold when Harrison came along during the early days of American involvement in World War II. When hostilities ceased, Ford Senior became an advertising executive. 'He was a pioneer of television commercials,' Harrison told Ian Brodie of the *Sunday Telegraph Magazine* in May, 1984. 'He invented the concept of the see-through washing machine to demonstrate the suds, and he was the first to use stop motion photography. He certainly seemed to have a lot more interesting job than a lot of the other guys' dads. This may sound silly, but it encouraged me not to want a real job.'

As a result, much of his childhood was spent in preparing not to have one. He was lazy, a slow, reluctant learner with no ambitions to rival his high-achieving father. He played a little baseball, fooled around with cars in a desultory fashion and kept himself pretty much to himself. He describes himself as a loner with a liking for books that never became a passion. Indeed he wasn't passionate about anything. Not for the young Harrison those joyous Saturday matinées at the cinema. 'I didn't spend much time at the movies. I didn't study Bogart's mannerisms, so I miss most of the references guys like Lucas and Spielberg toss around.' He doesn't sound in any way regretful. Nor yet did he waste time gazing into the night sky and imagining extra-terrestrials and intergalactic rockets like the young Steven Spielberg did.

He didn't even do what the other kids did in the 1950s, the age of soda fountains and rock and roll, girls in full skirts and ankle socks who didn't 'go all the way' and car crazy boys who wore jeans and slicked back their hair in the style of Marlon Brando and James Dean.

'There was nothing too remarkable about my childhood. I had no interest in games but I really can't remember what I did instead. I wasn't a cissy or anything like that. I probably went upstairs and read a book or cleaned up my room. We didn't go in for dressing up and play acting in my family. The idea that anyone could make a living out of acting only came to me later on.'

When he left high school, his grades were good enough to get him into Ripon College in North Wisconsin. It was a minor outpost by American university standards, and Ford was left to pursue his policy of non-achievement unmolested for the best part of three years. He acknowledges that his studies in English Literature and Philosophy were half-hearted, and much interrupted by long lie-ins and pizza breaks. 'Eventually it became clear to me that I hadn't a clue how I would make a living out of those two subjects so I just stopped going to classes. That was in my senior year. I was supposed to do a thesis on Edward Albee, but I didn't bother. Three days before my graduation, I had a total academic breakdown so I never even sat the exams. The college authorities threw me out.'

His parents, who had booked into a local hotel for the ceremonies, were not amused, especially when he told them that he was unsuited to a career in the military or business where most of his contemporaries were finding gainful employment in the expanding job market of the early sixties. In those days, an out-of-work twenty-one-year-old son, even one who'd grown into a callowly handsome six-footer, was a problem in a middle class family like the Ford's. Communities still expected respectability, and respectability equalled a job, a home and a family.

Although the means of achieving them weren't clear to him, Harrison had accepted the burden of these bourgeois expectations from an early age. Nor, indeed, was Ripon College to prove a total loss in this respect for it introduced him both to the stage and to his wife-to-be. He may have spent too much of his time asleep, but he found the 'adrenalin burn' the rest of his youth lacked in college plays which he discovered during his junior year.

'Standing up there in front of an audience of 600 people was the most challenging thing in my young life. Come to think of it, it scared me half to death, but I felt compelled to deal with that fear by doing it again. Eventually I realised that it was a career choice. I never came up with a suitable alternative.'

So it came to pass that he followed his ignominious ejection from college by a season of Summer Stock, the American equivalent of repertory. Initially he was based in the resort community of Williams Bay on the shores of Wisconsin's Lake Geneva, and later he travelled all over Illinois. He didn't get leading roles, but he enjoyed himself and people kept telling him that with his looks he'd be a natural, so he decided to give it a go. Although it wasn't the peak of his parents' aspirations for him, it came higher up their order of things than tree-trimming and being a buyer in a department store and it had more permanency than being a rigger for the Americas Cup yacht *Columbia*, the alternative money-spinners Harrison considered. Accordingly, he stood in the middle of America on a bleak September morning in 1963 and looked east, then west.

Stage or film? New York or California? There was only one way to decide. He pulled a coin out of his pocket and spun it into the air. It came down for New York. 'It was snowing hard although it was so early in the year so I tossed again and again, until it showed California. I knew I'd probably be poor and hungry. I didn't plan on being cold as well.'

Nor did he go alone, having married his long-term sweetheart, Mary, in the summer of his non-graduation. He'd known her through the Ripon days and she was prepared to share his dream of screen glory, so they loaded up Harrison's ancient Volkswagen and headed west. Realising that a dog might be a liability in Tinsel Town, he sold his pet Topy to his father to swell his meagre finances, then felt too guilty to accept the money.

Poor they certainly were, but the newly-weds had love and a sense of adventure to sustain them. Harrison's parents had instilled a belief in marriage in their son and he had no second thoughts about tying the knot of what he saw then as an indissoluble institution, at the tender age of twenty-one.

'I believed that life was made for couples, not for single men. A man alone hasn't enough strength to overcome the obstacles he finds confronting him. He needs constant moral support, a life jacket he can rely on in moments of distress. Perhaps love is above all a question of mutual support. I already believed this when I left college so there was no reason for us not to get married.'

The drive to California was a honeymoon, a voyage into the unknown with the Pacific as its final destination. They hit it sixty miles south of Los Angeles at Laguna Beach. Neither had ever seen the sea before and they spent their first warm West Coast night right there on the sand beside the ocean, amazed at the spectacle of water stretching to the distant horizon under the stars.

Laguna Beach, though chosen at random, turned out well for the young couple. Ford was able to polish his craft at the Laguna Playhouse where he worked for a season, rising through the ranks to more important roles, and the town was near enough to Hollywood to attract talent scouts. The one who came from Columbia's New Talent programme was intrigued by the boyish leading man in *John Brown's Body* and called him into head office for further negotiations. The Fords were on their way. Or so it seemed at the time.

In order to understand Harrison's early struggle it is necessary to understand the organisations he had to deal with. By 1964, Hollywood was a corporate jungle. The first generation of film makers, the Warner brothers, Darryl F. Zanuck, Sam Goldwyn, Cecil B. de Mille, Columbia's Harry Cohn, Paramount's Adolph Zukor and MGM's Louis B. Mayer had been the studio makers, but since World War II they had given way to the studio breakers, the lawyers and accountants, agents and salesmen, who presided over – and grew fat on – the decline of the system. The bodies on which they fed had the same names: Columbia, Paramount, Twentieth-Century Fox, United Artists, Universal and Warners, but their nature had changed. Forced by court decisions under anti-trust law to sell their chains, they made their money distributing their films through other people's cinemas, then invested it in their own film production programmes. However the increased risk inherent in the new way of doing business had made them cautious rather than innovative.

Whereas a thirties studio had a full stable of directors and actors on its books, and assigned them to its films by rota or whim, the sixties studio acquired its ideas from outside in the form of projects submitted by independent producers and directors. The tycoons could say yea or nay to the finance, but their scope for content control was much reduced. Instead of being creators, they had become a means to someone else's end. Nor did they have the marketplace to themselves any more. Television had seen to that and audience ratings, at their peak in 1946 when cinemas took more money in real terms than ever before or since, had declined steadily worldwide.

However, the studios had a history of tyranny to live up to, and they weren't about to let go without a struggle. Much of the destruction of their power had been wrought a decade earlier by actors like Burt Lancaster who had engineered star status for himself, then used it to clout the old regime over the head by setting up his own production company and making his own deals, long before his first seven-year contract with Paramount had expired.

But that too was history by the early sixties, an era when the only person who could still be tyrannised was the novice actor, a man with no prospects who could be comprehensively patronised by studio executives. Such a man was Harrison Ford when he walked nervously into Columbia's Gower Street headquarters and took the lift to the head of casting's office.

The story of what happened next appeals to his keen sense of irony. He tells it frequently and its details have been polished over the years, but basically it all comes down to a pressing need to answer a call of nature. 'Let me explain,' he says, with a glint in his eye. 'I was a boy from Wisconsin who'd arrived in Los Angeles not even knowing the names of the big studios. Now I was in one for the first time. I was ushered into the Presence, a little bald-headed guy, white shirt, white tie, thick cigar stub, over-heated walnut-panelled office, two telephones. He was sitting behind a desk, and there was a single chair in front of it so I sat down. Behind him there was an assistant, another little guy who looked like a racecourse tout. Again two telephones. They both totally ignored me for ten minutes while they made calls.

'Then the boss-man looked at me as if I was a bug in his soup, and demanded, "Who sent you here?" I told him. "Who the hell's that?" he asked the back-up guy. "I dunno," he replied. Then the boss asked me my name, my height, my weight, whether I spoke any foreign languages, had any hobbies. The assistant wrote it all down. "Okay," said the bald one, "we'll let you know if anything turns up."'

Exit Ford, crestfallen; but then fate took a hand. 'Normally I'd have gone straight down in the elevator and left the building, but when I pressed the button it didn't come and I realised I had to take a leak. When I came out of the john, the tout appeared in a panic shouting, "Hey, you, c'mmon, c'mmon, he wants you." I never knew precisely what changed his mind, but I guess an emergency had come up and they needed a guy in a hurry. I've always believed that if I'd gone down to the street, it wouldn't have been worth his while to follow me.'

Given his initial reception, it is hardly surprising that he was overwhelmed when he was shown back in and the boss said, 'You're not the type we're usually interested in, but how would you like to be under contract?' Of course the answer was yes. 'Sure, I was thrilled. Columbia wanted me. It proved a maxim I've always believed in: if you hang in there long enough, something is bound to happen.'

The pay was $150 a week, a handsome sinecure on which a couple could live comfortably, if not extravagantly, in the mid sixties. In other respects, however, Harrison was soon to discover that he wore shackles of his own making, and they weren't at all to his liking. Every day he had to show up at the studio in a jacket and tie, and attend acting classes. When the morning session was done, it was down to the executive dining room to mingle with the employers. There was a certain prestige in all this, a recognition of the fact that he was an actor, but it certainly didn't get him on the screen. It was also extremely boring, not to say soul-destroying.

'Everyone called you kid, mostly because they didn't know what your name was. This was 1964, but Columbia played it like 1924. They thought up these terrible promotional ideas for photo layouts. They'd put a Chevrolet Nova on Malibu Beach and we'd be summoned to play volleyball in front of it. You know, six starlets and six guys prancing around for *Argosy Magazine*. Then they'd print "photos by courtesy of Columbia Pictures" beside it. It was worse than a factory. Horrible really because you knew no one cared a damn about you. I went fucking nuts.'

Not only did he hate volleyball, but the Irish in him balked at being ordered around, while the Russian Jew was astonished at the purposelessness of it all. At the time, however, the studio seemed a better option than modelling, the most obvious alternative for someone with his physique. He was learning more about his chosen profession, in the negative sense at least, and there was always a chance that his number would come up. Meanwhile he bought a house in the Hollywood Bowl and started gutting the parts of it he didn't like. That eventually left him with the walls and the roof, at which point he bought tools and started replacing the rest. His interest in carpentry had begun.

This state of suspended animation lasted for eighteen long, frustrating months. Then Harrison got a part in a feature film, one day's work only, which he has since described accurately as 'nothing uplifting', before launching, as venomously as his natural graciousness permits, into another of his favourite anti-Hollywood tales. The obscurely titled film, *Dead Heat on a Merry-go-round* (1966), was a caper comedy written and directed by Bernard Girand, about an ingenious bank heist at Los Angeles airport. The perpetrator is not only a convict, but a con man who breaks his parole in the interests of self-enrichment.

Played with panache by James Coburn, he wins dames and influences people in a variety of disguises, but *Time* magazine was not impressed. 'Just fills the space between a frisky title and a tricky TV-comedy ending, but doesn't fill it with any revels that require a viewer's complete attention,' it stated wearily.

Among the things the writer didn't appreciate was the debut of Harrison Ford as a bellboy, a position so lowly that his name barely scraped onto the bottom of the credit list. He had a line though. 'Paging Mr Jones, paging Mr Jones.' James Coburn responded with 'Boy!' and Ford said 'Mr Jones' again. Then Coburn waved him over and he gave him a telegram. There is even a photograph of Ford, blond, boyishly sincere, in his Sheraton Hotel uniform, performing this feat. Nor was his performance neglected by his superiors, but astonishingly they were not amused.

'The guy who was vice president of Columbia at the time, called me into the office after that film. Now remember, all I had to do was deliver a telegram. No big deal. Well, he sat me down and he said, "Kid, you ain't got what it takes. First time Tony Curtis appeared in a movie, he had to deliver a bag of groceries, and I knew he had star quality. You ain't." It was only some time later that I understood he wanted me to impersonate a movie star, not a bellboy.'

Ordered ignominiously back to classes in the certain knowledge that he wouldn't get another part for six months at least, and probably a year, Harrison pondered on the strange ways of show business. His contract still had five and a half years to run, but the studio wouldn't let him act. 'In a way, acting was a last resort. It was only when I flunked out of college, and got married that I decided to give it a go. At this point, when I'd tried to take it up professionally, I discovered how wrong I was. It became clear to me that the one thing the world was not waiting for was Harrison Ford, actor.'

But what else to do? As yet, he couldn't come up with an answer so he hung in at Columbia until his second role a year later in a Jack Lemmon film called *Luv* (1967). Again it was a comedy, directed by Clive Donner, and based on a successful play by Murray Shisgal. However, it didn't translate to the screen, at least in the eyes of the *Monthly Film Bulletin*'s reviewer who recorded that 'a light but incisive comedy about the patterns and language of love in a Freud-ridden society has become an inept and lethally unamusing film farce.' Tough for Lemmon and co-stars Elaine May and Peter Falk maybe, less so for Ford whose name didn't even reach the credits this time.

Nor did he have to wait long for his next appearance in *A Time for Killing* (US title: *The Long Ride Home*), also in 1967. It was a project Columbia took over from Roger Corman and predictably, given those origins, it was a fairly savage low budget western with a message about the way in which war corrupts. Set in the American Civil War, it concerns a bunch of Confederate prisoners who escape from a Union fort, only to be pursued by Glenn Ford's commanding officer. Somewhere in the conflict can be found Lieutenant Shaffer, a young and unimportant officer played by one Harrison J. Ford.

The role was as minimal as ever, but again it brought the would-be actor unwelcome attention from his superiors. Perhaps, they suggested, it might do his image some good if he had his hair cut like Elvis Presley and changed his name. Harrison, they felt, was somewhat pretentious. 'I suggested Kurt Affair,' says the actor with satisfaction, 'and there was no more talk along those lines. Not that it mattered what I was called. I was going nowhere fast. That was obvious.'

Pretentious or not, the name 'Harrison Ford' had already made its mark on the film industry and there was an inscribed star set into the pavement of Hollywood Boulevard to prove it. Of course it didn't belong to Harrison from Chicago, but to another unrelated actor from the silent days, a handsome, dashing leading man from Kansas City who'd played opposite Norma Talmadge, Gloria Swanson, Clara Bow and Marion Davis.

His first film, *Up The Road With Sally*, was made in 1915 and one of the peaks of his career came seven years later when he co-starred with Lon Chaney in *Shadows*. As the twenties progressed, he specialised in comedies like *The Marriage Whirl*, *Up in Mabel's Room* and *The Girl From The Pullman*. As with many of the silent stars, the coming of talkies killed his career stone dead and he retired after a single attempt at the new medium, *Love in High Gear*, in 1932.

It was this long-forgotten gentleman player, like his namesake a very modest man, who caused the J. to divide Harrison and Ford when the name appeared in thirteenth position in the cast list for *A Time For Killing*. 'I hadn't heard of him until the Screen Actors' Guild contacted me and said I'd have to change my name which is why I added the J. for my first two films,' says Harrison Junior.

Later, he did some research and came up with the news that Harrison I had died on 2 December 1957 at the age of seventy-two. Although SAG was unable to confirm the death, Harrison dropped the initial anyway. As for the boulevard star, he is only too happy to share it. 'If they ever want to put an entry for me, I'll tell them they needn't bother. There's one already. I kinda like the idea of using the old guy's.'

Back at Columbia, Ford's contract was due for renegotiation. Mike Frankovitch, the Vice President in charge of production at the time, was away in Europe when Harrison's number came up, so the decision as to whether to take up the option fell on a colleague's shoulders. It was just Harrison's luck that it was the old enemy, the man who thought he hadn't got the Curtis quality, who faced him across the polished desk.

'"Kid," he said – what else? – "when Frankovitch comes back, I'm going to tell him he ought to get rid of you. I don't think you're worth a bunch of shit to us. But I know your wife is pregnant and you need the money, so I'll give you another coupla weeks. Just sign the piece of paper my secretary has. Okay kid? Now get outta here."'

At this point something snapped in a normally mild-mannered man. Tired of being patronised and pushed around by mediocrities, Harrison threw caution to the winds and told his persecutor where he could put his money. He was fired on the spot. Today it gives him great satisfaction to know that he's made it whereas the executive in question had to leave the business, but even at the time, he had no regrets. 'It was an odd era for the film business. All the studios were making their biggest pictures in Europe and back in Hollywood everyone was taking acid and smoking dope. Here I was, acting like a baby actor getting nowhere. That was the atmosphere when they let me go. Unfortunately, although I had the spirit to stand up for myself, I had nothing to back it up with. Mary was expecting our first son, Ben. I had to get another job.'

Three days later he did when he signed a similar contract with Universal. This may seem like jumping out of the frying pan into the fire, but he'd reached a point at which any change had to be for the better and, as it turned out, this one was. Universal had a full stable of long-running television shows like *The Virginian, Ironside, The FBI* and *Gunsmoke*, and there was often room for tall blond cannon fodder among the cowboys and the villains which was why they hired Harrison in the first place.

Initially Ford accepted all the offers eagerly and his face can be seen by the very observant in the *Gunsmoke* episodes, *The*

Sodbusters and *Wheelan's Men*. It was in these early days that it acquired its famous scar, the result of a car crash that occurred when he was trying to fasten his seat belt. The incident is very typical of Harrison, meticulously careful but slightly absent-minded, for he came to grief behind the wheel of his Volvo, the ultimate in safety-conscious cars, while attempting to take a safety precaution.

'I used to go down to the studio every morning from my home in Laguna Canyon Road. It was very winding and one day I thought I ought to be more careful so I reached with my right hand across to my left side to clip my seat belt on. At that point, I lost concentration and went slap bang into a tree. I guess I was lucky to be alive but I did look a dreadful mess. Later I ran into a bad stitcher. Fortunately it didn't affect my work because Universal weren't keeping me busy by this stage. I was filling in as an assistant knick knack buyer at Bullocks department store at the time. A scar was no hindrance there.'

As the decade progressed and the war in Vietnam claimed ever increasing numbers of his contemporaries, Ford had reason to be grateful that a car crash was his only injury. Lady Luck had her part to play in the fact that he was never drafted, but he certainly helped his own cause by marrying immediately after college when the conflict was in its very early stages, then becoming a father at a relatively young age. With single men readily available in the liberated sixties, married ones with families to support were high on the list of those who got the green light to stay at home, and so it proved with Harrison.

Months passed before he got himself a part in a Universal feature film, *Journey to Shiloh* (1967), based on Will Henry's Civil War novel, *Fields of Honour*. His name had crept up the credit order slightly into eighth place, behind James Caan as Buck Burnett, the leader of a septet of Texans looking for thrills in the Confederate army. Harrison plays one of them, Willie Bill Beardon, in a series of adventures that include witnessing the lynching of a runaway slave and the violent death of one of his band in a card game. In due course, the survivors are inducted into a Pensacola unit because of their skill on horseback and dispatched to Shiloh to face the Yankee armies.

Harrison's part in this rumbustious adventure yarn ends

abruptly when Willie Bill dies on the field of battle alongside his hard-riding mates, leaving Buck to flesh out the end of the story as a deserter who comes up against the military police, then wins a pardon from General Bragg. The film is described by Steven H. Scheuer as 'routine, but played with youthful energy', but Ford's role was too insignificant to be singled out for praise or blame. The *Monthly Film Bulletin* generalised as follows: 'The acting is often strident and the script too naïvely emotional not to fall into mawkishness at times,' criticism which might be taken to heart by its obscure director, William Hale, rather than by the performers, who had little say in this particular aspect of their destinies.

Next in line for the chronically undervalued services of Harrison Ford was a far better film maker, Michelangelo Antonioni. In 1966, he'd encapsulated the mood of a London that was just beginning to swing, in *Blow Up*, superficial, self-consciously arty and highly fashionable. Now it was Los Angeles's turn. The film was *Zabriskie Point* (1969), written initially by the director, then worked over by Sam Shepard at the start of what has become a distinguished career. Despite these good connections, the fantasy about alienation from our greedy, destructive world never looked like working.

It was Antonioni's first American project and he made the mistake of casting a wooden amateur, Mark Frechette, as Mark, a rebellious Los Angeles student who steals a light aircraft when he is suspected of shooting a policeman during a campus riot. Landing in the Arizona desert, he is picked up by an aimless girl and driven to Death Valley where they make symbolic passionate love among the sand dunes. Mark then gives himself up to the police and pays the ultimate penalty, leaving the girl to imagine the end of civilisation as we know it.

As usual the part played by Harrison Ford, loaned by Universal to MGM and Carlo Ponti for the film, was peripheral to these central concerns, but this time it mattered even less because the whole sub-plot in which he was involved landed up on the cutting room floor. When the film was released to a barrage of criticism, his absence from the finished project could be seen as an advantage, the more so because none of the actors who did appear have made any sort of name for themselves since.

In 1970, Universal interrupted Harrison's string of television bit parts once more to loan him back to his ex-employers at Columbia for *Getting Straight*, described by Leslie Halliwell as 'a modish comedy, far too long, far too pleased with itself and now irrevocably dated.'

Again it was a typical late sixties youth-orientated picture about student unrest and the alienation that caused it. Directed by Richard Rush, briefly fashionable at the time though his career has foundered since, it starred Elliott Gould as Harry Baily, a Vietnam veteran who returns to college to complete his Masters degree in Education, only to find that he has to tread a delicate line between the administration and his increasingly radical fellow students. Candice Bergen plays his girlfriend and somewhere in there you might just spot Jake (Harrison Ford).

Or you might not, because it was Jake's lowly credit rating, number sixteen in the line-up, and his cardboard cut-out character that caused Ford to cry 'Enough!' 'I was given tiny spaces to fill, nothing where I could take space and make my presence felt. Maybe those guys were right. I probably wasn't ready. But I was getting older. When I was twenty-one everyone thought I was seventeen, but inside I was ageing fast and I was going crazy. The studios had no faith in me as raw meat. The only thing they had faith in was something that looked like success based on something else.' Like Tony Curtis.

'In any case,' he continued, 'I wasn't temperamentally suited to being a studio actor. That meant doing every damned thing they told you. They were trying to eliminate individuality, and whatever intelligence I had told me that I was going in the wrong direction. I'd invested six years of my life in the business and I didn't want to give it up, but I knew I had to get away.'

The dilemma of what to do instead loomed large. Harrison, at twenty-eight, was still undisciplined and idle, a situation that several years of enforced under-achievement had done nothing to change. Since he'd arrived in Los Angeles, he'd generally taken the path of least resistance, allowing himself to be bossed around by men who certainly didn't have his interests at heart, and he'd paid for his passive acceptance of a regular pay cheque with a career he could now see was in a dead end. His expectations of it hadn't been enormous. He would have been quite happy with a television series – a character like Starsky or Hutch – to put groceries on the table. But a string of bit-part villains brought their own dangers in a climate in which fresh handsome faces waited at table in popular show business restaurants in the hope of filling just such slots.

'I invariably appeared in the same kind of roles. If there were two bad brothers, I was the sensitive one; but the studios were always looking for something new and I was worried I'd become over exposed, used up, with no prospect of building a long-term career. When I started, I thought acting was an awesome task, exciting and frightening and a wonderful way for someone with no degree to live. I suppose, being the son of an advertising executive in charge of Chicago's TV commercials, I should have known better, but I was not prepared for the disillusionment I found in the studio system. Yet I still wanted to be an actor when I grew up.'

Until that day should come, he decided he'd be a carpenter instead, an occupation for which he had equally little training, but one of the few for which he had suitable clothes. The work in progress on his house in the Hollywood Bowl had been even more extensive than he'd originally planned, but he'd been slightly surprised by the amount of satisfaction he'd got from putting it all back together again. Why should such skills not be made to pay?

Ford knew the right people and his first professional assignment was to turn a garage owned by Sergio Mendes into a recording studio. He had $100,000 to spend and his own fee was higher than the one he earned for his ill-starred appearance in *Dead Heat on a Merry-go-round*. The Brazilian musician lived in Encino, a suburb to the north of Los Angeles, three blocks away from a public library. One of their most regular customers at the time was Harrison Ford who took out carpentry books and carried them off to the site for reference purposes.

'I'd be up there on the roof reading the relevant page, hoping no one would come out and rumble me. No one had asked me if I knew anything about carpentry, which was lucky because I didn't. Sergio would wander out when he got out of bed, wearing a robe and smoking a big cigar, to see how I was getting on. I guess he wouldn't have had much faith in me if he'd seen me up there checking out the next step in a book, but that's how I taught myself carpentry, just as I taught myself acting, by submitting to the logic of the craft. My approach to both is almost totally technical.'

Fortunately it worked better in carpentry than it had among the studio sharks. The word of mouth on the Mendes job was good and Ford was soon regularly employed, remodelling houses, building fitted cabinets and bookshelves and making furniture for wealthy patrons in the canyons above Beverly Hills. He took great pride in his newly acquired skills, and his tongue-and-grooved pieces, now collector's items in the aftermath of celebrity, are worthy of the limelight that's been thrust upon them. Among his early employers were Joan Didion and John Gregory Dunne who certainly didn't realise that the bookcases they commissioned for three walls of the study in their beach house would soon be the envy of the film fraternity.

Others to profit from the Ford technique were Richard Dreyfuss, James Caan and James Coburn and it wasn't long before the carpenter was able to form his own construction gang and employ architects and builders. This gave him a whole new outlook on life, one based on the factor that underpins the great American dream: cash in the bank. 'I realised the correlation between money and respect. Take a lot of money off people and they'll treat you with respect. They'd ask, "How much is this going to cost me?" and I'd say, "I'm not sure yet, but I promise you that when it's done, it'll be done right." You have to have a certain kind of temperament for carpentry and a capacity for understanding people because they have no way of conceptualising what you're talking about. You have to carry them along and when you talk someone into something, and then rip their lives apart, you have to keep on going back to them gracefully to reassure them.'

Evidently the new philosophy that is as old as time worked. The customers were satisfied and the Fords didn't starve. Indeed they enjoyed a higher standard of living than they had since they'd left Chicago. And Harrison was a free man. 'It was such a relief after being tied up with the studios. I could see what I'd accomplished. It was great. I decided not to take any more acting parts until something came up that would give me a clear career advantage. I'd always believed it would take me ten years to get regular acting work in Hollywood. I'd assumed that just by hanging in there, the attrition rate would help me as the system took its toll on the other guys. Up to this point it hadn't, but I never gave up. It's a personal characteristic. I don't give up.'

Maybe not, but as he'd be the first to admit, he still had a lot of growing up to do and it was carpentry, rather than acting, that helped him to do it. The freelance life suited him, but it brought its own pressures. His only previous experience of organising himself, at Ripon College, had been a miserable failure and he'd readily succumbed to every diversion rather than concentrate on his studies. Then the studios had taken him over *in loco parentis*. His reaction to their ham-fisted control had been based partly on intelligence, in that he saw them for what they were: greedy, shallow and cynical about human values, but it also smacked of juvenile rebellion.

Photographs of him taken at the time show a callow boy with shiny hair and bright expectant eyes. Ivy League springs to mind, but you can also imagine him centre screen in his father's detergent ads. Ford agrees that his excessively clean-cut image was a disadvantage in the early years. 'I looked far too young to be interesting, and in a sense I resisted maturity. I had to learn my job and that takes a long time. I was a late bloomer which was fortunate because I couldn't have handled the position I'm in today when I started fifteen years ago,' he says with hindsight.

It was carpentry that gave Ford his first genuine taste of success, and the self-confidence that comes with it. He has always made it clear that he only considered becoming an actor once he failed academically and it is not hard to imagine that the twinges of remorse he felt about those wasted college days intensified as the years passed and his roles became ever more insignificant. Although he denies that money was ever a real worry, he took his responsibilities towards his wife and family pretty seriously, and that certainly included supporting them in a reasonable degree of comfort. Yet the work ethic, the cornerstone of his belief in middle class values, eluded him until he had to pick up his hammer and saw each morning and keep working until the job was done.

'Carpentry taught me about myself. When I took it up, it was my idea that if I didn't get a better part than usual, more money, better billing, I wouldn't do the part at all. I made the decision because anything was better than going around saying you were an out-of-work actor. I used to be extremely lazy, but nowadays I find I can't enjoy myself when I'm not working. My upbringing was oriented towards self-discipline, but it took me all those years to come to grips with it in my own life. Woodwork set me straight because you've got to concentrate. You daren't let your thoughts stray or you'll ruin it.'

Today, Ford can afford to look back on his studio days with wry humour, but at the time the pill was bitter, the constant fear of failure haunting. He is not, in general, a venomous man but he is glad the executive who fired him had to quit while he prospered. As for the studios, they still call him. 'It's just they don't call me "kid" any more. They don't care what I think of them, and they don't care what they once thought of me. They don't relate to that, but they do relate wholeheartedly to the success of films like *Star Wars*.'

He speaks with scorn that has to be heard to be believed, secure in the knowledge that his unlikely saviour, the unprepossessing George Lucas, is already waiting in the wings.

3   The Mentor with the Midas Touch

GEORGE WALTON LUCAS, JR and Harrison Ford have a few things
in common. They are from the same generation, for George
was born less than two years after Harrison, in May, 1944. Their
fathers are self-made businessmen, and they were brought up
in solid suburban affluence. Academically their childhoods were
undistinguished, and both had a liking for slipping off to their
rooms when they were small. It was what they did when they
got there that divides them forever into the moulder and the
moulded, the man with the empire-building imagination and
the man who would help him to realise those strange vivid
fantasies.

The elements that make George Lucas's films so much more
popular than anyone else's were all present and correct in his
childhood, but his early years were unmarked by the thrust and
commitment that would make him make them. As producer,
writer or director, he can claim five of the six highest-grossing
pictures in the history of the cinema, a meaningless phrase in
one sense, in that it takes no account of inflation, but a key
indicator of popularity in that no one else has had so many so
highly placed.

The Lucas quintet are the Luke Skywalker trilogy: *Star Wars,*
The Empire Strikes Back and *The Return of the Jedi*, plus *Raiders*
of the Lost Ark and *Indiana Jones and the Temple of Doom*, the
outsider – and overall winner to date – being Steven Spielberg's
E.T. Just as significantly, Lucas's first commercial success,
American Graffiti, is Hollywood's most profitable movie ever as
far as cost ratio to returns ($775,000: $117 million) is concerned.
The one thing the six films have in common, apart from Lucas
himself, is Harrison Ford. Only by understanding the man

who made him is it possible to understand the actor's current pre-eminence in his profession.

Competent writers, directors and producers are not exactly rare but an ideas man in Lucas's class comes but once in a generation. As the creator of Indiana Jones, Luke Skywalker, Darth Vader, R2-D2 and Han Solo, and the complicated environments in which they live, he will be immortal for as long as films are shown in cinemas. And that, if his Marin County-based company, Lucasfilm, has anything to do with it, will be for a very long time. Television may have influenced him, but his vision is essentially wide screen, larger than life, the ultimate escape into that maze of adventure that dominated what would otherwise have been a pretty routine childhood.

The Lucas family were Californian to the core and George grew up in Modesto, a small flat town set in an agricultural area to the south of San Francisco. In 1944, it had about 15,000 inhabitants, though it has increased eightfold since then. George was the pampered only son of George Walton Lucas, Sr, from a spectacularly unsuccessful working-class background, and Dorothy Bomberger, of German extraction and a member of one of the Central Valley's more prominent families. Despite the gap in their circumstances, the couple married before either was twenty, and had two daughters, Ann and Katherine, in the mid thirties, followed by George and his sister, Wendy, in the mid forties.

George Sr went to work in a local stationer's, L. M. Morris, and eventually took it over. An iron-willed, upwardly mobile businessman, he turned it into a prosperous enterprise, selling toys as well as typewriters and other office equipment to Modesto's well-heeled citizens. L. M. Morris ensured a fair degree of luxury for the Lucas family which lived initially in a one-storey ranch house on the outskirts of Modesto, then further out of town on a real ranch set in thirteen acres of walnut trees against the superb backdrop of the High Sierra.

George was a scrawny child with black hair, brown eyes and the Lucas ears, sticking out acutely from his narrow head (ears he would later use in films to suggest extra terrestrialism). As stubborn as his father, he flatly refused to learn the things that didn't appeal to him. As they included most school subjects, among them reading, writing and maths, a C average was good going and it frequently sank to D. Outside school, however, he displayed his obsessive nature in a variety of trivial pursuits, all of which were to stand him in good stead later.

His first passion, for comic books, sparked off a craze for drawing, mostly landscapes but always with people in them. Harrison Ford, more sophisticated in his tastes, reluctantly admits to a lukewarm youthful liking for Donald Duck and Mickey Mouse, but Lucas is not ashamed of his excessive preoccupation with vulgar imagery, even though it was so great at one time that his father had to build a shed onto the back of the house to accommodate the lurid paperwork. The crude designs and the simple messages of good and evil sparked off George's imagination and he and his friends constructed environments to match them, miniature cities and fields and battlegrounds, inspired by patriotic fervour in the aftermath of World War II.

Cartoons on television were a natural extension of comic books, and the young Lucas became an addict as soon as the first set was installed in Modesto in 1949. Fortunately, given that Lucas Sr refused to buy one, it belonged to George's best friend's family so he was able to take it over, staring transfixed at the adventure serials from the thirties, the days of Flash Gordon, Buck Rogers and others of that ilk. 'I was appalled at how I could have been so enthralled with something so bad,' Lucas told his biographer, Dale Pollock in *Skywalking*, 'and I said, "Holy smokes, if I got this excited about this stuff, it's going to be easy for me to get kids excited about the same thing, only better."' How right he was. Television made him appreciate graphics, zip-along action and visual excitement, with content coming a distant fourth, and his films reflect those priorities exactly.

It was never part of George's design for living to be the centre of attention, though the toys from his father's shop, and especially the finest model railway in Modesto, gave him an unsolicited degree of popularity when he was quite young. 'I could hang out with anyone,' he has said, but he didn't join gangs. Nor did he stand out from the crowd. 'Nondescript' is a word used frequently by adults who can't remember George Lucas's boy any too clearly.

As his teens approached, George Jr became even more of a recluse. His parents, who had the cultural aspirations of the *nouveau riche*, insisted on music and dancing lessons which he loathed. However, the musical message got through on another level, and the boy could be found hogging their record collection for hours at a time.

Later he assembled his own in his bedroom and played it from the end of school at 3 p.m. until bedtime. This was the era of Elvis Presley and Chuck Berry, Bill Haley and the Comets, Buddy Holly and Jim Reeves, *Oklahoma* and *South Pacific*. George loved them all. He also loved Hershey chocolate bars and Coca Cola, photography and Disneyland, at least until he discovered cars which were destined to become the greatest of all his youthful obsessions until they nearly killed him.

Pollock's theory is that cars gave the diminutive Lucas a sense of self-worth for the first time by making him king of the road. He was lucky in that his father, hitherto a stern taskmaster in the matter of financial rewards for chores performed, was prepared to buy him one when he was fifteen – before he passed his driving test. It was only a tiny Fiat Bianchina with a 'sewing machine motor in it', but George had always been good with his hands and supremely good at picking up any skills he felt he needed.

Before long, the car was modified beyond all recognition, with a roll bar replacing the roof he'd lost in an unscheduled flip-over. It was also ideally suited to auto-cross, the only kind of racing open to a kid of under twenty-one. Red cones were set out in a series of curves at fairs across the state and George Lucas whipped his little machine through them at a speed the more cumbersome American cars couldn't hope to match. By this means he accumulated racing trophies, found a hero in Alan Grant, the local champion, and became a force to be reckoned with in Modesto's teenage community.

It may have been speed and derring-do which attracted George to auto-cross, but there were solid advantages to hanging out with the car crowd. They were tough and George, who weighed in at less than eight stone when he left high school, was extremely vulnerable. 'Being with tough guys who happened to be your friends was the only way to keep from getting the shit pounded out of you,' he has said. He readily adopted the customs of the gang by wearing unwashed jeans and greasing his hair back in the style of another idol, Elvis Presley; and he added a devotion to girls to those he already had for rock 'n roll and cars.

In Modesto circa 1962 picking up girls meant cruising, driving round the streets in custom-built cars from the time school ended to the time the town shut down, at around one in the morning. On Saturdays and Sundays, George cruised full-time round the loop and back to the drive-in hamburger joint which was the centre of operations. If he didn't get out of the car, none of the girls knew how short he was so he was able to feel cool about saying 'hello' to them, something he was normally far too shy to do. Having low-life friends, he was able to meet low-life girls, all lacquered hair and blonde beehives and bubblegum and much more approachable than his middle class peers at Downey High School.

Not knowing that these experiences would soon be immortal-ised in *American Graffiti*, the Lucas parents were outraged by their 'beatnik' son and protested volubly about the juvenile delinquency they predicted for him. Nor were their fears entirely groundless, as George proved one sweltering June afternoon in 1962 when he wrapped the Fiat round one of their own walnut trees. It was a total write-off and only its racing seat-belt, which should never have sheared off at the base plate but did, saved him from certain death when he was thrown out, rather than being crushed inside the car.

For George Lucas, the accident was the end of the beginning. When he dragged himself back into the land of the living he was grown up, motivated, determined, transformed. At eighteen, an age when Harrison Ford left his distant Chicago suburb the better to waste the next three years of his life at lowly Ripon College, his future mentor became a man with a mission. 'I realised that I'd been living my life so close to the edge for so long,' Lucas told Pollock. 'That was when I decided to go straight, to be a better student, to try to do something with myself. You can't have that kind of experience and not feel that there must be a reason why you're here. I realised I should be spending my time trying to figure out what that reason is and trying to fulfil it.'

The first step in the new game plan was Modesto's Junior College, the only one prepared to interpret George's high school grades and the diploma that was delivered to him in his hospital bed three days after the accident ('Probably because my teachers felt sorry for me') as evidence of a wish for further study.

Despite his lack of background, his courses in astronomy, sociology and art history appealed and he applied himself to them with his characteristic iron-willed concentration, acquiring his arts degree in 1964.

He'd also developed an interest in filming – as opposed to driving – racing cars, using an 8 mm camera given to him by his father, so it was a natural progression to apply for the film school at the University of Southern California in Los Angeles. Further encouraged by Haskell Wexler, the Hollywood cameraman he met at drag race meetings, he was accepted and took up his place, albeit against his father's wishes. Lucas Sr seems to have been a stern man, extremely authoritarian and right-wing and totally determined to see his son installed at L. M. Morris, the business he'd built up for him. After working there for a couple of weeks as a delivery boy, George was equally determined never to set foot in the stationer's again.

'You'll be back,' said his father, with the chilling certainty of one accustomed to being in the right. 'No, I won't,' shouted George, glaring up at the figure towering over him. 'I'll never be back. I'll be a millionaire before I'm thirty.' It was a rash but prophetic challenge, as the child-man who threw down the gauntlet recognised at the time, especially for a would-be film maker in a business that hadn't as yet shown the slightest inclination to open its doors to the new generation. Nor would it do so. It would be up to George Lucas and his friends to batter them down.

It was at this point in his life that the ugly duckling became a swan, as undergraduate triumph followed undergraduate triumph. His peers included John Milius, John Carpenter, Bob Zemeckis and Randal Kleiser, to name but the best known of the set who were destined to become Hollywood's 'Dirty Dozen', but it was Lucas's films that won the student prizes, his screenings which attracted the most attention from colleagues and teachers alike. When he wasn't making them, he was watching other people's, catching up on the history of the industry he was to revolutionise, at the rate of five films per weekend.

Names like Godard, Kubrick, Kurosawa and Richard Lester, hitherto disregarded, began to mean something to him, and their influences can be seen in his work. At about the time Harrison Ford was delivering that disastrous telegram to James

Coburn, unaware of the brave new world that was being created for him a few miles away on the campus at Westwood, George Lucas was coming into his kingdom as of right.

'Suddenly my whole life was film,' he remembers. 'I really blossomed at USC. I didn't know anything when I went in there, but it helped me focus on film, and I loved doing that. It was all neat, new and exciting, and I devoted every waking hour to it.'

In the process he resisted drugs, all the rage as the hippie era got under way, and the Hollywood razzamatazz offered by certain fellow students with good connections. Nor was he one for beers with the boys, but he did form lasting friendships for the first time in his life and his peers detected 'a whackey sense of humour', an unsuspected trait in the habitually grave reserved young man. His work was so far ahead of theirs that his colleagues were forced to take note of the small, thin bespectacled figure whom their teachers hailed as a genius. Not that George could afford to be distracted by such plaudits. He'd persuaded his father to finance his college days but, true to his overpowering work ethic and his deeply ingrained suspicion of the arts which smacked to him of pinkoism, Lucas Sr only agreed to fund his son as a film maker for the duration of his USC course. Failure would mean an ignominious return to L. M. Morris.

This spectre, initially large, receded as his parents were forced to recognise George's talent. The abstract nature of his college work was reflected in his first commercial feature, *THX 1138*, a futuristic fantasy set in an Orwellian world, which he made in forty days in 1969, under the aegis of his first patron, Francis Ford Coppola. The film was misunderstood and mutilated by its distributors, Warner Bros, a barbarism that made Lucas swear he'd be his own master as soon as possible. It also caused a rift in his relations with Coppola who, in George's opinion, had condoned the sacrilege. Before he could be his own man, however, he needed the clout that only a box office success could provide. The time was ripe for *American Graffiti*.

By now Harrison Ford was chiselling his way around the Canyons, his expertise increasingly in demand, but fate was about to take a hand, for he and George Lucas were on a collision course.

4   Graffiti Artist

'WHEN I first met George Lucas, I had no sense of destiny,' says Harrison Ford, 'no feeling that this was the turning point. It was an ordinary office interview, fixed by my agent, a matter of routine. I don't even recall him very well. I don't think he spoke. He sat while other people talked. I had no impression of being in the presence of a wunderkind, nor of getting on particularly well with him. Presumably he said "yes" to me later.'

This apparently uncataclysmic encounter was engineered by Fred Roos, one of Harrison's few friends from his Columbia days. Roos had since joined forces with Coppola and had found himself appointed casting director on *American Graffiti*. It was to prove an awesome duty because Lucas insisted on holding an old-fashioned search for new faces. *Graffiti* is an ensemble film with a dozen major roles, and Roos's task was to discover about five unknown contenders for each of them, so that Lucas could select exactly the right combination.

Patiently he scoured the drama schools and community theatres in the San Francisco Bay area, assisted by the film's producer, Gary Kurtz, a man so dour as to make George Lucas look like a bundle of fun. Then the trio interviewed all the hopefuls, whittling them down to a manageable number for video tests at Haskell Wexler's Hollywood studios. This was a new technique at the time, but it allowed Lucas to fit faces to characters so as to find the blend he wanted.

With so many names to put forward, Roos had no difficulty including that of Harrison Ford, but this time it was a Harrison Ford who didn't really care whether he got a part or not who faced up to his interrogators. 'For once I wasn't there as a person who needed a job to put bread on the table. I had a real life behind me. When you're out of work and you walk into an audition, you're an empty vessel, but there'd been a significant change in my personality. I'd promised myself I wouldn't act again until I found something I really wanted to do and I'd kept to it. It meant I would only work three times in six years, but I got my pride back.'

Lucas's idea for *American Graffiti* was to encapsulate the four years that led up to his car crash in 1962, into a single sweltering night in the summer of that year. '*American Graffiti* is a musical,' he wrote in his story treatment in 1971. 'It has singing and dancing, but it is not a musical in the traditional sense because the characters in the film neither sing nor dance. The dancing is created by cars performing a fifties ritual called cruising, an endless parade of kids bombing round in dagoed, moondisked, flamed, chopped, tuck-and-rolled machines rumbling through a seemingly adultless, heat-drugged little town. The passing chrome-flashing cars become a visual choreography.'

The hub of this scenario is Mel's Drive In, modelled on Modesto's own, the ultimate hamburger joint in which the kids congregate to swap cars and pick up chicks, to see and to be seen. Lucas's secret weapon, designed to give this peculiarly Californian set-up a much more universal appeal, was music, a hit parade of fifties classics that would strike chords in anyone who'd been young at the time. They'd be heard over the car radios and introduced by Wolfman Jack, the archetypal disc jockey who would be the kids' cult hero. Ironically this ingenious notion almost caused Lucas's downfall at Universal when, after many negotiations, the studio finally agreed to put up the $775,000 needed to get the show on the road.

The story of the financing of *Graffiti* is almost as complex as the film's plot line, a series of episodes each of which lasts between two and three minutes, the time it takes to play a popular song. Lucas was not exactly hot after the box office failure of *THX 1138* and he'd fallen out, to a certain degree, with Coppola when the older man had refused to fight for him against the Warner Bros cuts in the film. Nor had their ill-fated association at American Zoetrope, Coppola's dream for a brave new film world outside San Francisco, helped their relationship. Lucas, ever the shopkeeper's son, was horrified at Coppola's extravagance and resolved to run his own ship, should he ever get one, on the draconian business principles that held good at L. M. Morris.

His first step on *American Graffiti*, a five-page outline, met with a total lack of interest from everyone except David Picker, President of United Artists, who offered $10,000 development money. Lucas, and his newly wedded wife, Marcia, then made the mistake of attending the Cannes Film Festival for *THX*, leaving Gary Kurtz to spend the whole sum on a first draft by one Richard Walters. 'This does not reflect my vision,' cried Lucas on his return, but it was too late. The bank vault was empty. He had no alternative but to write the next two drafts himself – blood from a stone for he was no author, a self-assessment that was corroborated by the industry when both drafts were turned down by every studio in town.

It was only when he enlisted the help of his old classmates, Willard Huyck and Gloria Katz, that the property became re-motely viable. They used aspects of the George they knew as role models for the four main characters: Steve, eighteen, the upstanding blond athlete and class president; Curt, also eighteen, the wise-cracking poetry lover; Terry the Toad, seventeen, the wimp who wants to get laid; and, to a lesser degree, John Milner, twenty-two, an over-the-top drag racer who is also partly based on George's fellow USC graduate, John Milius.

Working rapidly, Huyck and Katz put flesh on the bones of Lucas's work, but the concept remained his own. The rewritten material caused a ripple of interest in Ned Tanen, Universal's youngest executive, but only if Kurtz was replaced as producer by a more prominent name. In the end, and rather ungraciously, Lucas had to settle for Coppola as being less unacceptable than the others on the list he was given, with Kurtz as co-producer. The other rider, that all the fees for the rights to the songs came out of the total budget, was even harder to accept, especially as Columbia had already dumped the project because they reckoned that these could amount to $5 million. Drastic pruning was the order of the day.

For Lucas, cutting his list of eighty-five adolescent favourites to forty-five was self-mutilation on a grand scale. All his beloved Presley songs had to go – they were much too expensive – but the Beach Boys, whom Kurtz knew personally, obliged at nominal rates for 'All Summer Long' and 'Surfin' Safari' and gradually other music publishers fell into line. At $90,000 the final bill was more than 10 per cent of the budget, but once casting was completed, the film was ready to roll.

And there on that final cast list was Harrison Ford as Bob Falfa, 'the boy in the cowboy hat'. With him were other unknowns on their way to fame and fortune: Richard Dreyfuss, a cocky New Yorker with no movie experience, as the quick-witted Curt; Ron Howard, only eighteen but burdened with a child actor's reputation from his years as Opie on the *Andy Griffith Show*, as Steve; Paul Le Mat, an ex-boxer, as Milner; and Charles Martin Smith, a last minute choice for Terry the Toad. On the distaff side, Cindy Williams, like Ford a friend of Fred Roos, seemed over age at twenty-five for Steve's girl, Laurie, but managed to dress 'real high school' and scoop the pool. Others to make their first major appearances were Kathleen Quinlan as Peg; Candy Clark as Debbie; and the twelve-year-old Mackenzie Phillips as Carol. Falfa, though seen with several different girls, also had one of his own, played by Debralee Scott.

Though none have reached the current eminence of Harrison Ford, Richard Dreyfuss struck the big time first by becoming a Spielberg man in *Jaws* and *Close Encounters of the Third Kind*, then won a Best Acting Oscar for the Neil Simon comedy, *The Goodbye Girl*. Candy Clark had a considerable success in Nic Roeg's *The Man Who Fell to Earth*, Cindy Williams caught the hearts of the nation as Shirley in the TV series, *Laverne and Shirley*, and Ron Howard has made a big name for himself as the director of *Splash* and *Cocoon*. Yes, it was quite a line up. 'I had my finger on a whole range of hot young people that I thought had a future,' said Roos, 'but no one expected them to do what they've done.'

American Graffiti was filmed in five weeks in 1972 in Marin and Sonoma Counties outside San Francisco, a desperately tight schedule for a 110-minute ensemble picture. The pressure on cast and crew was further increased because it was all night work, with darkness falling around 9 p.m. and the unwelcome golden rays of the dawn appearing at 5 a.m. George Lucas, a day person by nature, was a driven man throughout, powering through the script at a demanding fifteen to twenty set-ups a session, when five to ten is better than average.

He was able to call on his natural technical flair for the many car scenes required by the drag racing and cruising, but his way with actors was unformed, to say the least, his concern for them self-evidently skin deep. With so many relative newcomers, he knew he needed to tell them they were doing a good job, but it certainly didn't come naturally and he often forgot. The cast had a running joke about George's response: either 'Cut' or 'Well, why don't we try it once more' at the end of a take, and a muttered 'Great, terrific' to any performer who asked if he'd done all right.

As the oldest cast member, Harrison Ford was the natural leader in a lot of the fun generated by a film about a group of kids having a good time. The mood of the movie quickly spread to the players and they spent their time between shots acting in character, aided and abetted by the car freaks who assembled nightly with their machines: 400 authentic late fifties and early sixties monsters, heavily chromed and finned, had been rounded up at $25 a night and their owners raced them round the streets whenever they weren't needed for the film.

Ford and Le Mat, in particular, swilled beer with their owners and, according to Dale Pollock in *Skywalking*, urinated in motel ice machines and ran climbing races up the Holiday Inn sign. Dreyfuss, allegedly as arrogant and aggressive in real life as the characters he often plays, and an East Coast 'foreigner' to boot, came in for a bit of stick from his peers, not least from Le Mat who threw him into the hotel pool, gashing his face just before his close ups were due to be shot, a highly unpopular move.

It was Dreyfuss, however, who led the Lucas-baiting, complaining about the Bermuda shorts and brightly patterned shirt he had to wear for Curt, and mocking the director for his characteristic reticence. But George was fortunate because the cast really pulled for him despite his abstraction. 'It was fun,' says Ford, 'like a party, but not a Hollywood party. It was a real low budget movie, even for those days. I only got a couple of hundred dollars a week. There were no dressing rooms. The actors sat in the same trailer as the costumes.'

He was earning considerably less than he had as a carpenter at this time, so it's hardly surprising that he treated the film like a holiday. For Lucas, however, it was the toughest thing he'd ever attempted. The film got off to a lousy start when the police in San Rafael, George's choice for the small town outdoor scenes, revoked their permit on Night Two, after a loss-of-business complaint from a bar owner. Half of Night One had already been wasted and a further $15,000 would be required to re-locate the unit in Petaluma for the crucial street sequences. Small wonder the director was in despair. Typically it was Coppola, with his producer's hat and his big spender's inclinations, who'd show up to tell George to relax, slow down, shoot as many takes as he liked and sort the finance out later. George, stubborn but practical, refused on the grounds that if his movie were to lay an egg, it would at least be laid cheaply and on time. This is the reverse of the normal relationship between producer and director in which the producer worries about the cheques and balances while the director holds out for as much cash as he can with which to put as many of his ideas as possible on celluloid.

Coppola, fresh from making *The Godfather*, a big budget epic full of meticulously chosen camera angles, was horrified by Lucas's way. 'The kid comes over, sets up the camera, puts everybody against the wall and shoots,' he commented, his outrage tinged with awe. This method left the actors, inexperienced as they were, to assist with the dramatic structure in any way they could, but with Lucas regularly printing the first take, they had to do it at high speed. The script was in no way sacred so they were allowed, even encouraged, to make up new lines, provided they tied in with the concept of the scene, a form of input that appealed greatly to Harrison Ford after the interminable spoon-feeding at the studios.

Coppola's intervention did have one happy result in that Haskell Wexler, the drag racing cameraman who'd helped George on *THX 1138*, was asked to replace the inexperienced operators who'd been hired to save money. Although there was no cash to spare for him, he generously came to the rescue and gave *Graffiti* its splendidly appropriate neon graininess.

As the days passed Lucas, on three fitful hours of sleep in twenty-four, became ever more silent, a slight, haggard figure husbanding his slender reserves of energy to bring his picture in on time and on budget. His cool cracked once when a sound man ruined a set-up in the vital moments before daylight would

demand a postponement. 'Boy, did I blow my top,' he remembers. 'I was yelling and the whole cast just stopped still and said,
"My God, he yelled!" It was a huge event because it had never
happened before.'

The last shot to go into the can was Falfa's climactic drag race
with Milner, an encounter that ends in a dramatic crash when
his car spins off the track, rolls over and explodes just as Harrison
Ford and Cindy Williams escape from it. Well, not Ford and
Williams in person, but their stunt doubles. Then came the
'wrap' party at which Lucas showed a twenty minute compi-
lation to the assembled cast and crew. When the lights went up,
it was the real Harrison Ford, not only one of nature's gentlemen
but thrilled to see himself play for real at last, who led the
cheering. 'Hey, this is great!' he shouted, turning to Cindy
Williams. However, Lucas, the perfectionist, disagreed.

There was considerably less euphoria some months later when
George and Marcia Lucas had completed the editing of *Graffiti*,
painstakingly – and painfully – reducing it from nearly three
hours to just under two. It was time for Universal, who'd left
Lucas pretty much alone during shooting and post-production,
to inspect their investment. Knowing that their executives, with
the exception of the project's backer, Ned Tanen, were old men
to whom rock 'n roll and cruising were as alien as moon walking,
the Lucases were justifiably apprehensive.

And how right they turned out to be. The day chosen for the
screening was 28 January 1973, a Sunday morning; the place,
the Northpoint Theater in San Francisco. Eight hundred members of the public laughed and cheered in all the right places,
but the Universal executives sat with stony faces, and the stoniest
of all was Ned Tanen's. As the final credits came up, he strode
out of the cinema and attacked the astonished Gary Kurtz on
the pavement. 'This is in no shape to show an audience. It's
unreleasable,' he raged.

Next in line for full frontal attack was Coppola. 'You boys
let me down,' Tanen stated unequivocally. 'I went in to bat for
you, and you let me down.' His opinion was backed up by the
other Universal executives but it was at this point, with Lucas
standing by in a daze, that Coppola redeemed himself for
deserting his friend over the cutting of *THX 1138*. 'This poor

kid has worked his ass off for you,' he told Tanen in an outburst of pure Italian fury. 'He's made a really terrific movie the audience loved and for no money at all. And you can't even say thank you to this kid, not even for bringing the picture in on schedule. I'll buy the picture back right now. I'll write a cheque right now. I think it's a great film and I want it back.'

This exchange went straight into Hollywood mythology, but unfortunately for Coppola, his passion was so intense that it convinced the doubting executives and they refused his cheque, denying him the *Graffiti* bonanza.

The victory was not unflawed for Lucas, nor yet for Harrison Ford, because Universal was determined to have its pound of flesh off the film its employees couldn't appreciate. Having previously been assured by the studio that the rights to 'Some Enchanted Evening,' the property of Richard Rogers and the Oscar Hammerstein II estate, were in the bag on grounds of friendship, Lucas had had Ford sing along to the *South Pacific* classic. Everyone agrees that Harrison is no Pavarotti but the scene had whimsical period charm. No matter, said Universal, the rights had suddenly become unavailable and the sequence had to go, along with two others totalling four and a half minutes.

It doesn't sound much, but it was enough to make George Lucas vow that he'd never work on another film without having total control. He'd invested three years of his life and received a niggardly $20,000 for co-writing and directing a slice of his past, only to have it tampered with by a handful of blinkered, self-seeking businessmen who'd never made a movie in their lives. And let there be no mistake, he genuinely believed that the cuts had ruined his picture. He'd known all along that it was rough round the edges, the result of too much haste and too little cash, but he'd edited it to the height of its potential. Anything less was an abomination, and the memory of it has haunted him ever since, even though the missing footage was partially restored for the 1978 re-release. Ironically, it was Hollywood's stab in the back that made Lucas into the towering independent he is today.

Harrison Ford's turn to see *American Graffiti* came up four months later on 15 May 1973. This time the preview was Tanen's; the venue, the Writers' Guild Theater in Beverly Hills, and once again the invited audience, largely kids, sang along with the soundtrack as they laughed and clapped. Most of the cast attended, but Ford walked out before the end, embarrassed perhaps by seeing himself so much larger than life for the first time, and a little disturbed by the beginning of the end of his anonymity.

Not that his portrayal of Bob Falfa, the dashing drag racer who has Milner beat but blows it, was destined to put his name in lights when *American Graffiti* opened in New York and Los Angeles on 1 August 1973 and across the country two weeks later. Tanen, who'd eventually admitted that he 'just didn't get it', was amazed both by queues stretching around the block nationwide – in the boondocks as well as the cities – and by the reviews which were generally ecstatic. Yet six months later, he was able to claim the best deal Universal – or anyone else in Hollywood – has ever made, a return of $50 for every one invested, a profit ratio even *Star Wars* wouldn't match.

Typical of the American reviews was Stephen Farber's in the *New York Times*. 'The movie deepens as it goes along. Its definitive, remarkably resonant portrait of adolescence transcends all generation gaps. Lucas has brought the past alive, with sympathy, affection and thorough understanding.' John Simon of *Esquire* insisted that it was not a simple exercise in nostalgia. 'It implies neither that things were ever so much rosier in those wonderful days, nor that they were so side-splittingly idiotic that we must love them for their campy, absurd charm like Gibson Girl calendars or tap dancing Pullman-porter dolls. Lucas and his co-scriptwriters merely ask us to look at this period, with judicious amusement, affectionately, yet critically aware that though its follies were different, they were neither bigger nor smaller than ours are today.'

When it came to distributing individual praise, the lion's share went to the quartet of boys spending their last Friday night together before widening horizons changed their lives and their relationships with one another for ever. Richard Dreyfuss was the most admired for his performance as the chubby, thoughtful Curt, the one who finds the way out of the charmed circle of his youth. Otherwise the acting was generally commented on in an ensemble manner, an accurate reflection of the film itself, leaving the credit for finding the players and getting them to perform, with Lucas.

'All the characters burst out of the stereotypes: they seem to have an independent life and by the end they are so real that it's painful to leave them,' wrote Farber. 'The whole movie is brilliantly cast and performed. Lucas's technical flair was already visible in *THX 1138*, but his work with the actors in *American Graffiti* is a revelation. His gifts are prodigious. At twenty-eight, he is already one of the world's master directors.'

The cast, having had creativity extracted from them at racing pace throughout the shooting, might have disagreed with this assessment, but John Simon did not. 'I shall not try to list the excellent but little known actors who pour themselves into these existences, scribbled like living graffiti on the walls of the night. Almost all of them are already experienced performers, yet we tend to be unable to place them, which gives them the combined advantages of professionals and amateurs. George Lucas had directed with a remarkably firm but unostentatious hand, two virtues equally rare in a young film maker.'

Female critics were less amused, most notably the formidable Pauline Kael of the *New Yorker* who accused Lucas of using women as 'plot functions', and not without justification since the final shot describing the fate of the characters ten years later encompasses only the boys, leaving the girls, presumably, to marry, have babies and settle down in the backwater in which they were born. In the early seventies, with Women's Lib sweeping America, this was dangerous ground and indeed Marcia Lucas had fought against the omission on ideological and practical grounds. However her husband, not only a male chauvinist pig but generally pretty uneasy with women, had been adamant.

Nevertheless it was clear, as the box office returns came in in the wake of the notices, that *American Graffiti* was a good film to be associated with. It picked up Academy Award Nominations for Best Picture, Best Director (Lucas), Best Original Screenplay (Lucas, Huyck and Katz), Best Supporting Actress (Candy Clark) and Best Editing (Marcia Lucas and Verna Fields) and although it won none of the coveted statuettes in the year in which *The Sting* scooped the pool, the exposure did no harm. Nor did the prizes it did pick up, a Golden Globe from the

Hollywood Foreign Press Association for the Best Comedy of the Year, and Screenplay Awards from the New York Film Critics Association and the National Society of Film Critics.

Although *Graffiti* allowed George Lucas to fulfil his promise to his father, that he'd be a millionaire by the time he was thirty, with two years in hand, it did nothing for the finances of Harrison Ford. With no percentage in the film, he was soon back in the Canyons working on other men's bookshelves, but there was a key difference. He was 'family' now, no longer a handsome would-be actor with a few insignificant credits behind him, but on first name terms with the men who were taking Hollywood apart and re-modelling it in their own image. The next to use his services was Francis Coppola, only five years older than George Lucas but the trail blazer for his generation in that he was the first film school graduate to make a feature, *Dementia 13*. That had been for Roger Corman in 1962, exactly a decade before *The Godfather* put the seal on his early reputation.

Two years later, while preparing *The Godfather II*, he found time for a more cherished project, *The Conversation*, the story of Harry Caul, a professional wire-tapper and the 'best bugger on the West Coast'. Harry is Catholic and therefore burdened with conscience, supremely efficient at his depressing calling but too obsessed with it to examine its wider implications. As it turns out, he is right because as soon as he breaks his own rules by acting on a conversation he overhears between two lovers in a San Francisco park, he is doomed.

Caul is played by Gene Hackman at his crumpled, seedy, brilliant best, another casting *tour de force* for Fred Roos, the co-producer on the picture. Once again the Roos connection paid off for Harrison Ford, who secured the small but vital role of Martin Stett. When Caul first hears the damning conversation, he takes the tapes to the Director (Robert Duvall) of the faceless corporation that employs him, then impulsively refuses to hand them over to his assistant, Stett. Later, the two men meet at a bugging equipment exhibition where Stett once again attempts to pressurise Caul into giving him the goods, and once again he is unsuccessful.

'I turn up as an evil young henchman in the movie,' Ford recalls. 'There was no role there until I decided to make him a homosexual.' His input was effective but, even combined with his sharp suit and loud checked tie, it failed to bring him any kind of individual recognition from critics who rightly concentrated on Hackman, at his hottest in the wake of his Oscar-winning performance in *The French Connection*, and on the film itself which got off to a good start abroad by winning the Palme d'Or at the Cannes Film Festival in 1974.

Coincidentally it was also extremely topical in the climate of the Watergate wire-tapping revelations, though that could have been no part of Coppola's intention when he first had the germ of the idea back in 1967. '*The Conversation* is a film of enormous enterprise and tension,' noted Jay Cocks in *Time*. 'It also gains, because of Watergate, an added timeliness, but it does not depend on it. More than anything, it is a film about moral paralysis, a subject that does not need headlines to lend it importance. The film is meticulously cast,' he added, almost as an afterthought, picking out the late John Cazale for special praise for his role as Caul's assistant.

The Director's assistant was not so fortunate, but *The Conversation* gave Harrison Ford another high class credit and the chance to work with Coppola, the most respected American director of the early seventies, in one of his best films: 'One no discerning film-goer should fail to see,' as Derek Malcolm wrote in the *Guardian*. It was an experience to cherish, for Coppola and Lucas were as different as chalk from cheese in every possible way except their passion for film. Where Ford had towered over the slight and retiring Lucas, he met the noisy, larger-than-life Coppola eyeball to eyeball and understood, perhaps for the first time, the true nature of conspicuous expenditure.

Coppola is nearly six feet tall and weighs in at over seventeen stone. He lives and thinks like a tycoon, whether his bank balance supports the thesis or not, rather in the style of the legendary John Huston, and Harrison was working with him at a time when his fee for *The Godfather* had given him a free rein, both commercially and privately. In personal terms, that meant a twenty-eight bedroomed mansion in San Francisco, with its own cinema and pool, plus a private jet and twelve cars. 'I don't think that's particularly opulent,' Coppola told the *Daily Mail*'s David Lewin. 'It's just informal and we have a staff of one. The anxiety has gone. Success liberates you – you don't have to go on unless you want to.'

For Ford, it was a whole new world, but his old one – with its bricks and mortar and woodwork, its prestigious extensions to houses designed by Frank Lloyd Wright and Lodner – still awaited him. Over the next three years, he accepted just two acting jobs, both for television. The first was a walk on in *The Trial of Lt. Calley*, a movie about the mass killer in Vietnam. His brief moment centre screen was as the witness who cried.

Dynasty, a lavish two-hour TV movie, made in 1976 long before Alexis Carrington was a predatory gleam in Joan Collins' eyes, gave him more to do as Mark, a scion of the Blackwood family. With that title, the film has to be a saga and the Blackwood parents, John (Harris Yulin), his wife Jennifer (Sarah Miles) and his brother Matt (Stacy Keach) are to be seen at its start setting off for the wide open spaces of Ohio where land was cheap in 1823.

John is one of those stubborn, God-fearing pioneers who'll farm his hundred acres if it kills him and his family, but Jennifer and Matt gang up on him – and eventually run away from him – to establish what they insist will be a far more profitable venture, a carriage business. The next important factor, as all students of such epics will appreciate, is the arrival of the railroad and the prospect of selling the farm – over John's dead body, of course – to the development company so they can run the tracks across it. This brings out greed in all the right places, including John and Jennifer's sons, Mark (Ford) and Carver (Gerrit Graham). 'The last half hour concentrates too much on Miles's ungrateful grown-up offspring,' said *Variety*, suggesting that Harrison had a certain amount of belated prominence in a production that would soon sink without a trace.

Dispirited, he returned to his work bench vowing that he'd never act again. The Canyons should have their carpenter. Enough obscurity was enough.

5   Intergalactic Cowboy

BY 1975 *Star Wars* rumours were running rife through the streets
of Hollywood. The George Lucas bandwagon was about to roll
again and *American Graffiti* had ensured that everyone would sit
up and take notice. No matter that the new project was a space
adventure, a very unfashionable genre at the time, nor that the
director's wife couldn't understand the plot, everyone wanted
to be in on it. That, of course, included every young hopeful in
town, the waiters and bellhops and bar tenders forever standing
in the wings for the chance that never came.

The one person it did not include was Harrison Ford, then
engaged in a wood and paint job for Sally Kellerman. Other
considerations apart, the people casting *Star Wars* had said that
no one from *Graffiti* would be considered. Once again, find new
faces was the order of the day. Worse still, the preliminary
selection panel consisted of Irene Lamb, Diane Crittenden and
Vic Ramos, rather than the obliging Mr Roos. The procedure
was the one that had worked for *Graffiti*, an endless sifting
through hundreds of actors for the perfect combination, and
Lucas joined forces with Brian de Palma, then casting *Carrie*,
which also required a group of young performers, to lessen the
strain.

De Palma is as chatty as Lucas is silent, which allowed
George the unaccustomed luxury of listening and learning as the
candidates, some thirty or forty a day, paraded their talents for
their allocated five minutes. Impassively he took notes on each
of them, then jotted down the names of the ones he liked on a
separate list for further consideration. Alan Ladd, Jr, the executive at Twentieth-Century Fox who had put his faith in *Star
Wars*, wanted bankable names for the leading roles of Luke
Skywalker, Han Solo and Princess Leia, but Lucas, as usual, had

other ideas. The faces must be fresh so that audiences couldn't be distracted by star-spotting and they must slot together as Dreyfuss, Le Mat, Martin Smith and Howard had done on *Graffiti*. The chemistry had to be right.

Mark Hamill had gone through the system for *Graffiti* when he was nineteen and failed at the first hurdle. Now he tried again. It was a nightmare. 'There were guys literally everywhere, in age from sixteen to thirty-five,' he recalls. 'They didn't let us read. You had to look right first. I walked in and Brian and George were sitting there. Brian said, "Tell us a little bit about yourself," and I went through the litany. George didn't say anything. I thought he was Brian's gofer or something.'

Fortunately the anonymity was mutual. Lucas didn't recognise Hamill either, and he added him to his list of fifty who would return for the videotaped readings. It was at this point that Harrison Ford came back into Lucas's life when he tripped over him – almost literally – in Francis Coppola's office. 'Francis's art director had inveigled me into installing a very elaborate raised door panel in his studio office,' Harrison remembers. 'Now I knew they were casting and I thought it a bit coy to be around there, being a carpenter, during the day, so I worked at night. Well, one day something came up and I got stuck and I had to work during the day. And, sure enough, that was the day that George was doing the casting for *Star Wars*.'

He was on his knees in the doorway when Coppola, Lucas, four other hot shots and the ever cocky Richard Dreyfuss walked in. It was not a happy moment. 'Dreyfuss came through first and made a big joke about being my assistant. That made me feel just great. I felt about the size of a pea when they walked through.'

However, it was an occasion on which Ford was to have the last laugh because Lucas, who'd found him supportive and easy going on *Graffiti*, asked him to help him out by reading the male parts opposite the contenders for Princess Leia. Harrison obliged, still believing there was nothing much in it for him. Several of the actors interviewed by Lucas for Han Solo were black and one of them, Glynn Turman, almost snatched the prize until the director reflected on the problems an inter-racial romance might cause him. 'I didn't want to make *Guess Who's Coming To Dinner*, so I backed off,' he has admitted.

Likewise he rejected the idea of having a Eurasian girl for Princess Leia. Carrie Fisher, the daughter of Eddie Fisher and Debbie Reynolds, was one of the first actresses to be tested and, like Hamill, she found the cattle-call gruelling and humiliating. 'The dialogue for the test was even more difficult than the dialogue that ended up in the film,' she says with a shudder. 'It was space triple-talk, killer lines.' Nor was the process helped by Lucas's refusal to allow the contenders to read the whole script until they'd signed their contracts, lest the plot should be broadcast around, which meant they had very little idea of what they were aiming for.

Lucas's concept of chemistry resulted in the final selection of two Solo–Luke–Leia trios: Ford, Hamill and Fisher, or Christopher Walken (like Ford an older actor with a boyish look), Will Selzer and Terri Nunn, a former Penthouse Pet. The groupings were in no way interchangeable. If Ford, Hamill or Fisher had been unavailable, George would have gone with his second choices. The discard heap was pretty impressive too. Nick Nolte and William Katt were Solo rejects, though Brian de Palma hired Katt for *Carrie*. Jodie Foster and Amy Irving were turned down for Leia, with Irving also finding a career-enhancing role in *Carrie*.

When it came to putting one trio above the other, Lucas preferred Fisher's youthful pertness to Nunn's tough worldly manner and Hamill's 'golly and gosh' enthusiasm to Selzer's more intellectual range. But why Ford? Opinions differ, but it is certain that the faithful Roos, called in at the end of the hunt for much-valued advice, had something to do with it. Dale Pollock suggests that Ford had become churlish reading for a part he knew he couldn't have, an anger that won him Han Solo. Alan Mackenzie, in *The Harrison Ford Story*, cites the actor's 'forthright and honest way of expressing himself that isn't a million light years away from Solo's lines in the movie' as a more likely reason.

Harrison himself is prepared to accept an element of desperation as a key factor. 'I knew I couldn't be in it, but good old Fred Roos did it again. He prevailed on George to see me after he'd seen everyone else. Three or four weeks before the final casting decision had to be made, I did a video test – same place where we did the *Graffiti* tests. Same kinda routine too. Just a couple of pages of script. No explanation. Just get in there and do it. In the end I did tests with all his other selections, about a hundred people in all. The beauty of the film is George's ensemble casting. When they'd tested everyone in the world, I got the part.'

Of course the rest of the world knows that Lucas, so dour, so driven, so immensely painstaking, would never have allowed indecent haste, let alone mere impatience to interfere with the realisation of his childhood dream, and in due course he told his own story. 'I liked Harrison from working with him on *Graffiti*. I thought he was a very talented actor and I enjoyed working with him. But when I considered him for *Star Wars*, I was afraid of being influenced by the fact that I liked him, that I was familiar with his work, that I was thinking of him for the part because of my previous associations with him. So I did test with a lot of others too. But I just couldn't find anybody who had his qualities as an actor and fitted my concept of the character as well as he did.'

Characteristically, Ford discounts the part his likeability played in the decision. However, he wasn't exactly over the moon about Lucas's offer when it finally came. Unlike George, with a childhood full of comics to draw on, Harrison's infant appreciation of the genre was minimal. 'I missed that phase when comics went through a big change in the areas of, I guess, more realism. At least they weren't talking about ducks and mice! But I was never very aware of those comics,' he comments, with the air of bewilderment of a grown-up venturing into unknown and unexpected territory.

Should he accept Solo, he asked himself; then he went home and asked Mary. 'Yes,' she said, still confident of a marriage that seemed stronger than ever after eleven financially uneven but happy years. 'We enjoyed it all, the hardships as well as the joy,' Harrison has told *Ciné-Revue*, 'and we knew that if and when success came, we'd always be together. I owe everything to Mary. Without her, I wouldn't be in the cinema today, because I wouldn't have accepted the role of Han Solo. When Lucas made me the offer, I hadn't been in front of a camera for three years. Mary wasn't only beautiful and kind. She understood my problems and it was she who gave me the confidence to accept. She pushed me back into the cinema.'

So the thirty-two-year-old unknown with the jinxed career and the happy home said 'yes', unaware of how inexorably, how painfully rapidly those adjectives would be reversed. He also spent some time working out how to make the best of Han Solo, the mercenary who comes good and therefore has a character as old as cinema, and then some. 'I liked his sense of humour. That was the best thing about him. As soon as I saw Carrie and Mark, it was obvious what the relationships would be – or could be. I knew nothing about science fiction, but it was apparent that the characters were very contemporary and the situations were simple – without meaning to be derogatory. It was simply straightforward, a clean human story. I mean, I didn't have to act science fiction.'

Just as *American Graffiti* had shown aspects of the teenage George Lucas, so *Star Wars* captures the mogul as a child, a child who pooled his pocket money with his sister Wendy, three years his junior, to buy ten comic books a week, a child who gazed so fixedly at cartoons on Modesto's first television set, a child who blocked out fantasy landscapes and constructed environments to flesh out his daydreams. When he'd made the futuristic *THX 1138*, Lucas had been accused of being cold and weird by Coppola and others, a reputation he'd managed to shake off with *American Graffiti*. Now he was out to prove just what a warm and lovable champion of good over evil he really was.

Nor was this entirely a pose. Compared with Harrison Ford, who has a degree of natural cynicism to mix in with his all-American naïvety, George Lucas is a primitive. He wishes people well in the wishy-washy liberal way that dominated his student days in the sixties and he genuinely believes that they need fairy tales to sustain them. It is his good fortune that his ideas are so instantly acceptable to the silent majority, not only in America but worldwide, and that he is able to put them over in ways which appeal to the child in all of us, as well as to children themselves.

Intellectuals may recoil from classic fairy tales as being too simplistic, but most people are not intellectuals. It is a straightforward equation that works in Lucas's favour, and there are executives in Hollywood who must wake up in the wee small hours haunted by their failure to recognise it. One of them is David Picker, of United Artists, the first man in the film industry to get a sighting of *Star Wars*. That was in 1971 when it was playing second fiddle to *Graffiti* in the package Lucas offered to the studio. Even in 1973, despite ducking out on *Graffiti*, Picker had first call on *Star Wars*, but once again he flunked the popularity test. Too expensive, he cried, and the special effects are well nigh impossible.

Next in line was Universal, Lucas's least favourite studio after its treatment of *Graffiti*. 'I hated them,' he remembers resentfully, 'but I had to go to them. Part of my deal to make *American Graffiti* was that I had to sign my life over to them for seven years. That's the way they work over there. They owned me.'

However, the gods smiled and Ned Tanen, still raging over *American Graffiti* a month before its triumphant release, said no as well, leaving George to wend his way to Alan Ladd, Jr at Fox with a simple request for $10,000 development money so he could write the screenplay. Lucas told him about his childhood dreams and showed him his plot summary, an obscure hand-written document telling 'the story of Mace Windu, a revered Jedi-bendu of Opuchi who was related to Usby C. J. Thape, padawaan learner to the famed Jedi.'

Not unnaturally Ladd was as baffled as Picker and Tanen had been, but he had admired *THX 1138* and had his judgement vindicated at a special screening of *Graffiti*. 'I thought it was a terrific movie; I felt I was seeing the work of a very talented man,' he commented. He also liked George on their first meeting, perhaps because the taciturn film maker was at his best talking about the history of adventure in the cinema, with particular reference to the kind of movies that Ladd, born into the Hollywood purple, had been involved with first hand through his father during his own childhood. So he said yes and, three weeks later, when Graffiti opened, there was no happier mogul in town.

Lucas too was content because the *Star Wars* deal, as expressed in a seventeen-page memo, gave him $50,000 to write the screenplay, $100,000 to direct the picture and 40 per cent of the profits, with $50,000 for Gary Kurtz as producer. The budget was set at a very modest $3,500,000 and the remaining rights for sequels and merchandising were to be finalised before the film started shooting.

Lucas's next task was to earn his first $50,000 by writing a script and, as always for him, it was a hard one. He'd researched fairy tales, mythology and social psychology; he'd read science fiction books, both contemporary and classic, and studied religion in an all-embracing trawl for ideas. Now the fruits of this labour had to be distilled and set down in black and white. With so much material to draw on, the first draft was a monster, as its author recalls.

'I wanted to make a fairy tale epic, but this was like *War and Peace*. So I took that script and cut it in half, put the first half aside and decided to write the screenplay from the second half. I was on page 170, and I thought "Holy smokes, I need 100 pages, not 500," but I had these great scenes. So I took that story and cut it into three parts. I took the first part and said, "This will be my first script, but no matter what happens, I'm going to get these three movies made."'

Herein lies the germ of the nine-part marathon saga *Star Wars* could still become. Lucas started in the middle with the fourth section, then made the fifth (*The Empire Strikes Back*) and the sixth (*The Return of the Jedi*), leaving the opening trilogy, which takes place twenty years earlier, and the closing one, set thirty years later, unexplored as yet. The robots C-3PO and R2-D2 are the only characters common to all nine parts.

The final screenplay, Lucas's fourth, emerged after two-and-a-half years of blood, sweat and tears, headaches, stomach aches and chest pains. He wrote in a specially constructed room, with a poster of Sergei Eisentein on one wall and one of *THX 1138* on another. Between them stood his exotic 1941 Wurlitzer which he only allowed himself to play when the day's quota was completed. He wrote all four drafts out in longhand on green and blue lined paper with hard lead pencils. His spelling and grammar were appalling, but gradually plot and characters emerged out of chaos.

Star Wars borrows liberally from Lucas's past, notably *THX* whose hero became Luke Skywalker, and from other people's imaginations, with *Flash Gordon*, in which fearsome technology is defeated by poorly-equipped humans, and Frank Herbert's *Dune*, among the more obvious influences. Luke Skywalker and Han Solo represent aspects of George Lucas, just as Curt, Steve, Toad and John did in *American Graffiti*. Initially Skywalker was an elderly general, but his creator came to realise that there would be more scope for character development if he grew towards his Jedi destiny. Accordingly he made him into a brash, wide-eyed eighteen-year-old marvelling at the world, just as he had done in his own childhood.

Han Solo is the older Lucas, the cynical businessman honed in the corridors of Hollywood, the loner who must look after himself first. He evolved tortuously from a green-skinned monster with gills in the first version to 'a tough James Dean-style starpilot, a cowboy in a starship: simple, sentimental and cocksure' in the version that Harrison Ford accepted. He is also the handsome dashing hero Lucas can never be, the unattainable fantasy figure who provides a focus for adult viewers by allowing them to identify with his flaws – he's essentially a gun for hire – as much as with his courage.

Princess Leia dominated early drafts, then dropped in age to eleven for a while before taking final shape as a tough, tomboyish sixteen-year-old, a suitable love interest for both Han and Luke. Solo was also given a pal for his adventures, the giant Wookie co-pilot, Chewbacca, who normally assists him in his smuggling operations.

These three contemporary characters are supposed to hold the centre of *Star Wars* together, but they face formidable competition from Lucas's more exotic creations, notably the robot double act, a variation on the classic contrast between tall and thin and short and fat pioneered by Don Quixote and Sancho Panza. In only slightly less inhuman form, there is the villainous Darth Vader, the embodiment of menace and evil in his black armour, and the avuncular sage, Obi Ben Kenobi, whose task it is to lead Luke into the Jedi brotherhood.

With the screenplay in acceptable shape at last and casting well under way, Lucas was in a position to make his bid for freedom at Twentieth Century Fox. It did his cause no harm that Alan Ladd, Jr had risen to head of production in the interim, nor that the studio was anticipating massive up-front demands from him in the wake of *Graffiti*'s cash returns. 'Suddenly I was powerful,' he said, with some amusement. 'Fox thought I was going to come back and demand millions of dollars and all those gross points, so I said, "I'll do it for the deal memo, but we haven't talked about things like merchandising and sequel rights."'

These included music rights, not valuable unless the film was a massive hit, the rights to make *Star Wars* toys and T-shirts which Fox considered more trouble than they were worth, and the ownership of any future films, a vital point for Lucas who believed in his saga, but not for Fox who were thinking in strictly one-off terms. Delighted by not having to pay out on the spot, they agreed to most of George's demands, though they retained final cut on *Star Wars* and first refusal on distributing any future films. Even so, Lucas was in business for himself to an unusually high degree. By trading cash for control, he built himself a platform for the independence he enjoys today, the independence that sets him apart from talented contemporaries like Francis Coppola and Steven Spielberg who still have to go to Hollywood – or to him – whenever they want to finance a film.

Having had his way with Twentieth-Century Fox, Lucas was prepared to give them a name to put on the cast list beside Mark Hamill, Harrison Ford and Carrie Fisher. The one he chose was Sir Alec Guinness, then in Los Angeles making *Murder by Death*. Boldly he dispatched the script to the living legend who looked dubiously at an unsolicited manuscript fronted by a drawing of a young man brandishing a sword. This was not the kind of approach he was accustomed to but, fortunately for his bank balance, he didn't let that stop him reading it. He considered the dialogue to be 'ropey', but was shrewd enough to allow himself to be caught up in the power of the narrative. He agreed to meet Lucas for lunch.

Though surprised by his host's youth, Guinness was sufficiently impressed to agree to go to work as Ben Kenobi, a decision that pleased Alan Ladd, Jr as much as it terrified the other actors. 'He gave me many sleepless nights,' says Harrison Ford, not entirely jokingly. 'I'd be thinking, "I'm supposed to be in a movie with Sir Alec Guinness. He'll laugh at me just once, and I'll pack up and go home." But of course he never did. He's really a very kind and generous person.'

Nor, in fact, did Harrison ever pack up his own equipment and take it home, as Sally Kellerman recalls. 'He left his ladder, pots of paint, his bag of tools and his overalls in my garage when he got the part in *Star Wars* and he's never been back to collect them. I've painted "Harrison Ford left these" on the garage wall above the tools, and people are amused and ask what it's all about.

'What happened is this,' she continued. 'My husband and I were paying him to do some work. He was a very accomplished carpenter and woodworker and he was also a very nice person, someone we loved to have around. We knew he'd get his big break one day, but we never expected it to happen right in the middle of a paint job in our kitchen. I wish him all success – and he deserves it, but I wish he would come back one day and finish putting up my bookshelves.'

Harrison may have felt secure enough to quit, but Lucas's problems with Fox were in no way over. His original story had been set in the jungle, but further consideration of such a hot, damp and pestilential environment persuaded him to switch to a desert location, and Tunisia was selected. Then there was the question of sound stages: up to nine were needed, a number unavailable in Hollywood, so Lucas and Gary Kurtz flew to Europe on a reconnaissance mission that included Rome, Paris and London, finally settling on Elstree in North London.

It was a decision that Alan Ladd, conscious of the cost savings that would result, approved wholeheartedly, but he was less supportive about Lucas's revised budget of $12 million, more than three times the amount he'd agreed to make the film for in their original memo. By the autumn of 1975, the *American Graffiti* profits had eliminated George's earlier debts and allowed him to invest $1 million of his own money in the *Star Wars* project, and it was at his own expense that he undertook the European tour. He also set up the Industrial Light and Magic (ILM) Company, a subsidiary of Lucasfilm registered in July, 1975 to devise the special effects for *Star Wars*. The man behind the magic, John Dykstra, chosen for his work as assistant to Douglas Turnbull on *2001*, was already installed in a warehouse in a suburb of Los Angeles where he was experimenting with the new computer-controlled cameras he would use to revolutionise his field.

In essence Lucas was going ahead without Fox's say so, risking his new fortune on his own talents, but it couldn't go on for ever. Reluctantly Fox went up to $5.5 million and Lucas came down to $10 million, before a compromise figure of $8.5 million was agreed. Lucas was paying for his lack of honesty during the initial negotiations when he'd given the studio a figure he knew to be unrealistically low for fear of having them back out on him. Now his carefully calculated and – he insists – genuine costings were seen as excessive. 'They assumed everyone was cheating them and padding their budgets,' he says, 'but we weren't. Ours stated the actual cost. When $8.5 million was agreed, we knew we were right on the edge and that if just one tiny thing went wrong, it was going to go over budget.'

The pressure was on and Lucas, though still without the absolute green light, hurried back to England to hire local talent for the rest of the cast: men whose faces would never be seen but who would, nonetheless, give movement and sound and life to Darth Vader, Chewbacca, C-3PO and R2-D2. The first two required giants, and Lucas met the Welsh weightlifter, six foot seven inch David Prowse, who had Frankenstein experience behind him, and asked him to choose between the parts. Prowse picked Vader, although he was told that his regional accent would not be suitable and that the villain would have to be dubbed, as indeed he was by James Earl Jones.

Peter Mayhew, even taller at seven foot two, was a hospital porter with rather less acting in his background, but he was to find that his feet, at size sixteen among the largest in Britain, would be to his advantage for the first time because they were just what George wanted for Chewbacca. Anthony Daniels, then twenty-nine and with a lot of experience of mime on stage, felt an instant rapport with the fussy, well-spoken C-3PO and with his diminutive creator, but Kenny Baker, the music hall performer selected for R2-D2, was less drawn to his metal shell and the squeaks that would come out of it. However, he allowed himself to be persuaded and another local, Peter Cushing, the cold-blooded master of Hammer Horror, completed the cast as the evil Fascist Grand Moff Tarkin.

Meanwhile, back in Los Angeles, the crunch was coming. Lucas's screenplay ran to 160 pages, about forty too long for a two hour movie by Ladd's book. George's old *American Graffiti* collaborators, Bill Huyck and Gloria Katz, had beefed up the dialogue a bit, particularly the repartee between Han Solo and Princess Leia, and it was looking good when Lucas finally came clean by admitting that $10 million was the minimum he could deliver it for.

The final decision fell to Chris Kalabokes, a financial analyst whose job it was to assess cost versus potential earnings. His answer was based on a folder containing Lucas's original, almost incomprehensible treatment, so it is a fine reflection on his judgement that he should have committed the studio, hard pressed and threatened by take-over as it was, to such a substantial expenditure. But he did. *Star Wars* might make $35 million, he projected, proving too that his judgement was in no way infallible!

6 The Jackpot that Jammed on Pay

FOR HARRISON FORD, Mark Hamill, Carrie Fisher and especially George Lucas, the seventy days it took to shoot *Star Wars* between March and July 1976 gave few hints of the glory to come. With the exception of Ford, they were Californian to the core, and even he had chosen Hollywood in preference to New York because of the climate. For all that, 1976 turned into the hottest summer in British history. Elstree was a nightmare, initially cold, always depressing, suburban and grim. The studios once used by Alfred Hitchcock were long past their prime by the mid seventies and, indeed, had not been used for two years before the *Star Wars* bonanza blew into town.

With a predominantly English cast and crew, the three leading actors were isolated from the mainstream by accent and attitude, but luckily they got on well together, forming themselves into a mini unit against the world. Hanging about in Elstree's dingy passages waiting for their scenes to come up, they devised their private jokes, so alienating the Englishmen still further, but their problems were as nothing compared to those of their beleaguered director.

From Day One, 26 March, everything that could go wrong had gone wrong. Shooting had started in the Sahara Desert in unseasonal and unwanted rain, the first to fall in a Tunisian winter for fifty years. The wind screeched across the flat landscape, blowing sand into everything, including the camera lenses, and it was bitterly cold. The crew was decimated by dysentery and the robots refused to co-operate, especially R2-D2 which stood still or fell over whether it contained the unfortunate Kenny Baker or not. The sandcrawler was blown to bits in the gale, but at least it functioned, which is more than could be said for the landspeeder, which belied its name by never moving at all.

Only Mark Hamill and Sir Alec Guinness accompanied the robot actors on this ill-omened jaunt, and Hamill at least found that the environment concentrated his mind wonderfully in these, his first scenes in his first feature film. Despite the wear and tear on his nervous system, Lucas too achieved his purpose by establishing his robots as the warm lovable jokers who would take the world by storm.

Everyone involved in the Tunisian experience felt that Elstree would be a piece of cake by comparison and at first it looked as if they might be right. The nine sound stages were filled with impressively gleaming sets which Lucas immediately had worked over so that they'd look 'organic'. Harrison Ford flew in from California on his first trip to Europe to be introduced to his spaceship, the Millennium Falcon, a full scale model that had been meticulously constructed by maritime engineers outside London and brought to the studios in sections.

The wardrobe department established the look required for each character, with Skywalker clad in rough cotton and Solo in a rather more fetching figure-hugging shirt and waistcoat in keeping with his maverick nature. Carrie Fisher came off worst in this area because the prudish George was determined to exclude sexuality from his vision. Accordingly he had her breasts taped and covered her from neck to toe in a loose white robe. 'Breasts don't bound in space, there's no jiggling in the Empire,' Carrie says wryly, recalling that breaking this painful news to her fell to Gary Kurtz. Lucas, forever inhibited with women, lacked the courage to discuss something so indelicate himself.

Throughout the shooting, he referred to Fisher as 'the Girl' and Hamill as 'the Kid'. Both characters were intense and serious, innocent and devoid of fun. Skywalker strides around wide-eyed as he tries to fulfil his destiny against enormous odds while Leia, a fast-talking toughie, is the antithesis of the heroines with cleavage Lucas had seen, but rejected, in his comic books. Han Solo, by contrast, had a zany appreciation of the strange world he liked to manipulate to his own advantage. He looks on Luke and Leia as his little brother and sister, lovable but often irritating and in the first film he treats them accordingly.

Solo's history is fairly detailed. He is an orphan abandoned by space gypsies and brought up by Wookies, a race of jungle mammals combining aspects of dogs, cats and gorillas who live to be 350 years old. Solo's early life among them explains Chewbacca's allegiance to him: he rescued him after he had been enslaved by the Empire. When he was twelve, Solo left the Wookie planet for the Space Academy, but his student days end abruptly when he sells exam papers and drag races space ships. Out on his ear, he becomes a spice smuggler, a small entrepreneur dedicated to private enterprise just as Lucas's father is. To counterbalance any negative aspects in this biography – Lucas is, after all, talking about heroes – Solo is a sworn enemy of the Empire, the totalitarian regime run by Darth Vader and opposed by Princess Leia's Rebel movement.

Solo is not involved in the establishing scenes for *Star Wars* which include the introduction of Leia, blaster firing, when her ship, carrying the stolen plans for the Empire's lethal Death Star, is captured by Darth Vader; and of Luke Skywalker, a farmer's nephew who discovers those plans when Leia's robots, C-3PO and R2-D2, pass his way. They take the boy to ask assistance from Ben Kenobi who tells Luke that his father was a Jedi warrior and instructs him in his destiny.

These events set the stage for the first of the big battles, with Solo and the Millennium Falcon engaged to carry Ben, Luke and the robots back to the Rebel base to rescue Leia and destroy the Death Star. Later, when Ben has given his life to save Luke's, Solo helps the boy hero to complete his duties so that the vital happy ending, the victory of mere humans over soulless technology, can be accomplished.

Mark Hamill is on record as saying, 'I have a sneaking suspicion that if there were a way to make movies without actors, George would do it,' but the director was well aware that there was no way *Star Wars* would be popular unless the public were fond of the leading characters. He also knew that they were cardboard cut-outs caught up in childish situations and that the dialogue was dire. 'You can't say this shit,' Harrison Ford was wont to remind him. 'You can only type it, and then not easily.'

★

That he was able to crack that kind of joke is indicative of the relatively easy relationship Ford had with Lucas. The two men had a deep dislike of England to draw them together, based apparently on an absence of decent hamburgers and the recalcitrance of the crew. 'The only damper on the pure fun,' says Harrison, 'was the almost unanimous attitude of the English crew, that we were totally out of our minds, especially George.'

For the locals, the small scruffy figure of George Lucas, shuffling around the sets in sneakers and faded jeans instead of stalking and bellowing as earlier Hollywood potentates had done, was extremely disconcerting. Worse still, he was accompanied by the taciturn Gary Kurtz, whose gifts are emphatically not in the field of public relations. The cameraman, Gil Taylor, a veteran of *Dr Strangelove* and *A Hard Day's Night*, resented their attitudes, and especially George's habit of moving the lights around without asking him, and his irritation was soon picked up by the rest of the technicians.

Nor was the potentially explosive situation calmed by union rules. The Association of Cinema and Television Technicians (ACTT) is an extremely privileged billet, with the clout to extract handsome salaries and impose draconian limitations, and the one it chose to impose here was the one Lucas least wanted: a 5.30 p.m. deadline. That was quitting time, no matter how near a scene was to completion and, until he adapted his schedules by putting the simpler shots near the end of the day, the film fell further and further behind.

This in turn increased the pressure on the young director, who once again fell victim to psychosomatic headaches and stomach pains. 'I forget how impossible making movies really is. I get so depressed but I guess I'll get through it somehow,' he wrote to Marcia, as things slipped inexorably from bad to worse. Frantically he deployed a second unit, cycling between sound stages in order to beat the deadline and maintain every possible ounce of his precious control. 'I cared about every single detail,' he moaned. 'I'd never done a picture that went on for so long. It was very trying.'

One of the things that saved him was the unflagging support of the actors, led by the courteous Sir Alec Guinness and Harrison Ford. Initially there had been trouble with Guinness who'd nearly walked off the picture when he learned of his impending death midway through *Star Wars*, but the quarrel had been patched up and he, unlike his compatriots in the crew, gave his all to the young American, although he hadn't much of a clue what he was supposed to be doing. Even on his lips, the dialogue sounds impossibly stilted, yet he kept faith throughout.

He was treated with deference due to a grand old man and invariably addressed as 'Sir Alec'. 'Was that out of respect or did he insist on it?' Harrison has been asked. 'Let's just say he prefers it,' the actor replied. Such tact stood him and Lucas in good stead. As the oldest of the American contingent, and the only one who'd had feature experience (Fisher's was limited to a single day on Warren Beatty's *Shampoo*), he was the natural leader and his relationship with Fisher and Hamill developed in much the same brotherly way as it does in the film.

He also knew about the Lucas method after *Graffiti*, and so was able to reassure the younger players that, despite appearances, it worked. Naturally they were disconcerted by a director who never spoke to them unless forced to, a situation that they came across first at a Chinese lunch just before work at Elstree began. It was supposed to be a celebration, but silence reigned supreme, a scenario they'd become all too familiar with as the weeks passed.

However, on the ever-changing sets, where painting finished on a section one minute and the cameras focused on it the next, they learned that working with Lucas had definite compensations. Instead of sticking the actors up against the walls and shooting them, as Coppola had accused him of in *American Graffiti*, the director allowed four or five takes per scene, and they were long ones, designed to allow the performers to develop their own ideas.

Neither dialogue nor situation was sacred, though George, mindful of time and money, wouldn't allow cameras to turn on adjustments he didn't believe would work. When, as often happened, he wasn't certain what *would* work, his suggestions suffered from lack of precision. 'Faster and more intense' were words heard frequently after a long and complex take which he felt lacked that indefinable something he wanted. Or he might say, 'Let's do it again, only this time do it better.'

'Very little time was wasted,' says Harrison, still being tactful. 'George didn't have an authoritarian attitude, like many direc-

The face that attracted Columbia's talent scouts: Harrison Ford poses for a studio portrait when making *Dead Heat on a Merry-go-round* (1966).

Dashing drag racer, Bob Falfa (Harrison Ford), and his girlfriend
(Debralee Scott) look for action in *American Graffiti* (1973).

Lined up for the kill with the Concho County Comanches in *Journey to Shiloh* (1967): (left to right) Don Stroud, Michael Sarrazin, Michael Vincent, James Caan, Paul Petersen, Michael Burns and Harrison Ford.

The film that hit the jackpot. Harrison Ford as Han Solo in *Star Wars*.

Back in Los Angeles, Harrison Ford obligingly signs photographs of himself at a party in Chasens, one of Hollywood's more celebrated watering holes.

tors. He didn't say, "Kid, I've been in this business twenty-five years, trust me." He was different. He knew the movie was based so strongly on the relationship among the three of us that he encouraged our contributions.'

For Harrison, so long a victim of Hollywood's baser ways, this was luxury indeed. '*Star Wars* was the first time in my whole career that I had a character where I could take space, not just fill it any more. George gave me a lot of freedom to change little parts of the dialogue that weren't comfortable. At times I threatened to tie him up and make him repeat his own lines, but I was wrong because in the end it worked. I really like working with him.'

Harrison's favourite example of collaboration is his dashing rescue of Princess Leia from the prison block of the Death Star. Solo and Skywalker wear the uniforms of the Imperial Storm Troopers and attract the attention of the officer in charge of the detention block. At this point, Solo has to convince the man that all is well. When he fails to stop the unseen official's interrogation, he fires his blaster into the control panel with nervous desperation cleverly combined with humour. 'We did it in one take and I never learned the dialogue for it because I wanted to show how desperate I was. I told George I wanted to do it all the way through the first time. I said, "Stop me if I'm really bad," but he didn't.'

Back in California, *Star Wars'* problems were increasing and multiplying, both at ILM, where Dykstra was still experimenting with a camera that would move round a model while keeping it constantly in focus, and at Twentieth-Century Fox, where Alan Ladd, Jr and his colleagues were suffering from ever higher blood pressure. The situation wasn't helped by Ladd's flying visit to London in May when he saw forty nearly disastrous minutes of badly edited footage. The studio had already abandoned their proposed Christmas, 1976 release date, and settled for the summer of 1977, but even that required a rough cut to be ready by the end of the year.

With the special effects techniques still elusive and the delays at Elstree, that seemed increasingly unlikely and Ladd was sorely tempted to pull the plug on the production there and then. Only his faith in Lucas dissuaded him, but by July, with *Star Wars* five weeks over schedule, considerably over budget and in need of two further weeks to reach completion, he felt he had no choice. 'You have three days to wrap it up,' he told the demented director. By hiring three crews, Lucas somehow contrived to put the remaining key scenes in the can, but the premature cut-off didn't help his paranoia. Once again he was convinced he'd been stabbed in the back.

Ford returned to his home in Los Angeles to await results, but for Lucas the race went on. He re-shot some of the Tunisian material in Death Valley in California, dispatched a second unit to the Mayan ruins at Tikal in Guatemala for the jungle scenes, and oversaw the special effects, visibly innovative at last, the dubbing of Chewbacca, Darth Vader and R2-D2 and the recording of John Williams' score by the London Symphony Orchestra.

By January, 1977 he had his rough cut ready to show firstly to some of the staff at Fox and secondly to a group of his own friends which included Steven Spielberg and Brian De Palma. Ironically it was the studio employees who were bowled over, the cognoscenti who looked on George with puzzled concern, especially De Palma who led the ribbing about 'Let the Force Be With You' and suggested re-writes all round. Only Spielberg thought differently. *Jaws*, his first record breaker, had put him at the top of the Hollywood class of 1975 and *Close Encounters of the Third Kind* was a potential rival for *Star Wars* in 1977, but he proved he knew a good thing when he saw it by supporting Lucas.

Next in line were the Fox executives, some of whom were invited to see *Star Wars* on 1 May 1977 at the Northpoint Theater in San Francisco, the same venue in which Coppola had had his classic confrontation with Ned Tanen after the first showing of *American Graffiti*. Once again it was a Sunday morning and the audience included a cross section of friends and relations. As with *Graffiti*, the reaction was hysterically favourable which gave Lucas the courage to face the screening for the Fox board of directors. Predictably, most of them hated the film without reservation.

Harrison Ford's opportunity came at a cast and crew screening at the headquarters of the Academy of Motion Picture Arts and Science in Beverly Hills on 21 May. The starting time was 10 a.m., and from the instant those famous rolling credits came up, the audience was ecstatic. For most of them, including Ford, this was the supreme moment, the culmination of those dark and difficult days in a foreign land, the realisation of a vision that made it all worth while. 'A long time ago, on a galaxy far, far away,' Lucas had written, and on this bright Californian morning everyone associated with the fantasy triggered by those emotive words recognised how strongly they were caught up in his dream. And if they were, why not others?

On this point, however, both Lucas and Ford were cautious. 'I knew the film worked,' said George, 'but I had no idea of what was going to happen.'

'I didn't recognise that we were into a winner,' Ford agreed. 'As I'd spent the previous seven years as a carpenter, I had no idea what success looked like. I was paid less for *Star Wars* than I was earning as a carpenter. I don't think I'd have recognised success if it had come up and bopped me on the head.'

In the corridors of Hollywood the arguments raged on. Ned Tanen, anxious no doubt about his rejection of the project, had a belated and horrible premonition that it would be the 'biggest hit ever made'. Fox's Alan Ladd, Jr agreed with this assessment but his colleagues were much less certain. Their market research showed that women didn't care for films with 'Wars' in the title and that no one had much time for robots and associated speechless hairy beasts like Wookies, nor indeed for science fiction of any kind. Lucas had begged the studio to call *Star Wars* a space fantasy, not a sci fi picture but, in need of a category and unable to think of another one, they hadn't obliged, with the result that cinema managers refused to guarantee more than a total of $1.5 million for the right to play it (a major movie could have expected a $10 million guarantee in 1977).

The moment of truth, for Lucas at least, came on Wednesday, 25 May when *Star Wars* featured in thirty-two cinemas across America. The doors opened in New York and Los Angeles at 8 a.m. for the 10 a.m. screening, generating queues around the block in both cities. George, still mixing the foreign language versions of his film, only emerged that evening to meet Marcia for a meal before returning for yet another night shift. According to Dale Pollock in *Skywalking*, they went to the Hamburger Hamlet, opposite Mann's Chinese Theater in Hollywood, unaware that *Star Wars* was playing right across the street. When they found their way barred by traffic jams and crowds they pondered as to what was up.

'We rounded the corner and saw *Star Wars* in giant block letters on the theatre marquee,' says Lucas. 'We just fell on the floor and I said, "I don't believe this." We sat there in the Hamburger Hamlet and watched the giant crowd out there, and then I went back and mixed all night. It wasn't excitement, it was amazement. I felt it was some kind of aberration.'

Star Wars grossed $3.5 million in nine days and recouped all its costs within two months, but this was the tip of the iceberg and its connections were only just beginning to be aware of how huge a hit they had on their hands. In the industry, it is still seen as a 'sleeper', a film that built steadily after its opening, then took off after it was hailed as a phenomenon in headlines across the country. The critics, generally cynical about gee-whiz adventures, saw it for what it is, a cunningly devised variation of the old 'A man's gotta do what a man's gotta do' chestnut – i.e. go adventuring to prove the worth of the individual and attain maturity by conquering evil.

Combine this with special effects that eventually proved sensational and you reach the fifteen to twenty-year-olds who make the bulk of the movie-going audience. And not only reach them but bowl them over so they come back again and again. 'It is enormous and exhilarating fun,' wrote Derek Malcolm in the *Guardian*, when the film opened in London on Boxing Day in 1977, 'for those who are prepared to settle down in their seats and let it all wash over them. Which, I firmly believe with the extra benefit of hindsight, is more-or-less exactly what the vast majority of the cinema going public want just now. Last year it was *Jaws*, which gave us more dangerous frissons and not long before that it was *The Exorcist*, with enough green slime to give us all nightmares. Inevitably 1977 was going to be the year of safer pleasures. *Star Wars*, let me tell you, wasn't given its U certificate for nothing. The only exclamation the producers want from you is "Wow!".'

After mentioning the Force, he continued, 'There are two funny (no, quite funny) robots, See-Threepio and Artoo-Detoo, an ace pilot (Harrison Ford) who represents our disbelief by proving a sceptic, a "walking carpet" who looks as if he's come straight out of a neolithic pantomime and an assortment of villains so unterrifying that it looks as if you'd only have to pinch them to produce a fit of giggles.'

Finally he commented on George Lucas's sources, 'These are legion. There is a space-age Western saloon, there's swash-buckling with laser beams, there's slapstick which reminds one of Laurel and Hardy and sentiment that reeks of *The Wizard of Oz*. There are lines which are almost, if not quite, taken from old movies, and direct allusions whipped from everything from *The Searchers* to *The Triumph of the Will*. It's an incredibly knowing movie. But the filching is so affectionate that you can't resent it. Whatever else you think about *Star Wars*, you can't call it the height of originality. The entirely mindless could go and see it with pleasure. But it plays enough games to satisfy the most sophisticated.'

Malcolm's review was typical of the more erudite newspapers. The scene from *The Searchers* he refers to is the one when Luke returns to his homestead to find that his uncle and aunt have been murdered by the Imperial Forces, while *The Triumph of The Will*, Leni Riefenstahl's incomparable documentary about Nazism, inspired Lucas's final victory parades. 'Was this a proper model for a Happy Ending?' some doubters asked. Others noted that Grand Moff Tarkin lives in a grey-green world, surrounded by cohorts in grey-green uniform, and that Darth Vader's forces could be seen as Storm Troopers. All this resulted in a certain amount of ideological confusion, especially among continental reviewers: French leftists described *Star Wars* as Fascist, while Italian right wingers diagnosed Communist leanings.

Probably Lucas himself came nearest to the truth when he admitted throwing the encyclopaedia at his film in order to make it into all things for all men. Religion in the form of the ethereal Force, self sacrifice, action, loyalty, an acceptance of a higher destiny, a touch of romance, they're all included. 'I mean, there's a reason this film is so popular. It's not that I'm giving out propaganda nobody wants to hear. I realised that for a film to have an impact, you have to come at things sideways. Head-on may be the attractive way to do it, but it doesn't have any effect unless you're very lucky. When you're going sideways, you can influence things more subtly because you're not attacking them.'

What was good for *Star Wars* was good for Harrison Ford,

but he didn't get anything much in the way of individual mentions for his part in the action. He came second in the cast list to Mark Hamill, but in general the three leading characters were lumped together, often disparagingly, with any plaudits available for human beings going to Sir Alec Guinness. Richard Roud's comments, also in the *Guardian*, summed up the general mood in this respect. 'There are so many things this film does not have, things that usually go to make the success of a film. It is not well acted (with the possible exception of Alec Guinness); its story is muddled and more than a little illogical. It is not – nor did it presumably want to be – particularly well-written. The special effects and the sets are good, but nothing compared with those in Kubrick's *2001*. There is hardly any violence, there is no sex at all, and its heroine looks like an ageing Jewish Shirley Temple.'

Lucas, however, has stood up for his performers. 'Everybody says, "Oh, the acting in George's films is terrible," but I don't believe that. I think it's very good, and one of the reasons for my films' success. I haven't done anything to make the actors wonderful, but they make the story work, they make the film popular.'

Be that as it may, Ford, Fisher and Hamill undoubtedly had popularity thrust upon them as *Star Wars* mania swept the world. It was at this point that the strength of Lucas's strategy at Fox became clear, because the film was accompanied wherever it went by an extraordinary range of goods. He may, as he claims, have originally envisaged a few wind-up R2-D2s, but the marketing men he employed to oversee this side of his business had done their jobs well. Manufacturers had to get licences to produce *Star Wars* spin-offs, and although there was a certain amount of ideological control – no sweet cigarettes, for example, and R2-D2 and C-3PO were not allowed to endorse alcohol or appear in girlie magazines – the scope was enormous, and artfully exploited.

Millions of *Star Wars* action figures were sold, not only the robots but the Fords and Fishers and Hamills who also found their distorted features on everything from T-shirts to bars of soap to jigsaw puzzles. Kids sucked intergalactic bubble gum as they read the novelisation of the *Star Wars* screenplay prepared by the young sci fi writer Alan Dean Foster, and the book climbed rapidly to the number one spot on the paperback best seller list. Bath time meant Darth Vader bubble bath and the satisfaction of unscrewing the villain's head to release the precious foam.

Painful imitations of Anthony Daniels' prissy English accent came from behind C-3PO masks from Minneapolis to Miami and hot drinks were poured from squat R2-D2 thermoses. The two-record album made more money than any score from a film that was not a musical in history, some $16 million, or getting on for twice the cost of the film itself. There were *Star Wars* ice creams, *Star Wars* breakfast cereals, *Star Wars* blasters – Lucas specified they should be made of rubber so as to minimise the damage – black digital watches, Citizens Band radio sets and, for richer fans, personalised jets that rose several hundred feet into the air.

Han Solo acquired a future quite different from the one he'd act out in *The Empire Strikes Back* and *The Return of the Jedi*, in a series of novels by one Brian Daley: *Han Solo at Stars' End*, *Han Solo and the Lost Legacy* and *Han Solo's Revenge*. He also appeared in a variety of comic strip guises, thanks to Marvel Comics. Blanket saturation was the order of the day, and how the public loved it.

By the end of August 1977, *Star Wars* had reached the magic $100 million quicker than any other picture, and it went on climbing, with re-issues in 1978, which reaped $46 million in five weeks, and in 1979, when the prize was $23 million in three weeks. In all, the film earned something over $525 million in ticket sales, which gave Fox $262 million. As for Lucas, once the studio's heavy costs had been deducted, he was left with a mere $40 million, later halved by taxation.

For Harrison Ford the success of *Star Wars* meant that he was a full time professional again. The fact that he never returned to Sally Kellerman's garage to pick up his tools is symbolic of his change of status. He knew he wouldn't need them, that he'd be offered more roles even before the returns came in. Ten months passed between the end of shooting and the première, but he made no more cabinets, even though the film hadn't had the chance to make him remotely rich, let alone famous. When it did break, the fame came first, and Harrison was quick to realise that maintaining the anonymity which became precious overnight would require a studied low profile. Now that he could call himself an actor, he would put his skills to private as well as public use.

'Fortunately I didn't have a unique physiognomy as Carrie and Mark do, so I'm much less recognised in the streets, about which I'm very happy,' he said at the time, setting the tone of many future comments. 'That could get heavy. It happens infrequently enough and people are usually very nice, because the film is very broadly accepted. That's a pleasure, but when they know where we're going to be and they're sitting outside the hotel asking for autographs, it can be a drag.

'Of course I didn't take the success of *Star Wars* personally, and in any case I've always made quite an effort to change my appearance from one film to another. In *The Conversation*, I made my character gay so no one would recognise me from *American Graffiti*. I know that if I walk down the street looking like Han Solo and acting like him, which I am very unlikely to do, then I'm going to be recognised. From the start, I decided I wouldn't do the things stars do to make sure they are spotted.'

Instead he lived quietly with Mary and their two young sons, Ben and Willard, in the remodelled house in the Hollywood Bowl and waited patiently for the riches to come to him. Lucas was in no way obliged to hand out his *Star Wars* profits except to Gary Kurtz and Sir Alec Guinness who received 5 per cent and 2 per cent respectively under their contracts. However, he was generous enough to show his appreciation to those who'd had faith in him. He gave shares in the profits to Bill Huyck and Gloria Katz for their unpaid labour on his screenplay, and to the composer, John Williams, the supervisor at Industrial Light and Magic, Jim Nelson, and his attorney, Tom Pollock. He also handed out cash bonuses, eighteen in all, worth between $2,000 and $10,000, to people who'd worked on the film, plus percentages in the *Star Wars* merchandising profits, valued at $50,000 each, to the men who'd designed the film. Left out in the cold was John Dykstra, who retaliated by taking over the ILM building to start his own company in, then used it to recreate his *Star Wars* special effects for the tatty rip off, *Battlestar Galactica*.

Lucas also wanted to reward his actors. He gave Harrison Ford, Carrie Fisher and Mark Hamill two percentage points to share between them which made them extremely happy. Others were less amused with their cash bonuses, notably Anthony Daniels who refused his. His initial liking for Lucas had been dissipated during filming when he discovered that the American wanted an employee, not a pal. Nor had he appreciated the lack of personal recognition given to a man behind a mask when the reviews came out. Barred from making public appearances by Lucas's wish to preserve the illusion of the robots, he hadn't been able to cash in on the publicity bonanza. Now he felt the proceeds were passing him by as well.

Predictably, when it came to prizes all the actors missed out. *Star Wars* picked up ten Oscar nominations for the 1978 Awards, but none of them were for performances. Lucas was nominated for Best Direction and Best Screenplay, and *Star Wars* for Best Film, but in the event these accolades went to Woody Allen and *Annie Hall*. On the technical side, *Star Wars* collected five statuettes: John Williams for the musical score; John Mollo for the costumes; John Barry for the art direction; John Dykstra and his ILM team for the special effects; and, most importantly in the Lucas household, Marcia (with Richard Chew and Paul Hirsch) for Best Editing.

Lucas apparently revelled in his wife's success, in the belief that for her it was a childhood dream come true, and wrote off his own failure on the grounds that he didn't really care very much. If this sounds over-saintly, it is worth reflecting that he now had what he'd always wanted, the freedom to control his own destiny. He had the money in the bank to draw up plans for the Skywalker Ranch where film makers could meet in a sympathetic environment outside San Francisco, far removed from the hell-hole of Hollywood, and the clout to put his sequels on the screen. With all that, did he need an Oscar? Realistically, he knew that the answer was no.

Harrison Ford didn't need one either. He used his percentage to buy a new family home in a canyon above Beverly Hills, and did it up while he waited a little longer. He'd had a lot of practice so the re-fitting came more easily this time. As he knew there would be two sequels to *Star Wars*, his long term financial worries

71

were at an end. 'Money had never meant very much to me,' he commented, 'but suddenly having it made it possible to live in a larger house and equip a new workshop on the premises. I don't think success changed me. I don't go to parties and I've never been involved in the Hollywood scene. Maybe if I had socialised a bit more, success would have come much sooner, because you have to know the right people. But by some irony, all the right people – like George Lucas and Francis Coppola – knew me, and I didn't even have to hustle for their attention.'

However, they weren't bosom buddies when the cameras weren't turning. Coppola, with his flashy lifestyle, represented values that Harrison rejected while Lucas, verging on the humourless and extremely obsessive, was hardly a congenial companion for a night on the town, let alone an evening round the hearth. 'I enjoy working with George,' says Harrison, 'and I presume he doesn't hate working with me. I consider him a friend, but we don't spend a great deal of time together when we're not working.'

Once the move was completed, the actor sat back for a while to consider his future. At last he'd got lucky, he was hot. The greatest mistake would be to fritter away his good fortune without building a solid career platform. 'When I knew *Star Wars* was going to be a big commercial success, that a lot of people were going to see it, the first and most important thing that occurred to me was to get something on film that would be a total contrast. I knew how Hollywood would react to that kind of film. They'd typecast me and then it would be impossible to break the mould. I believed I was capable of playing a lot of different types of characters and I was determined to take advantage of the offers being in *Star Wars* gave me. I was really lucky to have *Star Wars* as part of my life, but it was critical for me to look beyond it.'

And he did. Carrie Fisher appeared briefly in *I Want To Hold Your Hand* and John Huston's *Wise Blood* between *Star Wars* and *The Empire Strikes Back*, while Mark Hamill opted for near nonentity in *Corvette Summer* and Sam Fuller's *The Big Red One*. Meanwhile Ford laid his head on the block on five occasions, only to have it chopped off on four of them. Full-time actor he might be, but putting his name in lights would take a little longer.

7 Swings and Roundabouts

If HARRISON FORD had been gazing perceptively into his crystal ball, he would probably have realised that *Heroes*, a vehicle designed specifically to put Henry Winkler on the wide screen, was a chronic non-starter. All he saw, however, was Kenny Boyd, a mid-western farm boy who was light years away from Han Solo and an immediate pay cheque before the *Star Wars* golden goose came home to roost. Impulsively he said yes.

Henry Winkler had made himself into a household name on networked television as Arthur Fonzerelli, also known as The Fonz or Fonzie, in the vastly popular *Happy Days*, coincidentally a series that took its inspiration from *American Graffiti*. By recalling the good old days of freedom and irresponsibility, it appealed basically to young audiences but Winkler, like Ford, was looking for new fields to conquer.

He found them, as so many did in the late seventies aftermath of the Vietnam War, in the veterans market, in the person of Jack Dunne, still scarred – and belligerent with it – by his South-East Asian experiences four years after his discharge. The ironically titled *Heroes* takes him from New York via a veterans hospital to Eureka, California where he plans to start a worm farm with some former war buddies. En route, he falls in with Sally Field as a bride on the brink and persuades her to transfer her affections to him. During their overland journey, they visit Kenny Boyd's farm, a broken down place whose owner bears the indefinable stamp of failure, whether he's drag racing – yes, again – or attempting to make a living.

Kenny's part in *Heroes* begins and ends with this overnight stay in his dilapidated motor home. He is merely the most important of Jack's pals, one of three who will never join him on the worm farm, but the one who is alive and available to

discuss the wartime experiences that make them the outcasts
they are, during a long night of sorrow-raking. Jack's road to
self-realisation is the basis for one of those road movies that is
as old as Hollywood, and it is as deeply unoriginal and derivative
as that suggests.

Frank Rich, writing in *Time* when the film was released in
November, 1977, lists *It Happened One Night, Morgan – A
Suitable Case For Treatment* and *Five Easy Pieces* as obvious
sources, and criticises the director, Jeremy Paul Kagan, and the
writer, James Carabatsos, for their lack of insight, streams of
platitudes and the almost uninterrupted boredom they inflict on
their patrons. 'This film is as flat as an average made-for-TV
movie, though considerably more pretentious than most. Its
final ten minutes are a minor scandal. After wasting an audience's
time for two hours, the movie unleashes a gory cathartic fantasy
sequence in which the hero relives the horrors of his Vietnam
combat.

'The ruse does not work,' he continues, 'for at the end of
Heroes one does not pity the Vietnam dead so much as the
casualties in the movie's cast. Chief among them is Sally Field,
the film's love interest and an actress of considerable skill. In
Heroes, she plays a young woman who is also on the road to
find herself, but her character is so clumsily defined that she is
a blur upon the screen. Harrison Ford, the witty Han Solo of
Star Wars, fares no better – but such is Kagan's touch that *Heroes*
could probably reduce Robert Redford to the stature of Troy
Donahue.'

Rich set the tone for assessments in other parts of the world,
including the comment 'just plain awful' from Leslie Halliwell,
but Ford had no regrets. 'It was a good part, but Henry Winkler
was the real star of the film. I did it for short money. My part
wasn't big and I wasn't paid big money. Nor did it tell the
whole truth. The only kind of belief I can have is in something
that's well rounded, and this was not that kind of role. But I
had the chance to create something completely different from
Solo. Of course it wasn't as successful as *Star Wars*, but I knew
it would be quickly released and it'd give proof of my versatility.
Not a lot of people saw it, but the people in the business did,
and that was important to me.'

What they saw was a thoroughly researched Missouri farm

boy wielding an axe and driving an ancient souped-up racing car. *Heroes* is notable in that it is the first time Harrison was able to study the way in which his character would behave and use it to underpin his performance. The mid-western farm boy was switched to Missouri just ten days before shooting started, but Ford, whose Chicago accent would have suited the original scenario just fine, proved himself equal to the new dimension, such as it was.

'I got on an airplane and went to Missouri and bummed around for three days taping conversations. I went and met the actual type I was going to play – a guy interested in cars. I went into an auto-part store and told them I was a writer because if you tell them you're an actor, you spend the rest of the day talking about movies, and it puts a certain distance between them and you.'

Harrison Ford got third billing on *Heroes*, but it was back down the order for his next picture, the only one that could conceivably be considered career-enhancing between *Star Wars* and *The Empire Strikes Back*. Once again the caller was the faithful Fred Roos, currently engaged in co-producing and casting *Apocalypse Now* for Francis Coppola. Would Harrison play Colonel G. Lucas? Yes, he would, and in the name there hangs a tale.

It begins with the setting up of Zoetrope in the late sixties as a haven of independence for young film makers, with funds raised by Coppola from the sale of his own house. One of his first protégés was George Lucas, who'd worked for him on *The Rain People* in Nebraska as a production assistant. Now he was trying to set up his first feature under Coppola's patronage. Initially he submitted two ideas: *THX 1138* and a film based on Conrad's *Heart of Darkness* about the war in Vietnam which he and his fellow student, John Milius, had thought up when they were at the University of Southern California.

When Coppola approached Warner Bros with *THX*, he threw in *Apocalypse Now*, as they'd called their project, for good measure without Lucas's specific permission. George would receive $15,000 to write and direct his sci fi picture, with the promise of $25,000 for the war movie. During *American Graffiti*, *Apocalypse Now* stayed on the back burner, slated as a Lucas idea, but legally owned by Zoetrope since Warners had failed to take up their option.

With *The Godfather* and *Graffiti* behind them, both men were rich and famous when the subject came up again in 1973, but their relationship was nowhere near so close, due to disagreements as to the division of the *Graffiti* spoils. Nevertheless, Lucas still wanted to make *Apocalypse Now* and enlisted John Milius to write the script while Gary Kurtz scouted for locations in the Far East. The deal between Lucas and Coppola stipulated 25 per cent of the profits each, but Lucas would have had to split his portion with Milius, and so decided to go ahead with *Star Wars* instead.

Another year passed, and this time it was Coppola who raised the question of the Vietnam drama. It would, he thought, be a good idea to make it immediately and release it to coincide with the American Bicentennial in 1976. He offered George the original fee to write and direct it, whereas Fox had just given him six times as much for *Star Wars*. Lucas refused indignantly and Coppola ran out of patience. 'It was my picture, but I didn't have any control of the situation,' Lucas moaned in *Skywalking*. 'I don't hold anything against Francis though. He had every right to make it; he owned it. But I was quite upset at the time.'

Perhaps calling Harrison Ford's character Col. G. Lucas was supposed to propitiate the gods after this piece of moral piracy. If so, it didn't work, for *Apocalypse Now* threatened to engulf all those who were associated with it, with the exception of Harrison himself whose nine day stint in the Philippines, doubling for Vietnam, was trouble free. 'It wasn't a big role for me, just a quirky cameo as a US Army Intelligence Colonel. I had my hair cut short and presented another image, Vietnam style. When George saw the footage I'd done, he didn't recognise me until halfway through the scene, despite his name on my uniform. I hope I can maintain that anonymity because I think it's important, considering the incredible occurrence of the image of *Star Wars*.'

Most of Col. Lucas's scenes were shared with Martin Sheen as Willard, the hapless Captain with the shady Central Intelligence Agency background who is dispatched up river to Cambodia to dispose of Brando's maverick Green Beret Colonel Kurtz. The estimable Sheen was selected only after Steve McQueen,

Robert Redford, Al Pacino, Jack Nicholson, James Caan and Gene Hackman had turned Willard down, and his brave decision to go ahead was ill-rewarded by a near fatal heart attack in the depths of the Philippine jungle. Typhoon Olga didn't help either and *Apocalypse Now*, which didn't start shooting until March, 1976, the same month as *Star Wars*, eventually took two years to complete, at a cost of $36 million.

Coppola, bearded and flamboyant, managed to find parallels in the making of the film and its subject matter. 'We went into the jungle with too much money, too much expensive equipment, too little understanding of the conditions, and the jungle swallowed us up. What happened to the United States in Vietnam is what happened to us when we shot the movie in the Philippines.'

Harrison Ford may have been one of the few people to enjoy this experience, and there is no doubting his enthusiasm for his second Coppola project. 'Francis really is delightful,' he stated firmly. 'He allows you enormous freedom, just as George does. He lets you make a choice and then moves everything to support you, to make it work for you.'

Another cause for pleasure was Mr Coppola's pretty young assistant in these dark, steamy, difficult conditions. Her name was Melissa Mathison and their meeting would prove to be the final nail in the coffin of a twelve-year marriage that was winding down, much as he regretted it after Mary's conspicuous loyalty through the lean years.

'It was the cinema that separated us,' he told J. V. Cotton in *Ciné-Revue* in 1981, 'and I will never forgive it for that. That's why I'm ready to abandon everything in order to save what remains of my happiness: my two sons. Mary proved her love for me on many occasions. Each weekend, she'd bring the children to me at the ends of the earth, whether I was in Yugoslavia, London or Thailand. She never reproached me, but it became impossible because I knew I couldn't go backwards, couldn't break the contracts I'd signed to make other films, like the sequel to *Star Wars*. Mary was often far away and our love tore apart little by little.'

Some of the weekends in London and all those in Yugoslavia he refers to took place during his next film, *Force 10 From*

Navarone, a sequel to the highly praised *Guns of Navarone*, but made eighteen years later. It was the sort of desperate attempt to cash in on a decent film that should never have got off the ground. Its complicated credits reveal its mongrel origins, and the diverse provenance of the $10.5 million it would never make back, only too clearly. 'An Oliver A. Ungar presentation of a Guy Hamilton Production, a Navarone Productions Limited film for Produktion Navarone Mond Film Atypische Gesellschaft 1976' suggests the start of something bad. Rightly, as it turned out.

'Second Guns', as it came to be known with varying degrees of scorn and derision while it was being made, examines the further wartime experiences of Major Mallory and Sergeant Miller, respectively the action man and the cynic, and originally played by Gregory Peck and David Niven. As no plot time had passed, they had to be recast with younger men. Mallory was turned into a Brit by the late Robert Shaw, and Edward Fox, fresh from his first starring part in the title role of *The Day Of The Jackal*, made a suitable case of substitution for the wry and elegant Niven. That left a gap which needs must be filled by a tall handsome American so a Lt.-Col. Mike Barnsby was created to lead his US Rangers into battle.

Who better to play him, thought Oliver A. Ungar, a producer in the old fashioned mould, than Harrison 'Han Solo' Ford? It was a piece of casting in tune with the film's ragbag policy of gathering talent from recent box office draws, and Ford was joined by Carl Weathers, the black World Heavyweight Boxing Champion from *Rocky*, and Barbara Bach, a sultry beauty of little talent who was the current Bond bombshell. The director, Guy Hamilton, tall, suave and diplomatic, was also a refugee from Bond after four 007s in a row. He'd recently turned down *Superman*, which perhaps he would not have done had he known the fate that awaited *Force 10 From Navarone*.

'Second Guns' was made partly in Yugoslavia where its action was set, partly in Jersey substituting for Yugoslavia when gales and snow wiped out the January shoot in Rijeka, and partly in London. The story had to be tied to the original, which subjected it to constrictions beyond its control. It involves Mallory and Miller on a mission to destroy Nicolai Lescovar (Franco Nero), the Nazi spy who sabotaged their original derring-do. British

Intelligence suggests that he is now posing as a Yugoslavian resistance fighter and the War Office has no hesitation in returning its wounded heroes to the fray.

In the thick of it they meet Ford's Barnsby in an atmosphere of mutual suspicion, not least because the gallant Lieutenant-Colonel had hijacked an RAF plane to transport his commando unit to the field of operations. Thrown uneasily together, Mallory and Miller keep mum about their project and Barnsby reciprocates in kind.

Before the film was released, Ford was optimistic about its prospects. 'Mike Barnsby was one of those macho, tough guy parts that everyone thought I should be doing. He's a man of real capacity. He flies, he fights, he's got brains, but everything works against him. At the last minute, he gets the Robert Shaw and Edward Fox characters tacked onto his mission, so there's a lot of adversity in the relationship between them, until he begins to need them and they begin to need him – a nice kind of continuity of cross purposes that becomes established and finally resolved. An interesting character. I think it'll work.'

How wrong he was. *Force 10 From Navarone* was his first part in a traditional Hollywood-style movie, his first participation in a stars-for-stars'-sake line up. He may have come second in it, after Shaw, but he believed that being there at all would help his career. As *Star Wars* had been revealed in all its glory by the time he put on the uniform of Mike Barnsby, he was almost certainly incorrect, but that was his thinking at the time.

'It's fun to do supporting roles, because they're good character pieces,' he explained. 'The problem is that they don't usually write character parts as the leads in the movies. Unfortunately, you can't always play the supporting roles because of the complicated vision that people in this industry have. Hollywood only really takes notice when you're being paid the money and given the billing that a "lead actor" gets. That's why *Force Ten* was important for me to do. It was a package of big names that included me. It upped my price, gave me a certain value. If you're in the high-priced category, you've got a head start.'

Despite the frenzy of bridge blowing, dam busting, sheltering from aerial bombardment and traitor-shooting he was subjected to, Harrison had some good times on the picture, not least with Edward Fox who was reading everything he could find on

Edward VIII and Wallis Simpson in preparation for the Thames Television series, *Edward and Mrs Simpson*. What more pleasant way to while away a Sunday lunch in a comfortable hotel than by speculating on the true nature of that controversial lady and discussing the life and times of the king who barely was, with the sophisticated, obsessive Fox?

The illusion of living graciously while working gainfully was smashed for ever when *Force 10 From Navarone* was released in Britain for Christmas, 1978 to howls of rage. 'Oh, What A War Crime' screamed the *Daily Mirror* in a banner headline. 'Army Games with the goons of Navarone . . .' the text continued, and that was just the beginning of a litany of well justified complaint which the paper's anonymous correspondent wrapped up like this: 'If the industry can't make better war films than this, it is time a truce was called.'

Classier publications were quick to agree. 'It is appalling,' said Nigel Andrews of the *Financial Times*. 'Harrison Ford, Edward Fox, Franco Nero and the late Robert Shaw swashbuckle through this tale of an allied sabotage attempt in Yugoslavia in 1943 as if wading through mud.' Alexander Walker of the *Evening Standard* added another perspective: 'Their task: to blow up an important bridge. Their strategy: to make friends and drink, then fight the Germans. What follows barely admits a moment's credibility. The story is the kind that Alistair MacLean gets away with on the printed page, where the characters turn out to be not who you think they are three times over in as many paragraphs. On screen, it just sounds like a bit of lazy improvising.'

Given the chance to face up to this barrage of criticism, Harrison Ford excused himself to Alan Mackenzie in the officialese he resorts to in any emergency. '*Force 10 From Navarone* was an attempt, in a way, to objectify the sucess of *Star Wars*. It wasn't a personal success for me. It was George's movie, his success. Nonetheless, I wanted to take advantage of the chance to work. And it was a job I did for the money. And I was lost, because I didn't know what the story was about. I didn't have anything to act. There was no reason for my character being there. I had no part of the story that was important to tell. I was promised a rewrite, but it didn't come through. I had a hard time taking the stage with the bull that I was supposed to be doing. I can't do that, and I won't ever do that again. It wasn't a bad film. There were honest people involved in making an honest effort. But it wasn't the right thing for me to do.'

As an example of muddled thinking, this statement can have few equals, but Harrison abandoned neither the uniform nor the Second World War for his next project, and proved comprehensively, with the worst film of his short career, that he wasn't even learning from his mistakes. *Hanover Street* gave Ford fans their first sighting of their hero in his underpants, but the film was so terrible that very few availed themselves of the opportunity. However, it was the prospect of stripping off that tempted him when Kris Kristofferson wisely drew back from the brink and left the British project without a leading man at the last minute. Obligingly Harrison, who had intended to try to repair his marriage while restoring his new house, flew the Atlantic once again.

'I'd done *American Graffiti*, *Star Wars*, *Heroes* and *Force 10 From Navarone* and I hadn't yet got to kiss a girl on the screen. The characters I played were totally sexless, and here was a movie that was being touted as a love story. That was a clear, obvious reason for doing it so I agreed, expecting that the script which I didn't have total faith in would be changed as we went along. Well, it wasn't so and the making of the film was not a happy experience for me.'

The girl he got to kiss, Lesley-Anne Down, so perfectly cast as Miss Georgina in *Upstairs, Downstairs* and so unconvincing in other films, didn't help. She plays a nurse in bomb-torn London to Ford's B-52 bomber pilot, with Christopher Plummer as her cuckolded husband. The lovers-to-be meet at a bus stop, take tea together a few times and enjoy a roll or so among the damp wartime sheets. All too soon, the husband, a British Intelligence Officer, is sent on a secret mission behind enemy lines. Clearly he needs a plane to parachute out of, and whose should be chosen but his wife's lover's?

This contrived piece of plotting gives *Hanover Street* an action-packed finale to follow its tacky beginning and its steamy middle. The courageous pilot, no doubt feeling guilty though the expressing of such subtleties is not catered for in the script, roars to the rescue of the man whose wife he loves, on a high-powered motor bike, then leaps it over a 145 foot railway cutting at ninety miles an hour wearing a Nazi uniform and carrying Plummer on his broad back. Well, that's how it seems on the screen, though in fact it was Eddie Kidd, not Harrison Ford, who performed the stunt with a Plummer dummy aboard, for a fee of £10,000.

The man who must take the blame for *Hanover Street* is its writer-director Peter Hyams, who'd proved he could make a half-way decent adventure yarn with the ingenious *Capricorn One*. Having tempted Harrison Ford with top billing and lust in a brass bed, he refused to give him the scope for developing his character which he'd grown accustomed to in the Coppola–Lucas stable. The result was a conflict which did the doomed picture no good at all.

'Peter and I did not get along,' he says curtly. '*Hanover Street* is not one of my favourite films. In fact I haven't seen it and I don't like talking about it.'

The reviewers were less reticent however. '*Hanover Street* is the tear-dripping saga of a couple's tea-sipping romance in war-torn Europe,' wrote Frank Rich in *Time*. 'Why Columbia Pictures bothered to produce it is the biggest mystery to cloud the company since the departure of David Begelman. The movie has three types of scenes: briefing scenes, bombing scenes and tearoom scenes. Sometimes it is difficult to distinguish among them because every set in the film, indoors and out, is flooded with mist.'

And the actors had to take their share of the blame. 'Harrison Ford, who you may remember as the plastic and celluloid pilot in *Star Wars*, is here got up as a plastic and celluloid USAF bomber pilot stationed in England in 1943,' said the *New Statesman*'s Christopher Hitchens. 'He meets an English nurse, fetchingly enough played by Lesley-Anne Down and falls for her like anything. She's already married to a British Intelligence officer. No trouble at all is taken to contrive the coincidence whereby the two men are thrown together in the hell of a war and discover that a woman is only a woman, but a chap's a chap for all that. There are ghastly scenes of airborne jauntiness, with witless nose-gunners joshing each other on the intercom about the dangers of war. This is presumably intended to evoke *Catch 22*, but it fails embarrassingly.'

William Marshall, in the *Daily Mirror*, was more succinct but equally damning. 'This was the most unbelievable clap-trap featuring stupendously abysmal and embarrassing dialogue. Someone called Harrison Ford, delivering his lines like it was all a terrible mistake, took the part of the mutton-headed pilot.'

Yes, *Hanover Street* was a mistake all right, and Harrison still had one more to make before *The Empire Strikes Back* set his career on course for the eighties. As usual his motives were beyond reproach: just as he'd never made a romance, so he'd never made a comedy. Now he was offered one with what seemed like good credentials. Willing as always in this phase of his career to place his neck in a noose of someone else's devising, he said yes.

The Frisco Kid, which bears no relation to James Cagney's 1936 action adventure of the same name, was a project he'd first heard of during the making of *Heroes* when Henry Winkler was considering starring in it. Now it reappeared with Gene Wilder, so brilliantly funny in Mel Brooks' films like *Blazing Saddles* and *Young Frankenstein* throughout the seventies, as the immigrant Hasidic Rabbi who must cross America to find his flock – and his bride – in San Francisco. The director was Robert Aldrich, whose solid Hollywood reputation was based on blood, guts and extreme violence. Unfortunately, his previous attempt at comedy, *The Choirboys,* based on Joseph Wambaugh's novel, had failed, but no one seemed to have noticed that and he duly landed *The Frisco Kid.*

Like *Heroes,* the film involved a scenic journey across America from East to West. Avram Belinsky, Wilder's orthodox Polish Jew, arrives in Philadelphia with little money and less English to find he's missed his connection. This establishes him as a sucker and the rest of the film shows what happens to suckers when they find themselves adrift in middle America. They get robbed, they get left for dead, they get involved in gunfights, they get kidnapped by Indians, they get to work on a railroad gang, they get to learn to ride a horse and, eventually, to speak broken English.

And they get to meet Harrison Ford, lightly disguised as Tommy Lillard, outlaw, bank robber and the man who holds up Avram's train, then saves his life and ensures his safe passage to San Francisco and the unfortunate woman who awaits him.

Clearly Ford's role in all this is fall guy, the gunslinger with the heart of gold who has to field Wilder's jokes. Where the rabbi is anti violence and bloodshed, let alone bankrobbery, Tommy sees them as a way of life, perhaps the only way of life, and he uses a gun as naturally as another man would use a toothbrush. *The Frisco Kid* is a period film set in 1850, which made it another first in a career that hadn't gone back before 1940. For better, for worse, Harrison got to wear long johns and expose his hairy chest.

No doubt this was insufficient compensation for another pasting at the box office and in the newspaper columns. Susan Lardner led the charge in the *New Yorker*: 'There is no doubt that Wilder is charming, and he has often shown that he can be funny. In *The Frisco Kid* though, he must have trudged through his minimal paces in the hope that Mel Brooks would come riding to the rescue over the next mesa, and surely Robert Aldrich must be more at home steering Lee Marvin and Burt Reynolds around battlefields and prison yards than conducting a nubile rabbi across the country. Some of the dead weight of the picture is assumed by Harrison Ford, a young actor with a frowning charm of his own, in the part of the bank robber who becomes the rabbi's side kick.'

Nor were things noticeably kinder on the other side of the Atlantic where John Coleman wrote in the *New Statesman*: 'The film is essentially a string of episodes held together by the unlikely buddyism of rabbi and bank robber and tugged asunder by fairly consistent mis-timing. To get away with murder, both ways, the lightest of touches is needed. Wilder has clearly been encouraged to deliver a rounded character, which he does by fits and starts. His holy fool is often wily, as well as fearfully brave. Ford, on the other hand, as his reluctantly admiring and protective companion, is more two dimensional – and accordingly, more credible, closer to the requirements of farce.'

Damning with faint praise, perhaps, but it could have been worse. In any case, salvation was at hand. Harrison hadn't been contracted for the three *Star Wars* pictures in the first instance, as Carrie Fisher and Mark Hamill had, but George Lucas wanted him back. Ford, a little tougher now, had negotiated better terms and a 'more dashing' role for Han Solo which the tycoon had willingly agreed to. After all, he now had a lot of money, all of it his own, to invest in his and other trusted talents.

So ended one of the less happy phases in Harrison Ford's life. It is easy to believe that one of the reasons for taking on so much work, most of it in Europe, in the three years between *Star Wars* and *The Empire Strikes Back*, instead of returning to his carpenter's shop, was the break-up of a marriage which he'd always considered rock solid. For a man who believed in couples, there was a great deal of guilt involved in separation, and it is to his credit that he has never blamed anyone but himself.

'I probably wasn't easy to be married to,' he commented after his divorce in 1981. 'I respond to a sort of barometric pressure and this is a stressful occupation. In the dark spaces of my personality, I show it. I can be moody. I am independent, but not solitary. I like people in ones and twos – not parties. I am a very ordinary person. I don't go to anyone for advice or a shoulder to lean on. My questions are for me to answer out of my own experience.'

When the questions were answered, Harrison and Melissa Mathison moved in together and Mary, Ben and Willard set up home five miles away. Harrison has never spoken ill of his first wife, nor failed to acknowledge her wonderful support during the lean years. Their divorce seems to have been as amicable as possible in such painful circumstances and Ford has proved his devotion to his sons, by bringing them to European film festivals and on location whenever it doesn't interfere with their schooling.

'I cherish the time I spend with them,' he says sincerely. 'Of course it's marvellous for them to be able to share in this way in my life, but I don't want my fame to go to their heads. I am always very anxious to know that they're in class with their friends who, I hope, ignore the things they say about me. I really want them to believe that I'm not a star, just a father who loves his kids.'

As for Mary and Melissa, their discretion has become legendary. At this stage of his career, Ford may have picked his films poorly but, giving privacy top priority, his choice of women is beyond reproach. Neither has spoken out in public about their relations with Harrison, a remarkable case of silence in a town where mum is not often the word.

8   Love in a Cold Climate

THERE WAS never any doubt that *The Empire Strikes Back* would be made, but exactly who would work on it was open to negotiation. George Lucas was fairly determined not to write or direct it himself, but he knew that relinquishing control of any part of it was cutting an umbilical cord. It was going to hurt like hell emotionally. Since he'd become a living legend, he'd been involved as executive producer on the movie which, because he'd passed on *Star Wars*, he still owed Ned Tanen at Universal. Outsiders might imagine that an executive who'd shown the lack of judgement Tanen had over *American Graffiti*, then turned down his option, the biggest film in cinema history, wouldn't have had the gall to ask for more, but that would be to misunderstand the essentially whoreish nature of Hollywood. Twentieth-Century Fox's money had made Lucas hot; now Tanen wanted his pound of flesh. Pride was not an issue.

Ironically, the 'more' Tanen asked for was *More American Graffiti*, Lucas's first sequel and one of his rare failures financially and critically. It can be seen as the mogul's revenge on the studio which cut and ruined the original film. Or perhaps George cynically used Universal's money – $7.5 million, or ten times what *Graffiti* had cost – for an experiment he knew wouldn't work. Either way, *More American Graffiti* came out way below par. But there are certain extenuating circumstances.

For a start, Lucas's attempt to re-assemble the original cast for further, more adult adventures fell on deaf ears as far as Richard Dreyfuss was concerned. In the wake of *Jaws* and his Oscar for *The Goodbye Girl*, the cocky actor was demanding and getting star treatment. Lucas, whose firm belief it is that no one is indispensable, refused him special status on an ensemble picture which meant he had to scrap the key character of Curt.

That Dreyfuss was the only defector was a tribute to the loyalty Lucas inspired in the actors he'd set on the path to fame and fortune back in 1972. Even Harrison Ford, much further along that path than any of his colleagues, with the exception of Dreyfuss, was perfectly willing to resume as Bob Falfa, reincarnated some years on as a right-wing narcotics officer with a hippie-busting mission in life, though this was not, in the end, required.

Just as the loss of Curt meant the introduction of new characters, the loss of innocence in America in the late sixties when the sequel was set demanded new attitudes. The light-heartedness was gone. The futures of the four main male characters had already been predicted in the final credits of the original film. Now they had to live up to their grim destinies. The realities of Vietnam, small town failure and campus radicalism had to be faced.

'The story, when continued, is sort of sad and awful, and very painful,' said Bill Huyck, co-writer of the original with his wife, Gloria Katz. 'Plus the period is more serious. No way I wanted to get involved with it.' His defection left Universal with another problem which was solved by the appointment of B. W. Norton, Jr, a friend of the Huycks, as scriptwriter on the new picture. If he did a good job, Lucas promised, he could direct it as well, and so it came to pass. Unsurprisingly, though, he was never given a free hand. Lucas controlled both form and content, using different techniques and screen sizes for the four strands in his story, and he insisted on cutting between them in strict mathematical rotation.

The experiment was an ambitious failure, as George finally had to admit, 'I didn't have much of an emotional investment in the project.' It was in this frame of mind, with one dud sequel behind him, that he faced up to the dilemma of *The Empire Strikes Back*, but there was a crucial difference. This time – for the first time – his own money was at stake. Drained he might be, but somehow he had to make it work.

Step one was to hire Leigh Brackett, a veteran scriptwriter with a co-writer's credit on Howard Hawks's *The Big Sleep* to recommend her, to prepare a draft screenplay. She was noted for quick-fire repartee, and authorship of four sci fi novels did her credibility no harm. Already in her sixties, and fatally ill with cancer, she tackled George Lucas's dream after a single meeting in which he outlined the shape of scenes to come. By March 1978, she'd completed and handed in what was to be her final work. Two weeks later she was dead.

Once again the empty page haunted Lucas who could see no alternative to working the raw material himself. Due to go on holiday in Mexico, he confined himself to his hotel room while Marcia relaxed on the beach. Setting aside Leigh Brackett's version, he started afresh and eventually the deed was done. Hard it certainly was, but not quite as hard as he'd expected.

'As I worked through the nine-part saga, the stories themselves became easier to write,' he told Alan Arnold in *Once Upon a Galaxy: A Journal of the Making of The Empire Strikes Back*. 'The problem was coming up with the scenes and making them work. Sometimes what I had in mind didn't work dramatically. That's where the real struggle comes. After Leigh Brackett died, I was faced with the situation that somebody had to step in and do a re-write. That someone was me. But I found it much easier than I'd anticipated. It still took me three months, but that's a lot different to the two years *Star Wars* took. It was almost enjoyable.'

'There were times when I contemplated selling the whole thing to Fox to do whatever they wanted with,' he went on. 'I'd just take my percentage and go home and never think about *Star Wars* again. But the truth of it is I got captivated by the thing. It's in me. I can't help but get upset or excited when something isn't the way it's supposed to be. I can see that world. I know the way the characters live and breathe. In a way they have taken over.'

At this point, George had a stroke of luck in that Steven Spielberg put him in the way of Lawrence Kasdan, a diminutive bearded Chicago advertising copywriter whose way with words had already produced the as yet unmade screenplay for the Lucas–Spielberg joint venture, *Raiders of the Lost Ark*. The catalyst for Kasdan's employment on the project had been *Continental Divide*, a screenplay he'd drafted over a sandwich in his lunch break in a Los Angeles park. It was made into a film starring the late John Belushi, which, ironically, did the writer far more good off the screen by impressing Spielberg, than on it where it was seriously under-rated. On the strength of it, Kasdan was hired to write *Raiders* which, in turn, impressed Lucas so much that he employed him to script *Empire*, provided he'd share the final credit with Leigh Brackett.

By the time this deal was done, the vital question of who was to direct the sequel had been solved by the signing of Irvin Kershner, bald, in his late fifties and with a pretty uncommercial record behind him. However, he was a man of many parts, none of them Hollywood hack, which swayed Lucas in his favour. His early career had been as a professional musician. 'In high school, I played the violin and the viola. I studied composition and thought I'd be a great composer until I began listening to Prokofiev and Stravinsky. When I knew I wasn't going to be *that* great a composer, I began to be interested in the visual arts.'

At this stage his privileged Philadelphia youth was interrupted by the Second World War which brought him to England as an eighteen-year-old. After it, he turned to painting, photography and documentaries in that order. His first feature was *Stakeout of Dope Street* (1958), a low budget Roger Corman production which paved the way for more sensitive films he really wanted to make: *The Hoodlum Priest* (1961), *The Luck of Ginger Coffey* (1964), *A Fine Madness* (1966) and *The Flim-Flam Man* (1967) culminating in *Loving* (1970). Since then his career had been less impressive with only *The Return of A Man Called Horse* (1976), *Raid on Entebbe* (1977) and the John Carpenter-scripted *Eyes of Laura Mars* (1978) to show for the last five years.

Knowing that *The Empire Strikes Back* would have to develop the characters he'd established in only the skimpiest, two-dimensional sense in *Star Wars*, Lucas appreciated the insight and humanity of Kershner's sixties films, as well as his reputation for being a fast, precise worker. 'These films are incredibly difficult to make,' Lucas explained. 'Normally a director is concerned mainly with character and telling a story. In the *Star Wars* films that is important, but equally important are all the details. They're like little time bombs all over the set, thousands of them, and if you don't catch one, it could do you in. When the shot moves around and there's some little thing that isn't right, it could take the audience completely out of the movie. In a normal film there isn't that thin edge.'

Kersh, as he is known to his friends, was not unequivocally enthusiastic about picking up on George Lucas's juvenile dreams in the certain knowledge that he'd be working with used goods. 'I gave this offer a lot of thought,' he commented. 'Did I want to follow the most successful film ever made? Could I pull it off? Lucas kept saying that it would take at least two years and be very arduous. A lot of ego was involved, although my background in Zen kept telling me to forget the ego and take the assignment. I was grabbed by the fairy tale which Lucas had invented for the triple trilogy. I wanted to be part of keeping it alive.'

Lucas added his own impetus to the decision making process by saying, with more tact than truth, 'It'll be your film. The second part of this series is the most imprtant. If it works, we'll go on to do the third, even the fourth. If it doesn't, it'll be old hat and it'll destroy the real bloom on the project. So it's up to you!'

The director wasn't so naïve as to believe this *in toto*, but he was idealistic enough to be moved by Lucas's plans, then at the drawing board stage, for Skywalker Ranch, the Marin County film maker's Utopia which would reflect Kersh's own mistrust of Hollywood. 'It was an extraordinary dream,' he told Dale Pollock. 'All the billions ever made in the film business, and no one has ever ploughed it back into a library, research, bringing directors together, creating an environment where the love of films could create new dimensions. When I saw his dream, I trusted George.

'Everyone looked askance when it was announced that I would direct *Empire*,' he added. 'No one had expected me to, but I wanted to make a better picture, more stylish and more fun than *Star Wars*.' In the event he didn't, but he signed, even before Leigh Brackett died, and started work on pre-production with the screenplay far from finished. The bare bones of the script were hers, the flesh was Lucas's, but the skin, the texture, came from Kersh and Kasdan in a whole series of sessions devoted to the bouncing of ideas. Kasdan would write a section, then argue the toss with Lucas and Kershner for hours before shaping the final version. In this way, Kersh got the input he required, Lucas kept overall control and Kasdan got his credit. Everyone should have been happy.

Lucas's strength, as displayed in *Star Wars*, lies in the speed of his story telling, a quickness of the plot that can deceive the brain into believing that there's more up there than there actually is. Kasdan, as his own 'auteur' films, *Body Heat* and *The Big Chill*, have proved, is more of an analyser, a canny mixer of motivation with slick presentation. Kershner, whose interests include aesthetics and philosophy, favoured a more intellectual approach, as he stated quite firmly. 'These films are morality plays. They have many of the elements of the medieval morality play. They are also fairy tales, with the qualities of a fairy tale. A morality play is at its best when it has mystery, when it is not clear-cut or simplistic. There must be elements of ambiguity. The characters must emerge more fully in *Empire* than in *Star Wars*. In the first movie, the situations were so powerful you didn't really have time to watch the characters. They were totally in the service of the story. In the new film, they are still in the service of the story, because the narrative must flow, but they are more defined. They have rivalries, jealousies, sexual tensions.'

One who was glad to hear it was Harrison Ford, reassembled with the rest of the cast as pre-production got under way. His new contract stipulated a more wide-ranging Solo, and Lucas was as good as his word. In *The Empire Strikes Back*, the unfledged central trio move into their *Gone With The Wind* mode, with Leia as the irresistible Scarlett O'Hara, Han Solo as the handsome, roguish Rhett Butler, the ladies' man no full-blooded woman can say no to, and Luke as the wimpish but saintly Ashley Wilkes, forever bound to do the decent thing. Well, that was the theory anyway, and although the passion was never delivered, it was at least hinted at.

Even so, Harrison Ford had to take a lot of Solo's development on faith for he was still very much an employee, albeit a slightly more confident one after his five post *Star Wars* pictures. 'There's no place for personal triumph in a film like this,' he says wryly. 'I don't even know why Solo is pursued by bounty hunters throughout *The Empire Strikes Back*. I can imagine, but basically, I just work here, you know what I mean . . . In fact I didn't get the script of *Empire* until three weeks before we started shooting.

One of George's real strengths is not giving you all the information you need, yet at the same time not denying you anything essential. You have a feeling that you want to know more at all times.'

Lucas deliberately worked on the need-to-know principle in order to protect his precious plot twists, so much so that some of the actors never received the whole script and had to wait for the completed film to put their contributions into context. However, none of the original team turned down a second stint in the dream factory. Maybe it wasn't the most fulfilling work in the world, but it paid well and even Anthony Daniels, by far the angriest (because of his enforced facelessness) when the *Star Wars* tidal wave broke, was tempted back into C-3PO's irksome gilded shell by the offer of a small percentage.

As for Sir Alec Guinness, now rich far beyond the expectations his distinguished career had given him, he was determined to do his brief scenes as Luke's mentor from beyond the grave, despite a potentially blinding eye infection which limited the time he could work under the bright lights.

The most eminent human newcomer was Billy Dee Williams as Lando Calrissian, a handsome gambler and an inveterate conman who would cheerfully betray his friends in order to save his planet, Bespin, from the depredations of the Empire. The black character was Lucas's response to accusations of racism in *Star Wars*, a charge based on the fact that the villain, Darth Vader, was clad in black and used the voice of a black actor, James Earl Jones. Lando's purpose, therefore, was to be even smoother and more dashing than Han Solo. His base was Cloud City and the screenplay specified that half of its residents were to be black as well.

Williams, selected by Lucas after his performance in *Lady Sings The Blues*, was less than enchanted with what he saw as Lucas's racial window dressing, but eventually he allowed himself to be persuaded to accept his share of the bonanza. 'Lando could be played by a black or white actor,' he rationalised. 'The part requires a universal, international quality which I have. He is an alternative to the usual WASP hero.'

Once over that hurdle, Lucas felt free to give rein to his phenomenal imagination with a whole range of other-worldly creations. The most novel was Yoda, who compensates for his tiny stature with eight hundred years of experience as a Jedi master-teacher. His task is to assist Ben Kenobi, now disembodied, to instruct Luke in the further implications of the Force as an incentive to either good or evil, depending on the motives of whoever is wielding it. *The Empire Strikes Back* also introduces the Emperor himself as a hooded figure emanating ill will, a counterbalance to Ben Kenobi's benevolent apparitions.

Other innovations are the snow planet, Hoth, with its specially adapted transporters: the plodding, implacable snow walkers, known as AT-ATs (All Terrain Attack Transports) who serve the Empire, and the Tauntauns, part camel, part kangaroo, who bound effortlessly over the icy surface on behalf of the Rebels. Keen to set a completely different tone right from the start, Lucas began his story in this cold desolate place where the Rebel forces, with Luke and Han in attendance, are hiding out after their triumphant destruction of the Death Star at the end of *Star Wars*.

Accordingly, when the cameras finally turned on *The Empire Strikes Back* on 5 March 1979, the venue was Finse in Norway, a village with seventy-five permanent residents, most of them snow clearance and railway workers. During the winter this remote place, chosen for its photogenic 6,000 ft glacier, could only be reached by train or helicopter. The film company took over the one seventy-bed ski lodge for the duration and installed Mark Hamill and his pregnant wife, Marilous Carrie Fisher, Irvin Kershner and Gary Kurtz, re-employed as producer at his own request despite the problems his lack of decisiveness and personal charisma had caused on *Star Wars*.

This time there was good reason for his habitually gloomy countenance. The early scenes, designed to establish Luke Skywalker in the thick of the battle of Hoth once Darth Vader's probes find the last Rebel stronghold and he lands his troops for a massive assault, required bright spring sunshine, glittering frosty mornings with clear blue skies. Instead, the blizzard raged outside, avalanches blocked the railway line, all trains were turned back and the temperatures plummeted to an average of ten degrees below zero.

For several days, cast and crew were mostly confined to barracks, though they made experimental sorties in the environs of the ski lodge to test the mass of equipment and tracked vehicles imported from Sweden and Switzerland during the previous months, plus their own Arctic clothing. Mark Hamill had the worst of the first two days when he was required to lie face down in the snow, impersonating Luke severely injured after an encounter with an angry Wampa, a bestial native of Hoth. When that was completed, with the summit of the glacier still totally obscured by clouds, Kersh looked around for more sequences to shoot in the whiteout and came up with Han Solo's rescue of his friend from this predicament, a scene originally slated for Elstree studios. To keep the cameras turning, he decided to summon Harrison Ford to Norway after all.

The journey was complicated: a flight to Oslo and a train to the ski resort of Geilo thirty miles to the east of Finse where the actor was unloaded and told to proceed as best he could. Two hairy taxi rides took him to Ustaoset, twenty-three miles from his destination where he picked up a snow-plough for the rest of the trip. After sitting in the engine compartment for several hours while the vehicle forced its way through the drifts, he arrived at midnight. The show could go on.

The next morning found him exhausted but ready in his Han Solo costume, a professional approach that greatly impressed the unit publicist, Alan Arnold. 'He looked a bit dazed and bleary eyed,' he recalled. 'He had gotten very little sleep, but he could not have been more courteous. His manner reminded me of something I had not encountered since dealing with actors from the past, romantic stars like Cary Grant, in particular, who were trained in the old studio style attitude to publicity. I have seldom seen it in the younger generation of actors who tend to be self-conscious, probably because a fair number of them are inarticulate. Yet here was Harrison – urbane, self-assured, and charming after having been up half the night. What a pleasant change.'

That first week in Norway set the tone for *The Empire Strikes Back*, a film that proved at least as tumultuous to make as *Star Wars* and rather more than twice as expensive. There were sixty-four sets and 250 scenes to be shot in four months for an estimated $18.5 million, most of them at Elstree, now enhanced by the addition of a 250 ft by 125 ft by 45 ft sound stage built by Lucasfilm to house Solo's spaceship, the Millennium Falcon. The unseasonal blizzard meant that Kershner and Co. arrived a day late in North London with frost-bitten cheeks and little else to show for their ordeal. Meanwhile the second unit stayed on in Finse until the snow melted to make good the deficit by putting as much of the all-important chill factor on film as possible.

Lucas himself awaited his minions at Elstree, determined to see how it felt to sit on the sidelines from the very beginning, though even sitting was difficult because he refused to have a chair with his name on it. As the days passed, it became clear that Kersh was making a slower, more lyrical film than George intended, one that explored the motivation of the characters at the expense of his beloved non-humans. *Empire* had been meticulously storyboarded, scene by scene, but Kershner was prepared to deviate from this form of prepared text. He particularly enjoyed working with actors, playing out their scenes and letting them project themselves in a variety of ways. 'That was his strength and his weakness,' Kurtz explained. 'George would never do that. He'd stick to the storyboard and fix it in the editing room. It worked to our advantage because Kersh's scenes were often better than planned, but they also took a lot more time.'

As time became more of the essence, the inevitable strains between director and executive producer, the creator and the man who was paying the bills, increased. Lucas forced himself to return to California to supervise the special effects at Industrial Light and Magic, but as the weeks turned to months, the messages from the West Coast became more urgent; and their tone was always the same: get the thing done and forget the frills. We'll fit it together later.

In due course, the mogul returned to Elstree, where he bent over backwards to give his employee the time he wanted while saving his own financial bacon. 'Generally I enjoy not directing,' he said, somewhat ambiguously, of this delicate balancing act. 'It's a great relief and a lot of pressure off me. This is the good side. I'm not really as emotionally distressed as I'd be if I were directing. Once in a while, when I'm on the set, I get a little restless as if I were directing, wishing I could go in there and get it done. I like what Kersh is doing creatively. I don't have a strong feeling of wishing it were being done in another way

– well, perhaps once in a while – and I much prefer that
somebody else do the work.'

And yes, he could speed it up, he knew he could, and he
knew he should because the budget was getting out of hand. A
few weeks into the production, Kurtz had to tell Lucas that
Empire was costing $100,000 a day and that the final bill would
be $22 million, yet when George went back to the Bank of
America in Los Angeles and asked for his production loan to be
increased by $6 million, the answer was an abrupt no. Only by
persuading a new backer, the First National Bank of Boston, to
take over the Bank of America commitment and guarantee a
loan of $25 million could he meet the immediate demands of
his $1 million a week payroll. Even this was a temporary solution
because a further $3 million shortfall brought a swift backing-off
from the Boston bankers, now well aware that the original
pre-production budget of $15 million was close to being
doubled. They were adamant that they'd only put up the completion money if Twentieth-Century Fox guaranteed the loan.

This was the humble pie solution Lucas wanted least in the
world, but he had no alternative and Fox duly received a
vastly improved distribution deal. Ironically their go ahead came
through so slowly that First National Bank of Boston gave
Lucas what he wanted without the guarantee, but by that time
it was too late. Fox had cut itself in. It's easy to cast Kershner
as the villain of this piece, but in fact the operation was on a
vastly increased scale at Industrial Light and Magic as well,
where 605 special effects were shot, twice as many as for *Star
Wars*.

Human nature being what it is, Lucas found it easier to put
the blame on his fellow men rather than on obdurate Tauntauns
and AT-ATs so it was back to England, and this time he forced
Kershner and Kurtz to listen. Scenes were cut, sets ruled out
and the cast persuaded to rehearse on their one rest day a week.
In June, a rough cut was ready, but if anything it upset the
harassed tycoon even more. 'I felt it wasn't working at all,' he
commented gloomily. 'Here I was, way over budget, running
out of money, and I had a movie I thought was no good. Or
perhaps it was just a lot better than I wanted to make it. And I
was paying for it.'

So too were the cast who found Kersh increasingly on the defensive. Ford, Hamill and Fisher shared fewer scenes than they had in *Star Wars*, and so found themselves even more alone in a foreign land. For Harrison, *Empire*'s highlights were his moments of tentative lust with Fisher, the first of them aboard the Millennium Falcon in which they escape from the planet Hoth. Bending over the machine's damaged hyper-space drive unit as they hide out in a dense asteroid field, Leia and Han brush against one another and the pilot takes advantage of the situation to give her a swift kiss. This merely confuses the tomboyish Leia, still with her breasts taped in deference to the Lucas sex ethic, but with a new plaited hairstyle described as 'thirties Nordic'. In the circumstances, C-3PO's untimely intervention is not unwelcome as it gives her the opportunity to sort out her awakening sexual awareness in the cockpit on her own.

After several more daredevil Falcon flights, Solo is betrayed by Lando Calrissian and turned over to Darth Vader who tortures him so that Luke can demonstrate his post-Yoda increased awareness of the Force by picking up the pain vibes telepathically and rushing to his pal's rescue. Only when he is sure that his trap has been properly baited does Vader hand Solo over to his henchman, Boba Fett, for his final punishment by carbon freezing. As Leia and Chewbacca watch the grim process, the Princess blurts out, 'I love you.' 'I know,' Solo replies cockily, as he is lowered into the pit.

This key exchange, which attracted a lot of comment when *Empire* was released, came about as a result of an extended bouncing-of-ideas session between Kershner and Ford. Harrison was keen to acquire a punch exit line, preferably one that would leave his return in Part III open to negotiation. 'In the script, my line read, "I love you too." But that was too much on the nose. If you didn't have something else there at that point you would not get your full pay-off in that scene. You know, there's a sense of dread and mystery there, and there's no satisfying conclusion in "I love you too." I wanted the moment to have another complexion. Kershner agreed. At one point, I said to him, "I think she ought to say, 'I love you,' and I'll say, 'I know.'" That's beautiful and acceptable and funny.'

One who did not agree was Carrie Fisher, a nervous waif-like figure haunted in those days by her famous parents and her own self-doubts. 'I was nineteen when I made *Star Wars*, chosen at random, and told to lose weight, which at the time was a problem. This time around, for *Empire*, I was told to gain weight. The only film I'd ever done before *Star Wars* was *Shampoo*. But they decided to go with me anyway, a strong girl with a low voice and a self-righteous nature.'

But faced with Ford's deviations, the low voice was raised to a pitch of near hysteria. 'I would just like to be there when you decide to change things,' she reproached Kershner, who replied, 'You weren't here to be there.'

Fisher: 'I was in the studio.'

Kersh: 'Okay, okay.'

Fisher: 'I yelled at Harrison about the changes.'

Kersh: 'Don't yell at Harrison. Yell at me.'

Fisher: 'There's no reason for me to be mad at Harrison.'

Kersh: 'Alright, alright.'

Fisher: 'But when he came to me with the changes, I got mad at him and it screws us up.'

Kersh: 'Where is Harrison?'

Fisher: 'He's downstairs. He's very angry with me and he has a total right to be. I should not speak to him in that way.'

And so the wrangle went on, a ritual clash of egos between people under pressure, each with a job to do and wanting to get the best deal out of it. Harrison, older and tougher, won this round, but he found that he was still answerable to George Lucas. 'Occasionally I feel very sure about changes, like the "I love you," "I know" scene,' he explained later. 'I knew that my last speech had to be a strong character line and I managed to persuade Kersh to give me that line. I'm grateful he did. When George finally saw the sequence cut together, he said, "It's a laugh line. I'm not sure it belongs there. This is a serious dramatic moment." I said, "I think it really works. It relieves a grim situation without generating laughs or diverting the drama. It makes Solo's plight more poignant and memorable."'

In the end he did convince George, but he never convinced Larry Kasdan who put his outrage into print in America's *Starlog* magazine. 'Han and Leia's relationship is not at all what I had envisaged. I could be the only person who feels this way, but I thought their romance had a touch of falseness about it. Han and Leia's scenes were among what I was proudest of in my

98

script, but they hardly remained. Their being changed had a lot to do with the circumstances of filming, Kershner and the actors' feeling about doing their roles again. I was one of the people who wasn't crazy about Harrison Ford in *Empire*.'

All of which worried the actor not one jot. 'Writers sometimes have to live with a script so long that it begins to suit them too well. They can't see the validity of changes,' was his succinct retort.

And that was that. Not exactly *Gone With the Wind*, as it happened, but a touch of true romance to liven up the endless quasi-violent exchanges and feats of derring-do. 'People who are expecting a repetition of the emotional experience of the first film are not going to find exactly that,' Ford summed up. 'The audience that saw the first film is more sophisticated now, three years later; in the same way, the techniques are more sophisticated. And the demands upon them are slightly more than they were in the first film. This film is much more emotional, and some of the emotions are extremely difficult to deal with. The accomplishment of saying something true about those emotions is great.'

He added that he was pleased the kids he watched watching *Empire* didn't say, 'Yucky!' when he kissed Leia in the Millennium Falcon. Fisher too responded gamely when asked to endorse this particular part of the product, though she expressed a preference for the more combative scenes. 'I like it whenever Harrison and I yelled at each other,' she said, 'but he is very good at kissing. All actors have the opportunity of taking kissing lessons at drama school. Naturally we all choose to do so.'

Harrison, of course, hadn't been to drama school, but it was a nice attempt at graciousness, especially after the arguments over their screen romance.

On a personal level, *The Empire Strikes Back* came at a trying time for Harrison. He lived quietly in a flat in London, turned up on time and approached his task with his customary professionalism, but his mind was often elsewhere. 'I'm reshaping my life,' he told Alan Arnold on the set at Elstree. 'I'm getting a divorce. There's no continuity at the moment. My lifestyle isn't trendy. I'm the kind of guy who thinks he's rich if there's a $5,000 cheque in the mail. There's so much I want to do, but first I want to return to California and become my own person again. People know me as an actor. Right now that's all I want them to know about me.'

Once *Empire* wrapped, Ford was free to go and set up his new life with Melissa Mathison. Their modest house in Benedict Canyon above Beverly Hills was built in 1941 'Because they built things properly then. After the war, builders started taking short cuts.' It was deliberately difficult to find, at the end of one of many indistinguishable cul-de-sacs with 'no outlet' warnings at their entrances. It is also far removed from the ostentatious mansions pointed out by the driver on the daily stars'-homes-spotting coach trip. Indeed, it is so modest that Ben and Willard were forced to practise basketball in the street when they came to visit their father.

As befits a carpenter, its style is more Alpine chalet than fairy tale palace, with dark cedar complementing red brick, the whole dominated by two massive chimneys. The grounds run to a patio, but no pool and no tennis court. The scar-producing Volvo has long gone, replaced by a sleek black Porsche, but in a town where anyone who is anyone has designer number plates, Harrison's is an unmemorable combination. As always, anonymity has top priority.

'I got back home after four months on *Empire*,' he remembers, 'and found the entire house, which had hardwood floors, had just had its first coat of stain the day before. The floors were actually still wet when I came in. The work was supposed to have been a two-month job and it still wasn't finished. So we lived in the basement for weeks and I'd get up every morning to work on the house until we finally got into it. Didn't get into the house for about a month after I got back. But that was a good re-entry into reality. I didn't mind at all.' By the end, wood surfaces gleamed and sash windows opened effortlessly. The carpenter for the canyons had not lost his touch.

Meanwhile up at Lucasfilm outside San Francisco, George was doing what he loved best: overseeing the editing of *Empire*. The finished product cost him $33 million once interest payments were included, and his main preoccupation was whether it would do 30 per cent of *Star Wars* business. If it did, he would be in the clear. If it didn't, he expected to be in hock for life. 'What the hell. I can always go and make documentaries,' he said which, though undoubtedly true, was essentially bravado. His plans for Skywalker Ranch were far advanced by this time, and they were all riding on *Empire*.

The new deal with Fox gave Lucas total control over the advertising for the film, and the centre of his campaign was the relationship between Leia, Han and Luke, which he saw as the classic triangle: given the choice between a good guy and a bad guy, the girl invariably chooses the bad guy. 'We had a hard time getting girls to see *Star Wars*,' he reasoned. 'I wanted to say that this one was more female-oriented and had a love story. I wanted a broader base.'

In the event he need not have worried. So that there should be no time of the day or night when fans couldn't see *Empire*, the film was booked around the clock at the Egyptian Theater in Hollywood, with an opening date of 21 May 1980. Three days before, the enthusiasts began to mass on the pavement outside the cinema, and their response when they got inside was deafening. So was the general public's. Within three months, Lucas was in the clear; within six, he was rich. *Empire* sold $365 million of tickets around the world, second only to *Star Wars*, and this time he owned the movie. The shareout with Fox reflected their respective input much more equitably, but not as equitably as it would have done if First National Bank of Boston hadn't demanded its pound of flesh and handed the studio a fortune, which it had very little ethical right to, on a plate.

For critics and public alike, the most startling revelation in *The Empire Strikes Back* was the enormity of the Lucas undertaking. For the first time it was revealed that there would be three trilogies, with *Star Wars* as part one of the middle one. 'John Williams' vaulting theme music starts with a crash, planets by the zillion glisten brightly in the black firmament and then, across the screen, the following words emblazoned: '*Star Wars* . . . Part Five . . . *The Empire Strikes Back*.' Can George Lucas really mean it? Part Five? Is Lucas going to spend the rest of his life making these things?' David Denby's reaction in *New York Magazine* was typical as critics worldwide braced themselves for the non-stop onslaught to come.

Most of the scribes winced a bit at the repetitiousness of it all. 'Once again we're pitched into one of those flimsy-on-a-grand-scale science fiction plots,' Denby continued. 'The forces of the Empire, led into battle by the Emperor's black-caped, black-helmeted henchman, Lord Darth Vader, attempt to annihilate the Rebels, who are scattered and weak, but held together by possession of the Force, a mystical power at the heart of things. As before, the Rebels are led by Princess Leia (Carrie Fisher) and her bantering paramour, Han Solo (Harrison Ford), along with that perpetual neophyte virgin adventurer, Luke Skywalker (Mark Hamill).'

Nor did Kershner escape unscathed, although *Empire* was greeted appropriately enough as a Lucas film. 'The quality is already beginning to diminish,' wrote *The Times*'s Nicholas Wapshott. 'Lucas provides the story and is executive producer, but he has delegated the screenwriting to Lawrence Kasdan and Leigh Brackett and the direction to Irvin Kershner . . . There is very little humour. The Laurel and Hardy of C-3PO and R2-D2, the mismatched robots, are kept apart for most of the story. Too much is said and not enough left to visual explanation. The escaping princess and her earthly companions become dull, the frightening Darth Vader and his gang less fearsome and more attractive than they should be. The new characters, a glum plastic puppet and a black space pirate, do not grip the imagination. Quite simply, Lucas has done it all before and better. Without his intelligence and the novelty of meeting the *Star Wars* menagerie for the first time, the film fails to involve and seldom charms.'

Audiences, of course, did not agree and Lucas could afford to be generous once again to the men and women who'd made his dream sequel come true. This time the handout was an astonishing $5 million, divided not only between the cast and crew who'd worked on *Empire*, but among all the employees of Industrial Light and Magic and Lucasfilm. Everyone from the janitors upwards received a bonus cheque calculated on length of service rather than specific contributions to the new money spinner.

And of course the end was not in sight. *The Empire Strikes Back* stops in mid-fantasy, a device borrowed with due forethought from the old Saturday morning serials Lucas had been brought up on. A third film was inevitable.

'I have no real defence for that argument,' Harrison Ford replied when attacked on the open-endedness of *Empire*, 'but what obligation is there to tie up every question with an equal answer? The cliffhanger is because the trilogy was really constructed in the classic form of a three act play. Naturally there are going to be questions in the second act which have to be resolved in the third. I guess it really depends on what you do a movie for. I figure there was at least $11 of entertainment in *Empire*. So if you paid four bucks and didn't get an ending, you're still $7 ahead of the game.'

His own status after the release of *Empire* was much richer, but otherwise unchanged. Once again he wasn't singled out for praise or blame in the reviews and Han Solo, in his carbon frozen state, could come or go as Lucas pleased, as Mark Hamill was quick to spot. 'George is very clever. He's not going to compromise himself by making us indispensable. None of us will do a *Star Wars* picture against our will. George will see to that. Look at what's happened to Harrison. He wasn't sure whether he wanted to repeat his role as Solo, and he's not at all committed to do it a third time. So George has left him in limbo in this one. As Lando Calrissian says after Han is hauled up from the carbon freezing chamber, "He's in a perfect state of hibernation." So George has given himself the option. Han is not vital to future stories. It's up to Harrison, I guess, as to whether Han comes back into the saga.'

As Harrison supervised the staining of his floors and adapted himself to the strains of being a divorced father, he pondered this question of sharing the limelight. All around him, the *Empire* gravy train rolled on and the shops were once again filled with souvenirs, many of them depicting him with varying degrees of accuracy in his Solo guise. But was he getting his just deserts?

Carrie Fisher suggests that he thought not. 'The merchandising, it's very funny,' she explained wryly. 'Harrison gets so upset: "Mark gets to be a puzzle, why don't I?" Those kinds of arguments. And we'll go, "Wait a minute! Why don't I get to be on a pencil box for chrissake! I mean if I'm gonna be in this and I'm gonna end up being two sizes of dolls, and a belt and a cookie and a hat, then why don't I get to be on an eraser too?"'

She was joking, of course, but was there an undercurrent of true jealousy? Probably the answer is yes. If Han Solo was to be of lasting use, it was as a means to an end, a stepping stone to recognition as an actor. The character, Harrison knew, didn't have it in him to do it on his own; his contribution to his career was to lead him on to greater things. He felt that the more exposure he got, of whatever kind, under whatever humiliating commercial circumstances, the more likely this progression would become.

It is fair to say that while Harrison is grateful to Han Solo, he has little emotional involvement with him. '*Star Wars* and *Empire* aren't the sort of films where you reflect on the finer points of character,' he told me once, 'because you can't violate the demanding tempo. One thing I do like is Solo's sense of humour. I don't like people who don't have one, nor do I like portraying them. Sure it's fair to say that Solo is two dimensional, but I was happy to serve the films in that way. It made no difference to the way I approached my work.'

Through the late summer and autumn of 1980, as *Empire* put his name in lights across America, scripts were placed in the Ford mailbox, but Harrison continued to chisel away at his new home. He'd learned something from those five interim failures: read first, sign later – or not at all. In due course his patience was rewarded. The script that really had his name on it was *Raiders of the Lost Ark*.

9   Licensed to Thrill

LATE MAY, 1977: two short, compact Americans dig in the golden sand in front of the Mauna Kea Hotel on the Big Island of Hawaii. It is an appropriate location for the making of cinema history, a long, low luxurious building filled with art treasures and sculpted into a hillside overlooking a small bay. Around it stretches black volcanic rock, scarred and pitted and bleak, for the oasis in which it stands is as artificial as any movie set. Every scrap of soil for the golf course, the sweeping lawns and colourful flower beds, every grain of sand for the beach, has been brought from somewhere else.

The two Americans are rather younger than the rank and file of wealthy compatriots who surround them. The one doing most of the talking is bearded, prematurely greying and ecstatic. When he'd arrived in Hawaii, George Lucas had been taut as a piano wire, but the night before he'd taken a phone call during dinner from Ashley Boone, Twentieth-Century Fox's Marketing Chief. *Star Wars* was doing great business in its first week. 'Wow . . . gee . . . that's amazing!' the child-man replied, falling easily into the vernacular of his youth. Back at the table, he loosened up and began to talk and laugh. Once he was started, there was no stopping him. Like a dam breaking, the tension flooded out and new ideas took its place.

His companion on the beach, normally the more outgoing of the two, is a worried man. Steven Spielberg, unbearded, as yet, untouched by Lucasfilm, is taking a break from *Close Encounters of the Third Kind*, but he still has a long way to go on what is proving to be a pretty obdurate picture. Nevertheless he celebrates his friend's success – the men have known each other for ten years – with proper enthusiasm by building a castle with him, an elaborate multi-turreted affair down on the shoreline where the sand is hard. When it is finished, the men watch it resist the waves for thirty minutes. For them, it is a cliffhanger, a period of shared emotion that becomes a symbol of their partnership. Nowadays, whenever one of them has a movie coming out, they build a sandcastle. If it proves sturdy, success is guaranteed. Obviously they build very strong sand castles.

As they plied their buckets and spades and patted their ramparts into position, they talked. Spielberg recalled how the United Artists executives had offered him a movie after *Sugarland Express*. What, they'd enquired politely, would he like to direct most in the world? 'James Bond', he'd replied without hesitation. Theoretically the gift was in their parish because the studio had always been associated with the durable secret agent, but they recoiled in horror. Bond was British, and that was how he was going to stay, even from behind the cameras. Spielberg went away and made *Jaws* for Universal instead, but the yen to direct a high-intensity epic adventure remained.

'I've got something better than Bond,' said Lucas, secure on his adrenalin high. And he told Spielberg what it was; a three part series about a globe-trotting archaeologist, dame's delight by night, intrepid adventurer by day. His era was the thirties, his background academic, his adversary in Part I, Hitler himself for his incredible feats of derring-do were to be underpinned by history. 'We'll call him Indiana Smith,' Lucas added. 'Indy for short.' Indiana was the name of Marcia's female Alaskan malamute, and it caused a short ripple of laughter before construction work proceeded with the deadly earnestness George Lucas had once given to his childhood environments. But somehow it stuck.

Lucas's grand design was to combine Hitler's recorded fascination with religious objects, especially those that could be made to nourish his sense of omnipotence, with the mythology surrounding the Ark of the Covenant, the gold-encrusted wooden chest containing the broken tablets of the Ten Commandments that is mentioned in the Old Testament. Missing from the Temple in Jerusalem since Solomon's time circa 1980 BC, the Ark could conveniently be found almost anywhere. Why not in the lost city of Tanis, a fertile field for archaeologist Dr

Indiana Smith? And why not gear the action to a race for the Ark between the Nazi dictator and the professor?

Why not indeed? Spielberg added a final touch to his draw-bridge, sat back on his heels and looked keen. 'That sounds real exciting,' he said. 'I've always wanted to bring a serial to life that blends Lash LaRue and Spy Smasher with elements of Edgar Rice Burroughs. I've always wondered why Hollywood hasn't done anything to revive the genre of narrow misses and close calls.'

Unfortunately there was a fly in the ointment. Although the overall plan and most of the details were Lucas's, some of the key ones were not. His first collaborator on *Raiders of the Lost Ark* was Phil Kaufman and it was he who'd suggested the Hitler–Covenant link-up back in 1975 when Lucas was still unsure whether he'd go with *Star Wars* or *Raiders* first. The two men had worked for several weeks on story development, and Kaufman was slated to direct. In May, 1977, he still had his rights.

Some six months after Sandcastle Day, having sneaked a preview of *Close Encounters of the Third Kind* and been bowled over, Lucas rang Spielberg, and this time the news was better. 'You remember the movie we talked about at the Mauna Kea? Well, Phil's not directing it. Nor am I. I've retired from directing. It's yours if you want it.' Spielberg did, and although both men had films to complete first, *Raiders of the Lost Ark* took on a more positive shape from that moment.

'The reason I turned to Steve was that he'd gotten very excited about it when I mentioned it,' Lucas explained. 'The picture would still be on the shelf if Steven hadn't expressed an interest. I was eager to have him direct it because he's an extremely good director, especially with action and suspense, and that's primarily what this film is. What inspired me to make it was a desire to see this kind of movie. You sit back and say, "Why don't they make this kind of movie any more?" And I'm in a position to do it. So I'm really doing it more than anything else so that I can enjoy it. I just wanted to see this movie.'

Spielberg's first contribution to the project was the appoint-ment of Larry Kasdan as scriptwriter; his second, to change the hero's name to Jones on the grounds that Smith was too common! Kasdan's brief was specific: his work must reflect the twin visions of two very hot movie makers. 'Either he's chasing them, or they're chasing him,' was Lucas's summary of the plot of a film he wanted to remain true to the thirties serials that inspired it. It was not to be a spoof, but a genuine action adventure. If audiences wished to laugh, they were not to do so at the expense of the characters or the situations. As for Spielberg, he wanted a rollercoaster ride, a non-stop crash and dash for nearly two hours. This one really had to move.

For Kasdan, working on only his third screenplay, it was a tough nut to crack, but he exudes natural self-confidence and he set to work with a will. Four months later, the first draft was done and the trio went into lengthy – and very noisy – tape-recorded input sessions designed to pack the action still further. Although the film is one third Spielberg, one third Kasdan and one third Lucas, it remained true to George's original vision and Indiana Jones reflects his fantasy: tall, sardonic and wisecracking, the ladies' man that he could never be. Indy also shares certain characteristics with Han Solo. He is a bounty hunter, though his speciality is antiquities; he is an amoral rebel, but George gave him an ethical streak as well. 'He must be a person we can look up to,' he enlarged to Dale Pollock. 'We're doing a role model for little kids, so we have to be careful. We need someone who's honest and true and trusting.'

Spielberg had envisaged an altogether more downbeat character, a heavy drinker some way away from the Cary Grant style playboy George had in mind. The result was a compromise, and so too was the casting. 'We wanted an unknown, originally, a total unknown,' Spielberg explained. 'Conceitedly, George and I wanted to make a star out of Johnny, the Construction Worker from Malibu. We couldn't find a construction worker in Malibu, so we began by looking at more substantial people in the film business.'

The search convinced Lucas, Spielberg and Kasdan that Tom Selleck was tailor-made for Dr Indiana Jones. Quite why this should be is not clear, though Lucas, inevitably, wanted someone relatively cheap who could be locked into a three-picture deal, and Selleck, in his pre-*Magnum* days, certainly fitted that bill. The television actor had very little experience of film work, but he tested for Indy and got him. However, as he warned at the time, CBS television had already put him under contract for *Magnum* after a successful pilot, and their schedule might prevent him taking up the offer.

Lucas was confident he could overcome such wrinkles, but the television company executives proved surprisingly obdurate. No, they wouldn't postpone their series until their leading man had made *Raiders of the Lost Ark*. With the benefit of hindsight, this appears to be a pretty foolish decision because their asset would have appreciated considerably in the hands of Lucas and Spielberg before they got him on the box. It was ironic, too, that they had to put back *Magnum* in any case when the Screen Actors' Guild strike shut down production in America, including Hawaii where Selleck awaited the start of his gun burst. Meanwhile *Raiders*, free from such union restraints, rolled in London, leaving one very sad actor who could easily have fitted in both roles, stranded in mid-Pacific.

'When I lost *Raiders* through no fault of my own, I thought, "Well, that was my shot. From now on, I'm a TV actor,"' Selleck said morosely. 'I felt entitled to get something out of it and kept telling people, "That was my part, you know."'

With the tall dark actor out of the running, the controlling triumvirate put their heads together again and came up with another name: Harrison Ford. Lucas had objections on grounds of cost and identification with Solo, while Kasdan did not number himself among the actor's warmest supporters after the dialogue alterations on *The Empire Strikes Back*, so it was Steven Spielberg who swung things in Harrison's favour.

'They could find me if they wanted me,' was Harrison's viewpoint, as he pursued his pre-*Star Wars* low profile tactics while auditions proceeded in the Lucasfilm offices, and eventually the phone rang in the new house in Benedict Canyon. 'It was George and he told me what I'd heard for a long time – that they were making this film. I assumed they had someone for the part so I was surprised when George called me and asked me to talk to Steven. Then I read the script and called Steven. I was enthusiastic about both of them: the script and the director. A good start, right?

'The only question I had in my mind about it was, because both *Empire* and *Raiders* were written by Larry Kasdan, that there was some little similarity in the characters,' he continued. 'Or in the dialogue, not the characters. Steven agreed we should make a definition between the two and not give Indiana Jones the kinda snappy dialogue which, in cases, was a little Han Solo.'

Such details were worked out at a meeting in Spielberg's house in a work room dominated by video games, just as George Lucas's is by his Wurlitzer. These guys are not called 'Movie Brats' for nothing and Harrison, his youngest son Willard, and his girlfriend Melissa Mathison, found themselves playing pinball while the men discussed the project.

'Steven was bubbly and enthusiastic,' Ford told Derek Taylor in *The Making of Raiders of the Lost Ark*. 'He seemed he might be fun to work with. So I agreed and took the part. And he was a lot of fun to work with. I enjoyed the film as much as anything I've ever done and it's been hard work as well, which I like.'

Yes, the protestant work ethic, so notably absent from his lackadaisical youth, had come into its own by this time and Ford was more than ready to make the big contribution now that the chance had come. 'Indiana Jones was clearly the most dominant single character in any of George's films,' he assessed, 'quite at variance with his theories about movie stars and what they mean.'

With the windfall in the bag, he freely admitted that he 'got the part by default,' and Selleck too came out of the affair well when *Raiders* was released. 'Now I've seen it, it's hard to imagine anyone being better than Harrison Ford. He was quite wonderful,' he said, with conspicuous gallantry in the circumstances.

Faced with Spielberg's certainty about Ford, Lucas gave in graciously, according to his fellow executive producer on *Raiders*, Howard Kazanjian. 'When George described his character, the artist came up with three or four very good-looking pictures. He was a rugged individual, with a bullwhip, a gun and a leather jacket and hat. We knew that was our character. But we had difficulty finding an actor. You can find a guy who looks good and is tough-looking, but he can't act. Eventually we realised that Harrison was Indiana Jones, and fortunately he agreed to do the part.'

Spielberg confirms this account. 'We were stuck,' he admits.

Two faces of space pilot Han Solo in George Lucas's Star Wars trilogy: with Carrie Fisher as Princess Leia (above) in *The Return of the Jedi* (1983) and (below) enduring the cold on the ice planet, Hoth, in *The Empire Strikes Back* (1980).

The Wookie, Chewbacca (Peter Mayhew), towers over the Star Wars triumvirate: Princess Leia (Carrie Fisher), Han Solo (Harrison Ford) and Luke Skywalker (Mark Hamill) in *The Empire Strikes Back* (1980).

Harrison Ford as Kenny Boyd, a Vietnam veteran facing an uncertain future as he turns his hand to maintenance outside his dilapidated motor home in *Heroes* (1977).

Harrison Ford as David Halloran on a secret mission behind enemy lines in *Hanover Street* (1979).

Lt-Col. Barnsby (Harrison Ford) awaiting his chance to bash the Hun in the World War II drama, *Force Ten From Navarone* (1978).

A moment of passion with Lesley-Anne Down for Harrison Ford's bomber
pilot in the World War II romance, *Hanover Street* (1979).

'We had three weeks left to cast the part of Indiana Jones and there was nobody close. Then I saw *The Empire Strikes Back* and I realised Harrison Ford is Indiana Jones. I called Lucas and said, "He's right under our noses!" George said, "I know who you're going to say!" "Who?" I asked. He said, "Harrison Ford. Let's get him." And we did.'

With a script and a star in the bag, no one worried too much about where the money was coming from. Separately Lucas and Spielberg had put Hollywood back on the map. A collaboration between them would surely have the Midas touch. The original budget for *Raiders* was a modest $7 million. Presumably the studios would slit one another's throats to be the first on the bandwagon. Wrong again. Proving that there's truth in the maxim that a man is only as good as his last film, the executives pointed the finger at Spielberg's *1941*, the rumbustious but diffuse comedy starring the late John Belushi that contrived to run amok by doubling a $16 million budget, making it the sixth most expensive film ever. Worse still, it never looked like reaching its break-even point of $60 million in rentals, netting a paltry $47.2 million around the world.

Its joint backers, Columbia and Universal, were not amused, especially as the blame for running over schedule was Spielberg's. They'd given him a new toy, a French Louma Crane, which could take a camera into spaces where no crew could hope to fit. It could shoot from half an inch above the ground for miniatures. It could track round obstacles for chase sequences. It could move between heads and shoulders in a dense crowd of people. It was limited only by its user's imagination, by no means a severe enough check, in commercial terms at least, when the man playing with it had the visual genius of Steven Spielberg. In a frenzy of excited experimentation, he ran it for every angle it was worth while the dollars slipped through his fingers. Hollywood wasn't ready to let him loose again just yet.

George Lucas, the shopkeeper's son, had no such blots on his copybook, but he did have his own ideas on control, to which end he devised what was dubbed 'a killer deal' for his agents, Tom Pollock and Charles Weber, to present to the studios. When its terms were released, Hollywood blanched, not least because it knew someone would capitulate and so set a precedent none of them wanted to live with. Michael Eisner, President of Paramount, was that someone, perhaps because his studio was one of the few giants to miss out on the Spielberg–Lucas cake to date. He agreed to many of Lucas's demands, though he stood firm on the severe financial penalties he would impose if *Raiders* went over schedule or over budget.

That, of course, was fine by George who was at least as determined as any studio to put the shackles on extravagance. First he worked out a contract for himself and his protégé: Spielberg would get $1 million as director; Lucas $1 million as producer; and Lucasfilm $1 million as the production company. Spielberg would receive a percentage of gross profits; Lucas's share was to come later, out of net profits.

Once that was agreed, Lucas devoted himself to making sure Steven saw things his way. The film was to be made in eighty-five days, most of them in Tunisia and Elstree, with a small second unit travelling the globe to shoot establishing footage in some of Kasdan's more exotic locations. The idea that Indy and Co. travel to Cairo and Nepal was implanted in the audience's minds by the judicious use of maps. Whatever Spielberg said he needed, Lucas halved – at best. A four-engined Flying Wing bomber became a two-engined bomber, saving $200,000. Two thousand Arab extras became 600; the 200 acres they were supposed to dig in order to represent the Nazi excavation of the lost city of Tanis became seventy. This time the saving was $750,000.

Lucas taught Spielberg to create illusions of grandeur while cutting costs to the bone, and the younger man learned his lessons well. It was a fairly severe exercise in self-discipline, for his natural bent is expensive. He likes to move his camera around, using it to its full potential. It is, after all, what he's been doing since he was a scrawny, wimpish child who stared wide-eyed at his mother's birthday present to his father: an 8 mm camera. 'She got it for him to record memories on film, and I had to sit, as I'm sure everyone has, through home movies,' Steven recalls with a grimace. 'Where the camera's going up and down and you can't see anything. Where you drive by the Grand Canyon at forty miles an hour and it's a big blur. My father really was an awful photographer. I'd just stare at the screen and say, "Gee, you're not holding the camera steady enough. This doesn't make any sense." So one day he gave me the camera and said, "You be the family photographer. You take the pictures." That was how it began.'

After that, the Spielberg holidays were radically changed as Steven subjected his parents and his three sisters to draconian direction with unremitting enthusiasm. They'd arrive exhausted and fretful at a camping site, only to be forced to let their son out, drive away and return so that he could film the car coming in before they unloaded it and set up the tents. In an already unhappy household, the strain was considerable but Steven's only passion was film so they indulged him. An academic failure and a loner, a no hoper in a series of high schools dominated by sports jocks, he saw his narrow suburban world through a lens darkly.

When he was twelve, he was given his first camera, a simple Kodak, which he used to film elaborate train crashes meticulously staged on his model railway. He also terrorised his sisters into acting out lurid melodramas, dressing them up as Nazis and making them simulate excruciating death scenes for his ever-turning camera. 'I used film, I think, to escape into another world. Away from my parents. They weren't getting along and there was a lot of noise in the house at night. It was an escape for me. A great escape.'

In some ways, he's been escaping ever since, using his intuitive grasp of the medium to put over the message. Spielberg is no Lucas when it comes to business. Rather he is rich despite himself, because of his phenomenal talent. 'I hate to talk like a mercenary,' he told his biographer, Tony Crawley, 'But George said, "Let's make the best deal they've ever made in Hollywood."'

Once that deal had been set, Spielberg found reality thrust upon him with a vengeance. 'This is a B movie,' George would say, in the tones of someone who'd have preferred it to be a C movie. 'They used to make four of them a week, at each studio, for fifteen years through the thirties and the forties.' To his credit, Steven took his medicine like a man. He made *Raiders* George's way, in practical terms, but the flair and speed and the instinctive grasp of what would make audiences cheer were all his own.

Their association was made easier by the many things they

had in common. Lucas was Californian, whereas the Spielberg family moved from Cincinatti, where Steven was born, to New Jersey, then to the nondescript Phoenix suburb of Scottsdale, Arizona where he spent his adolescence. However, both their families were solidly upwardly mobile and relentlessly middle class. Spielberg's father, Arnold, was a computer engineer, a somewhat avant-garde profession in the fifties. Apart from his fortuitous lack of expertise with the movie camera, his greatest contribution to his son's sparkling career seems to have been waking him up at midnight when he was six and driving him to a field on the outskirts of town to watch a meteorite shower, a scene Steven recreated so effectively in *Close Encounters of the Third Kind*.

Like George, Steven was an unprepossessing child who did badly at school, but eventually used his idiosyncrasies to make himself popular. He too was fascinated with the cinema, but his parents restricted his visits to things they thought suitable, mostly Disney and the Saturday morning serials which inspired *Raiders of the Lost Ark*. Westerns were among the many forbidden genres, so he made his own, a four-minute film with two schoolfriends dressed as cowboys and no horse. He couldn't afford one after he'd paid for the film itself with money earned from whitewashing the neighbour's fruit trees.

While Lucas was going through his drag racing phase, Spielberg was learning his craft on his home ground. Action was in his blood and his teenage productions, meticulously story-boarded and accompanied by his own music (he was a self-taught organist) often featured his class mates as GIs, with the school bully cunningly appeased by the role of dare-devil hero. 'I enjoyed dressing them up,' Steven remembers, 'but it was difficult to keep them interested. I could only shoot on week-ends. Monday through Friday, I was in school. Saturday and Sunday, when I needed them to come over to the house and be in a movie, they really wanted to go out, have a good time. For the first few weeks, they loved it. They were great! After that, other interests developed. They got into cars. They got into girls. They wouldn't turn up and I'd replace actors, rewrite characters out of the movie. That was the major problem.'

He had no time for cars or girls. When he was seventeen, his parents divorced and his mother, Leah, took her children to Los

Angeles. Steven's grades weren't good enough to get him into the film school at USC where George Lucas, three years his senior, was already showing signs of his prodigious talents. Instead, Steven studied English at California State University at Long Beach, mostly to avoid the Vietnam draft. Just as Lucas had, he used the time to catch up on the movies his parents had disapproved of, making himself into a film buff in the process.

Spielberg also shares Lucas's natural temperance, his stern sense of purpose and his meteoric rise, which gives the two men a considerable basis for mutual respect. 'The important thing for me is that George and I have been friends a lot longer than we've been working together,' he said at the start of *Raiders*. 'George and I have been working together for only a year. We've been friends for eleven and it's very important that nothing get in the way of that friendship. This movie is the proving ground of whether we – not just George and me, but all our friends – can continue to make movies together without feeling envious or competitive or resentful.'

It was a danger Lucas, too, was well aware of. 'You never know in a situation like that, but I figured we could survive it. Steven is unique. The most naturally talented director I've ever met. I had to learn everything I know. Whatever talent I have is in a whole different area, being in tune with a mass sensibility. My talent is not particularly in making films.'

Once it was established that so long as Spielberg worked fast and cheaply, Lucas would allow his creativity full rein, *Raiders of the Lost Ark* began to take shape. Harrison Ford was joined at the top of the cast list by Karen Allen, a freckled New York stage actress who was chosen to play the tough Marion Ravenwood, the only major woman's role in the film.

'Steven Spielberg and Frank Marshall came to New York to meet actors,' she recalls. 'They asked me to come and read for it so I did and then later they asked me to come and do some screen tests for it. They gave me a scene from *Raiders* – the scene where Marion and Indiana Jones first meet. So I did screen tests and I did several different ones with different actors. It was from there they decided to cast me in the role.

'A few things convinced me to take it,' she continued. 'First, it was different from anything else I'd done. I liked the idea of dressing up and of escape. And the moviemakers were out simply to delight the imagination. I was completely freed up. I could do no research for the part. How do we know what an American girl living in Nepal would look like? She's not going to be thirties stylish. At first, I thought that flaming red hair would fit such a fiery heroine. But Steven blotted out my freckles, gave me a jet black wig and that was it.'

When casting the lesser roles, Spielberg employed a novel method of putting candidates at their ease. Initially they weren't given the script, but invited to join him in a large kitchen where they helped to make cakes or biscuits. There were lots of other people around as well and, as the conversation developed, one of them would pick up a camera and take a few shots. In this way, the director hoped to see them at their most relaxed. Later he gave them short scenes to act out in the conventional way. By this method, he selected Paul Freeman for the villainous Belloq, Ronald Lacey for Toht, the expansive Welshman, John Rhys-Davis for Sallah and the universally popular Denholm Elliot for Brody.

With 'who' out of the way, the diminutive moguls were free to turn to 'where', and this time the choice was easier. Although they prepared budgets for doing the studio work in California as well as at Elstree, there can have been few doubts as to which would win, as the British slant to the cast suggests. Sterling was low against the dollar in 1980 and the grim North London studios had certainly been lucky for Lucas, just as he had been for them. He had friends in the right places now, people he could call on with absolute faith in their abilities and their loyalty to his films. He'd become accustomed to working within the prickly British union regulations. He was no longer the small town boy from Modesto chancing his arm on his instincts, but a man of wealth and international stature. Maybe he still preferred hamburgers to French cuisine, but London had moved on too, and fast food outlets were springing up all over. Maybe they weren't as authentic as in Marin County, but Lucas knew he could survive another London experience.

Nor was cost the only preoccupation, as Lucas's fellow executive producer Howard Kazanjian explained. 'We wanted to maintain secrecy and that was certainly more easily done in London than in the United States. Suddenly it'll happen that everyone in the States knows what you're doing, what the story is about, and then you see your story on television before you can get your movie out. So the need for secrecy was one of the main reasons we came here. And also, of course, it's close to Tunisia, and the script called for that part of the world.'

For Harrison Ford, the choice was less than happy. His love nest in Benedict Canyon was as he wanted it at last, and as such, far too good to leave. Besides, he'd had enough of Elstree to last a lifetime and he'd have dearly loved to make a film in Hollywood so as to be near his sons and to settle into the new domesticity. However, he recognised that when the stakes are high, you have to pay the ante. When Steven Spielberg flew out of Los Angeles for London, Harrison settled into the first class seat beside him.

During the ten hour flight, the two men more than paid off the cost of their tickets by working over the flesh and bones of Indiana Jones. There'd been no time for Larry Kasdan to rewrite the script in a less Han Soloish manner, but Spielberg was enthusiastic about letting Ford put words into the mouth of his character, and it was never too soon to start. 'Steve and I went through the script, line by line,' Harrison says of the extended story conference. 'By the time we got to Heathrow, we'd worked out the entire film.'

As the odd couple stepped down onto the damp tarmac, it was exit, temporarily, Han Solo; enter, triumphantly, Indiana Jones.

10   Bullwhipper Extraordinary

GEORGE LUCAS's grand design for *Raiders* can be most simply described as Ark swapping. Indiana Jones' deadliest rival is a fellow archaeologist, Belloq, a Nazi henchman who travels the world plundering significant artefacts to appease the Führer's passion for all things occult. Jones wants them too, to sell at a handsome profit to American museums, not in itself a particularly noble aim, but some way ahead of the propagation of National Socialism.

The two men meet first in the Peruvian jungle where Jones is running a gauntlet of booby traps in order to acquire a solid gold idol. No sooner has he completed the tricky task than Belloq is onto him, snatching the prize and setting the first chase sequence in motion as Indy escapes. In true Bondian manner, these alarms and excursions give way to the academic hush of the National Museum of Washington where Denholm Elliot's Brody enlists Indy for a secret mission. The Germans are excavating the lost city of Tanis in order to find the Ark of the Covenant in the belief that possession of it will make their armies invincible. However, they need the headpiece of the Staff of Ra to throw light – literally – on its precise whereabouts. Jones's assignment is to beat them to it.

The Staff is apparently under the jurisdiction of an old pal of Indy's in Nepal, one Abner Ravenwood, owner of a sleazy bar in the foothills of the Himalayas, and it is here that the hero meets up with the heroine, the hard-drinking Marion who is running the Raven after her father's death. It is characteristic of this sort of epic that the couple don't hit it off immediately but circumstances throw them together and they are obliged to become partners in a whole series of escapes and imprisonments, of which the most dramatic is in the snake-infested Well of

Souls. Indeed, Marion is kidnapped almost as often as the Ark as the action moves from Egypt to the ship, the *Bantu Wind*, to the Mediterranean island on which the final confrontation takes place.

Clearly the originality in all this is zero, but the structure is meticulous. Lucas divided his screenplay into sixty two-page scenes, and put in six key cliffhangers, one every twenty pages. 'It's a serialesque movie,' he explained. 'It's also basically an action piece. We want to keep things interspaced and at the same time build tension. The opening sequence has to seem to go on for one-third of the movie, then we give the audience a chance to rest before we hit them with the next cliffhanger.'

The most novel challenge in all this for Harrison Ford was certainly physical. He describes himself as 'something of a powderpuff when it comes to sport,' yet he was forced to recognise that the swift-footed, bullwhip-wielding Indiana Jones required high-frequency action on his part. 'Hell, if I hadn't done some of the stunts I wouldn't have been in the film at all,' he says sardonically.

His first task was to learn to crack the ten foot bullwhip around convincingly. As it was Indy's trademark, as distinctive and characteristic as Cagney's rat-a-tat dialogue or Bogart's cigarette, the whip work had to be good and Ford had to practise long and hard. One of the problems was a wrist broken in a fall from a ladder at Valerie Harper's house during his carpentering days. 'It never quite came back,' he explained, 'as I realised when I started bullwhipping. I might not have noticed but for that.' In order to strengthen it, he carried a small, heavy metal ball which he rolled around in his hand as he waited for things to happen, a therapeutic device that bound the tissues together to make the whipping easier.

Then there was the question of technique. 'Well,' he shrugged, 'there's not a lot you can do. The stunt co-ordinator showed me how not to whip the hell out of myself, but after half an hour, he finished because it's really something you have to do for yourself.'

In the event, he had a little more time to prepare himself because the first scenes to be shot on *Raiders* were whip-free. They were acted out off the coast of France near La Rochelle, where the Nazi submarine hijack of the *Bantu Wind*, the ship carrying the Ark to America, was staged over five perishing days in July, 1980.

'I'm famous for not doing sport,' said Harrison, 'and I hadn't been fit for about thirteen years. By inclination, I don't do a thing. I don't work out. I certainly don't jog, but I do have a good constitution. As for the submarine, swimming to it didn't involve danger, only discomfort.'

Having got his feet wet, so to speak, it was back to Elstree where four of the huge sound stages had become the Raven Bar, the Peruvian temple, the Well of Souls and the Map Room where the light shines through the medallion to show where the Ark is hidden. Many film makers believe that the best psychological approach to their work is to shoot the toughest scenes first on the principle that nothing that comes afterwards can ever be quite so bad again. With this in mind, Spielberg launched into his Elstree programme in the second week of July with more than 6,000 snakes as extras.

Recognising that a man with a weakness, especially one that he overcomes, can line up an audience on his side even more effectively than one without, Lucas and Spielberg had given Indiana Jones one of the most common in the world: snake phobia. Now the reptiles had to slither up and be counted so that he could display his mastery over his terror. The need for abnormal numbers of snakes had been foreseen several months earlier and an animal handler hired to supervise the hatching of the masses in Holland, with the result that each of the 6,000 common – and harmless – grass snakes had been earmarked from birth for EMI studios. They were joined in the bottom of the Well of Souls by assorted pieces of judiciously coiled garden hose and a sprinkling of deadlies: cobras and constrictors, to add an element of real danger.

Their arrival sent electric currents of anticipation through the studio corridors as the crew, many of whom sympathised with Indy's nightmares, braced themselves for action. 'They're here.' 'They're not here.' 'I hear they eat whole goats.' 'Don't they have their stings removed?' 'They can easily escape.' The rumours had been flying around for days. Fortunately for Harrison Ford, he didn't share Indy's phobia. 'Snakes don't bother me at all. When I was a kid, I worked in a boy scout camp as a nature councillor. I used to collect them. Used to run and catch every snake we could. And I'm amazed that that's the most frightening scene in *Raiders* for most people.'

Had it been spiders, however, it would have been another matter. 'It's not that they're creepy,' he added, 'but inside my house they multiply, and then their kids have kids. Ugh. All those spiders.'

Ironically it was on the home front that the snakes got their own back on Indiana Jones. *Raiders* had just come out and was showing to packed houses when Harrison was bitten for the first time in his life. 'Hard to believe, isn't it? A damned snake in my own garden.'

Poor Karen Allen, who had to stand beside her partner through much of the ordeal, was considerably less sanguine about spending the next five days of her life knee high in coils. 'It's okay for Harrison,' she said, not without bitterness. 'He has on his boots and gloves, and leather clothes, but I have naked arms and nothing on my legs or feet. In the beginning it was tough because I just couldn't stand the snakes on my feet, but I got used to them.'

Too used to them, at one point, because when she had to scream in terror, Spielberg felt that her degree of shrillness was inadequate. His response was simple, quick and extremely effective: he crept up behind her and dropped a snake down her back.

The director, of course, was loving every moment of the high drama. For him, 6,000 snakes weren't nearly enough, but at least they were giving him the chance to display his own mental toughness under pressure by posing two really serious problems. One was a fundamental error in the script based on ignorance of the true nature of the beast. 'George, Larry and I didn't know that snakes love fire. Cold-blooded, they warm to it. Cobras and pythons will strike at flames. So we have to find something else that they hate – a smell, a pesticide. I'll have to have the insert team come and get little groups of them to move away. This is the most aggravating part of the film so far. They could slow us down a couple of days. We just didn't know.'

Problem two was a serious shortage of serum. No one in their right mind would put stars on whose backs millions of dollars were riding into a pit full of cobras without taking elementary precautions, but Britain is a country in which the adder is the only venomous snake and serum is a rarity. By Snake Day Five, a Friday, the man who'd promised it two months earlier had failed to deliver and the call went out to France and the American Embassy. Spielberg shot round the cobra vacuum while the messages became increasingly frantic and on Saturday, the vital phials of fluids arrived from India via France.

One of the cobras soon demonstrated that having the antidote plus an ambulance, two male nurses and a doctor on standby wasn't overkill, by wiping out one of the pythons. It was the one that had been trying to bite people all week, but this time it chose the wrong target, and the cobra's revenge was swift and fatal.

As if to compensate for its bad behaviour, and the delays the serum had caused, the key cobra delivered brilliantly when its big moment came on the following Monday, as producer Frank Marshall explained. 'What do you know? It hooded first shot. Glen Randall, the stunt co-ordinator who did *The Black Stallion*, said they had to wait two days to get their cobra to hood on the right spot. He couldn't believe it. Ours hooded straight off.'

The next day the main unit moved onto another stage, the Raven Bar, leaving the unfortunate Marshall to conquer his own snake phobia by overseeing the second unit. As a Spielberg man with a duty to Lucas to make sure the whizz kid kept to his schedule, he had to pick up any pieces left along the way. In this instance, that made him responsible for covering up the snakes-in-the-fire plot deficiency by devising ways of shooting fleeing reptiles, an assignment that gave him plenty of time to prove that anyone can get used to anything if they really have to. 'Once you see other people, like snake handlers, not worrying about it, then you touch one,' he commented drily. 'Eventually I got to be real comfortable with them. Some of the shots I did were a real challenge.'

Meanwhile Harrison, fuelled by constant cups of strong, black, unsweetened coffee, was casting off his natural inertia as the intrepid archaeologist bounded through catacombs and whipped up a storm in the Raven bar-room brawl. He had a stunt double on hand, the Irishman, Martin Grace, the only man to stand in for both Sean Connery and Roger Moore on the Bond films. He'd done some of Harrison's snake sequences when the going got deadly, but it became a matter of pride for the actor to do as much of the running, leaping and fighting as possible himself. Not that there weren't times when he cursed his own pride. Take the rock, for example, the co-star of that electrifying pre-credit chase that set the tone for the film.

Harrison was convinced he could outrun it. Spielberg disagreed, but Glenn Randall, the stunt co-ordinator, felt the actor would do okay. It was two against one, and the director didn't use his power of veto. 'We decided that the more action scenes I could personally do, the easier it would be for the audience to identify with and believe in the character,' Ford explained. 'But if I didn't trust the stunt guys who were manning the safety devices and looking out for me, I would never have done it. No way. As it was, I looked a little scared in the rock scene, didn't I? I'd have been crazy not to be. It wasn't a real boulder, but it wasn't cardboard either. It took 800 lb of plaster to make it roll right. And had I tripped, I could have been in big trouble.'

After ten confrontations with the rock, which was shot twice from each of five angles, Harrison was still running, but not so hard as Spielberg was sweating. 'Harrison raced the rock ten times and he won ten times and beat the odds. He was lucky. And I was an idiot for letting him try!'

When it came to the statue however, Ford decided that discretion was the better part of valour. The Jackal God stood twenty-nine feet high before it was toppled through a wall by Indy so that he and Marion could escape from the Well of Souls. Made out of plaster of Paris and attached by one lead to hydraulic rams that would tip it in a preordained direction through a breakaway wall, it had to be manned throughout, but this time it was Martin Grace who took the risks. Luckily, as it turned out, for the observant watcher will notice that 'Indy' loses his footing as the Jackal begins to go.

'Yes, it went too soon,' Grace told Alan Mackenzie, 'and that's when you have to think very fast. I was actually still hanging down when it started going. I should have been on my position. Stunt people are usually very fast thinking. In situations like that, you have to think very fast and get it together. We've got the sort of lightning reflexes, very sharp minds and that's a great combination to come up with the goods!' The implication, of course, is that Ford would have been injured, perhaps seriously, whereas Grace emerged unscathed.

1980 was not one of Britain's finer summers so it was with relief that the unit drove out to Luton airport to catch their charter flight to Tozeur, a Tunisian oasis town inhabited by 13,000 people and 200,000 palm trees. The plane touched down on the sand strip and the cast were duly whisked away to the Sahara Palace Hotel, an enclave of tranquillity and luxury outside the ramshackle town of Nefta, and the new *Raiders* headquarters. After a day of settling in, operations began briskly at Sedala where the lost city of Tanis, meticulously recreated from the visions of George Lucas as storyboarded by Steven Spielberg, awaited the director's attention.

As the sun beat down, it was possible to appreciate the logistics involved in keeping cast and crew going in such a remote place. Iced bottled water and soft drinks were constantly to hand and elaborate international meals were served by English caterers. Even so, it was impossible to prevent the constant attentions of 50,000 flies or the spread of dysentery among people working at full stretch for twelve hours a day in intense and unaccustomed heat. Soon Elstree began to seem like a paradise lost.

Only Spielberg was spared, due in no small part to his strict diet of British canned foods: baked beans, spaghetti, meat, fruit, cheese, macaroni. Dull it certainly was, but no flies and no possibility of unhygienic preparation made it safe. While Steven, in any case no gourmet, was standing, the show could go on. And it did. He alone never got sick.

Harrison Ford succumbed early on and never recovered, but he managed to keep working, even if he had to take short unscheduled breaks on occasion. It was during the Tanis sequences that he did the one stunt he really was lucky to walk away from. The scenario calls for Indy to have a fight in and around the propellors of the Flying Wing aeroplane. The engines are running full tilt and one set of wheels is chocked which makes the plane go round in circles.

'The bad guy is supposed to throw me down in front of the wheels and I am supposed to roll over backwards to get away from them,' Ford remembers grimly. 'All day long the technical crew was having trouble with the plane. It weighed a couple of tons, so they were powering it with low-gear, high-torque electric motors – the kind that can push through a brick wall without slowing down. They had to stay out of camera range, at the end of a cable fifty yards away. I still wanted to do this fight myself. I'm able to add bits of character touches to moments like these, and when the audience recognises the actor, it adds credibility to what is normally straight action stuff. We rehearsed the scene several times, then decided to shoot it.

'Everybody's ready and the take begins,' he continued. 'I go down and start to roll away – and my foot slips, right under the rolling plane's tyre. Everybody was yelling, "Stop! Stop!" while the tyre crawled up my leg. Luckily the brakes worked – inches before my knee was crushed, but I was pinned to the sand. I'm not normally a worrier. I know they're not going to kill the main character in a $20 million film. I also know Indy wouldn't look good with a peg-leg. Still, I was a lot more careful about stunt work after that!'

Mixing daring with caution became a way of life during those long hot Tunisian days. No, he would not become paranoid. They weren't really trying to harm him when they made him hang onto the rear of a truck, then fall off it, only to cling on by scraping over the gravel on his stomach. It couldn't be dangerous, could it, because the picture still had several weeks to run. Or could it? 'The stuff that turns out to be dangerous is the stuff that no one thinks about,' he summed up. 'It's not the obviously dangerous stunts, the ones you protect yourself for, calculate and worry about, so that all the angles are covered, that get you. It's the stuff you didn't think was dangerous that sneaks up on you.'

In any event, he survived and received his just reward for so much unforeseen activity in the shape of an excellent collaboration with Steven Spielberg who remained true to the promise he'd made on the plane from California, to let Ford shape Indy in his own image. Indeed the tall calm actor and the short, hairy, hyperactive director, physical and emotional opposites in every way, contrived to capitalise on their differences and make themselves into a formidable mutual-admiration society in the process. Spielberg, not himself a scriptwriter as Lucas had been for *American Graffiti* and *Star Wars*, had little respect for the written word and was perfectly prepared to substitute new dialogue as he went along. Or to let Harrison do so whenever it made him feel more in character.

'My only impulse to change lines comes when the words are impossible to get out of my mouth,' said Ford, telling only part of the truth. 'The process of film making involves so many situations and personalities that it becomes a very liquid medium. The physical presence of actors and crew are concrete factors, but the script should relate to them more like a road map of probabilities than a rigid blueprint.'

When we met shortly before *Raiders of the Lost Ark* came out, Harrison was eager to elaborate on the joys of the Spielberg experience. 'Steve allowed a collaboration that was a lot of fun. He was always willing to let me do another take if I insisted I could do it better. With some directors you have an extraordinary exchange of ideas with one leading to another and another. Steve and I worked that way. With others, you have to win a whole argument to change anything. But Steve's receptive. If I had a bit of an idea, he'd add to it and I'd add to it until we built it into something better – or something so outrageous, we both collapsed laughing on the floor.'

Spielberg, when asked about his leading man, was able to respond in kind, and no one thought he was lying when he said, 'He never does a scene or plays a moment without feeling justification for that moment, even if it's just getting into the truck and punching the sergeant out of the window. There has to be a justification to play that scene. He never burns out. He tapers off the fun of the first take. Doing anything for the first time is usually better than doing anything for the twentieth time. After twenty takes everything becomes rather studied but you can get the details right. The biggest danger is that you get it on one take, you can't believe you got it on one.

'So you stop trusting yourself,' he continued. 'Harrison says, "I must be able to do better. It couldn't have been that good." And I say, "I don't know. It was great, but we got it the first time. That's kinda odd." So we do it ten times and then I'll say, "It was number one. Why'd we spend an hour doing ten takes? It was number one."'

Undoubtedly Spielberg is an easier director for an actor to work with than Lucas. He is a bubbling ebullient enthusiast who takes his licence to thrill seriously, but finds time and energy to encourage his players. Where Lucas responds with a curt strangled, 'Great. You were great!' when asked to comment, Spielberg communicated easily and directly. 'Harrison is giving the performance of his life,' he told anyone who would listen on Day Sixty-one of *Raiders*. 'I'm sure he'll top this in his next film, but at least up to now, this is the best I've ever seen him. He's just amazing every day. It has to look effortless and it does.'

One of Ford's most effective pieces of input wiped out three well-worked pages of Larry Kasdan's script, saved the unit three days' work and proved to be a brilliant piece of improvisation. The scene was intended to be the ultimate confrontation between the scimitar and the bullwhip, the huge curved sword in the hands of a massively intimidating Arab against the snaking lash wielded by the fleet-footed Indy. The first morning scheduled for shooting these precisely storyboarded, highly energetic events, found Ford at a particularly low ebb, unable to stand up straight and obliged to use such speed as he had to head for the bathroom a good deal more frequently than he'd have liked.

Could he ever forget it? 'I was into my fifth week of dysentery at the time. The location was an hour and a half's drive from where we stayed. I'm riding to the set at 5.30 a.m. and I can't wait to storm up to Steven with this idea. I'd worked out we could save days in this lousy location this way! Beside which, it was right and important. What is more vital to the character's mind is finding Marion. He doesn't have time for another five minute fight. He hadn't unholstered his gun as yet. But as was very often the case, when I suggested it to Steven – "let's just shoot the fucker" – he said he'd thought the same thing that morning.'

'Yeah,' Spielberg agrees, 'I said, "look, let's all be heroes. Shoot the guy and save the girl." It was towards the end of the shoot and I was exhausted.'

Not, of course, that Spielberg, the perfectionist, would ever have allowed mere convenience, let alone personal considerations, to interfere with his film making unless his finely tuned instincts told him the changes were appropriate, but on this occasion he knew they were. Gunning down the Arab in the Cairo marketplace may not have been cricket, but Indy was no fresh-faced idealist either. Rather, he was mature, grizzled, amoral and well able to put expedience above honour and make it stick. 'He may be a swashbuckling hero type, but he has human frailties,' Ford explained. 'He does brave things, but I wouldn't describe him as a hero. He teaches but I wouldn't describe him as an intellectual. I wanted to avoid any elements that might be too similar to Han Solo. Indy doesn't have any fancy gadgetry keeping him at a distance from enemies and trouble. The story is set in 1936, after all, and he's right in there with just his battered trilby and bullwhip to keep the world at bay.'

When the film came out, the scene was highly praised for its snappiness and the unexpected element in it that made the audience laugh, just as the carbon freezing exchange, 'I love you', 'I know' between Solo and Leia in *The Empire Strikes Back* had done. The bullet solution also kept things moving which, of course, had been the prime consideration throughout.

Another Harrison Ford comic coup concerned the sequence when Indy impersonates a German by putting on a Nazi uniform which doesn't fit at all. 'I'd already been in a certain number of films with scenes of this type,' he told Bertrand Borie in *L'Ecran Fantastique*, 'and it always struck me how each time the borrowed garments fitted the borrower like a glove. It's completely idiotic. So I suggested we should make it into a joke and Spielberg added to that basic idea. We worked together on it because it's never the idea that is funny. It's the way of putting it on film. No one can claim all the creativity in such and such a scene: making it work has to be a group effort.'

As actor as opposed to action man, it was the professorial side of Indiana Jones, an unlikely combination of flamboyant adventurer and bespectacled academic, that gave Ford most pause for thought. Nothing in his career to date, including his own desultory college days, had prepared him to give a lecture to dozens of rapt students in a huge amphitheatre. As he recalls, 'It is one of the rare moments in the film which demands a *raison d'être* in that it's not part of the general tone: suddenly the comic adventurer becomes a totally serious professor, visibly interesting to his students and attractive to the girls among them who have nothing in common with a girl like Marion. Put like that, it sounds very simple but in front of the cameras it's less so.'

For Spielberg, *Raiders of the Lost Ark* was a test that didn't find him wanting. The ghosts of *1941* were often joined on the sets at Elstree and Nefta by the reality of George Lucas who was apt to sit silently in the background, chin in hand, watching his more outgoing friend speculatively, and ever-ready to curb the more exuberant flights of his imagination. Clearly this put their friendship under considerable strain, as Lucas admitted. 'You never know in a situation like that, but I figured we could survive it.'

That they did was due in equal parts to Spielberg's desire to respond to George's economic policy, and Lucas's readiness to keep a low profile. 'I'll always consider *Raiders* to be my film as a director, but George's film as a creator,' Spielberg comments. 'I needed the picture to exorcise myself from the kind of technological rut I was falling into, where I couldn't walk away from a shot until it was 100 per cent what I intended. To be able to walk away and say, "That's good enough for what we're trying to do here," was the most important film-school lesson a professional production had ever taught me.'

Another thing Spielberg learnt on *Raiders* was the subtle art of delegation. He shot all the close-ups, but his second unit, masterminded at times in the desert by a beetroot-faced Lucas with a severely peeling nose, but more often by Michael Moore, supplied much more of the supplementary footage than is normal, even on an epic. Better still, Spielberg was able to accept the contributions gracefully. 'Mickey Moore kept to 85 per cent of the basic storyboards. But for every sketch in the truck chase, he must have gotten me three or four shots I'd never planned on. Much better than my original sketches. He started shooting a week before we arrived in Nefta. I directed all the sequences that involved Harrison. Everything involving wider shots using doubles, Mickey did.'

Steven's reward came even sooner than anyone expected when *Raiders* wrapped after seventy-three days, twelve ahead of the schedule and under budget. The original slated cost of $7 million had swollen to $22 million, but that had been anticipated and Paramount's draconian penalty clauses were never invoked. It was appropriate that Lucas, who'd always believed that any deficiencies in shooting could be made good in the editing room, finally got his chance to add zest to *Raiders* at that stage. Spielberg had been guaranteed final cut, but as soon as his rough was completed, he gladly handed it over to his friend.

George watched it with his wife, at which point Marcia Lucas proved her worth, and that her Oscar for *American Graffiti* was no fluke, by spotting a terminal weakness. Where George used editing to beef up the action, her strength was giving more humanity to the characters. Yet here was a film ending with the girl out of sight. Frankly, she told George, it wouldn't do. Once the omission was pointed out, it became so glaringly obvious that neither Spielberg nor Lucas could live with it so Steven went to San Francisco to shoot a new one, with Marion waiting for Indy on the steps of a government building.

Both men were well satisfied with the results. 'I've got to tell you, you're really a good director,' Lucas told Spielberg on the phone after seeing the rough cut. It would have been presumptuous coming from anyone else, but Spielberg was delighted with the compliment, and with the accompanying prediction that *Raiders of the Lost Ark* would be the runaway box office success of 1981. Lucas had passed out of his doubting phase. Nowadays he knew what would sell, and of course he was right. *Raiders* earned $335 million worldwide, a figure only topped at that time by *Star Wars* and *The Empire Strikes Back*.

Spielberg's share of the cake was $22 million, more than he got for *Jaws* and *Close Encounters of the Third Kind* combined, and Lucasfilm got $21 million, though Lucas himself had to be content with a modest $2.5 million. As for Paramount, they'd spotted the gold in them there mountains and mined it to the tune of $49 million, more than doubling their $22 million investment. And they still have the right to distribute the film in perpetuity. As was now customary with Lucasfilm, the cast and crew split a further $7 million. Harrison has neither confirmed nor denied his 7 per cent share but, if it is anywhere near accurate, he would have been $10 million the richer when the receipts came in.

So everyone was happy. 'I probably had more fun on that picture than any other,' George commented, with the hindsight of a man who has been totally vindicated. 'I had all the confidence in the world in Steve and I was not at risk financially. I was hoping it would come in on budget, but if it didn't . . . well, for once I wasn't at risk.'

Characteristically, Spielberg looked at the situation from a more directorial angle. 'The thing to keep in mind about *Raiders* is that it's only a movie, not a statement of the times, the way things were in 1936. It takes all the licence of an exotic entertainment that aims to thrill and scare and strike one with a sense of wonder – with the cleverness of the hero pitted against an enemy of despicable class and wit. A gravy train movie! I don't make intellectual movies. George, however, is really an intellectual. The one thing we always have in common is that we just love audience films, slightly taller than life . . . and seen through youngsters' eyes.

'By the time I made *Raiders*,' he went on, 'I was getting tired of long complicated production schedules. I look at the logs of my favourite films of the thirties and forties and almost all of them were made in forty to sixty days, sixty-five to seventy days tops for a movie like *Northwest Passage*. My crew wanted an A movie, I wanted a B-plus. I brought them down to my pulp level. There were two ways I could have made this movie. I could have done it as a neo-Brechtian *film noir*, with multiple shadows out of Carol Reed or Orson Welles, like *The Third Man* and *Touch of Evil*. But then I realised that what for me could be a turn-on could wreck a gravy train movie. Why impose production values – visual noise? I just worked to tell the story, but I was happy making this movie, largely because of George Lucas and Harrison Ford. Both were full-time collaborators.'

18 July 1981 was *Raiders* Day in America, and the public's response in 1,078 cinemas nationwide was instantaneous and ecstatic. So, too, was the media's reaction with a *Newsweek* cover and a major feature in *Time* to whet appetites, undoubtedly the most effective boost a film can get in a country that has no national newspapers. However the critics, struggling as usual between enjoyment of a spectacle and a sense of self-image which suggests that fun can't be art, had their reservations.

'Spielberg is like the young Howard Hughes,' wrote David Denby in *New York Magazine*. 'He needs big screwy machines to fire his imagination (the planes in this movie are like the strange giant things that Hughes built in the thirties). When he doesn't have a big set to play with, his ideas go flat. The dialogue that Lawrence Kasdan has written for him is full of unplayable B movie turds like, "What exactly is the headpiece to the Staff of Ra?" A shoot-out in a Nepalese tavern is just standard movie violence; a chase through the Cairo bazaar is as dull as the one in *Sphinx*. When action fails, everything fails because pop moviemakers have nothing to fall back on.'

Andrew Sarris in *The Voice* put the other point of view. 'There are two sight gags in *Raiders of the Lost Ark* that are alone worth the price of admission, but I refuse to describe them until everyone has had a chance to experience them. One involves a prodigious Arab swordsman and his ridiculous fate; the other an unusually menacing coat hanger. Overall, however, *Raiders* is in no way a spoof. It is a rousing adventure yarn, full of high spirits and affectionate irony. I recommend it wholeheartedly and wholeheadedly.'

For Harrison Ford, it was reincarnation time. He might reasonably have expected to find himself with a strong public identity at last, but in fact he was hailed as the eighties answer to a host of thirties and forties stars. Humphrey Bogart, James Stewart, Lee Marvin, Errol Flynn, Robert Mitchum, John Wayne, Clark Gable: audiences were invited to pay their money and spot the likeness. The most obvious and popular choice, and the one given credibility by Spielberg himself, was Bogart as Fred C. Dobbs, a similarly battered adventurer in *The Treasure of the Sierra Madre*, but the critics were persuasive, not to say inventive, in supplying alternatives.

'With his stetson and stubbly beard and leather jacket, Harrison Ford occasionally evokes the young, modest James Stewart,' David Denby summed up. 'Like Stewart, Ford doesn't get the chance to build much of a character. There are no real people in the work of Lucas and Spielberg, and that may be the reason I always feel a little unsatisfied – as if my responses had been hollowed out – when their movies are over.'

The booby prize for the most arcane comparison must go to Sarris however. 'One of the biggest surprises in the film is the extent to which Harrison Ford incarnates Richard Arlen in his grubbier days on the poverty row of adventure movies. I had not thought that Ford had it in him to convey such a marvellously weary doggedness of spirit as he confronts the inexhaustible wiles of the world's villains. And who are the greatest villains in the world? The Nazis. The limitless, unambiguous evil of the Nazis is a convenient "given" with which Spielberg can fashion a satisfying romantic spectacle involving Ford's Indiana Jones, an academic adventurer, the type who would rather perish than publish. The opening shots of Jones stomping through the jungle with the cameras following behind is as muscularly kinetic as anything seen on the screen since the pre-credit shot of Toshiro Mifune from the rear in Akira Kurosawa's *Yojimbo*.'

Yes, critics certainly like to be seen to be movie buffs, but Harrison was quick to disclaim all the distinguished role models ascribed to him. After all, he still hadn't seen *Casablanca*, had he? Not all of it anyway, and he hadn't a clue what Lucas and Spielberg were on about when they started out-pointing one another on the history of the cinema. All he knew was that he'd clawed his way to the top of the cast list and the film was a major hit, which made him a star. Not that he cared about that either as he didn't believe in them, but it was a vindication for the years of rejection and struggle.

'I used to be self-effacing in front of executives and movie makers,' he told me shortly after *Raiders* came out. 'I was grateful for a job, most any job, but now I know I have other options and when I ask for the money I want, they pay it. I receive a lot of propositions. I'm pleased to have the opportunity to make the choices from amongst as broad a range of material as I can get.'

Of course *Raiders* had its minuses as well as its pluses. Indy's hat, for one. Spielberg had finally found the model he liked at Herbert Johnson's, London's most exclusive hatter, and ordered two dozen copies at £49 each so that Indy need never go bare-headed. And how Ford hated the battered brown Grosvenor, especially in 120 degrees of heat. Tunisia, too, was something of a turn off, not least because of the dysentery. 'That does spoil a nation for you. To see it from a toilet seat. It'll do it every time. It was just a very tough location.'

However, the perils were worth it because he was proud of the finished result. '*Raiders* is about movies. It is an intricately designed tribute to the craft. I'm quite in awe of the film, and the way it was accomplished. Steven set out to make an epic film, technically complex, on a short schedule. He didn't waste any time in retakes. He was fast and efficient, and that's the way I like to work. My responsibility was to define the character for the audience, to make the film as good as I could.'

Spielberg agreed both on the responsibility and its accomplishment when he said, 'Harrison is a very original leading man. There's not been anyone like him for thirty or forty years. He carries this picture wonderfully.' But the last word belongs to Derek Taylor:

'Not to lay on too much syrup,' he wrote in *The Making of Raiders of the Lost Ark*, 'I should say Harrison Ford did much to make the film a very happy and human adventure on screen and off. Such leading men are priceless. There were many moments when I tried to imagine how it would have been if Indiana Jones had been played by a mean fellow with either an inflamed ego or hangovers or contrived crises over script, directorial mannerisms, God knows what. Harrison was so crucial to the film and so rarely off screen that had he been unpleasant, things could have been really miserable.'

Written from the heart by a man who'd knocked around movie sets for years, it sounds like a proper tribute to a perfect gentleman.

11   Brave New World

'A MAN who is tired of London is tired of life,' wrote Dr Johnson, but Harrison Ford comes high on the list of those who don't believe him. By the late summer of 1981, he'd made four films there, all of them out of the same dilapidated Elstree dressing room. Once Lucas and Spielberg had recognised the technical expertise on the cheap in darkest English suburbia, Harrison had perforce to follow them, but no one said he had to like it, and he didn't.

'You gotta travel on, travel on,' he stated world-wearily, the picture of a man in a suite in the Savoy who wished he was in a fast food joint in California. 'This is a wonderful country, very pretty, and I admire the people. The crews are as good as any in the world. There are far more craft services here because of the old apprentice system. Young people learn their trade from the ground up and, as a carpenter, I appreciate that. But from my point of view, living in hotels or rented houses, I'm a prey to the tourist economy which is pretty dispiriting just now. London generally ain't what it used to be, is it?'

So it was back to Los Angeles and home sweet home, where the sound of ripping paper filled the smoggy air. Harrison, having earned a break, was able to lounge around thinking about carpentry, reading the newspapers and wondering where his next cup of coffee was coming from, but Melissa Mathison was as busy as she'd ever been in her life because Steven Spielberg had finally persuaded her to write the script for *E.T.* The idea for the film had come to him in 1976 while he was making *Close Encounters of the Third Kind* in Mobile, Alabama. What if, he asked himself, an alien stayed on earth and made friends with a wimpish lonely boy like Steven Spielberg?

He was encouraged in this fantasy by the late François

Truffaut, playing Lacombe in *Close Encounters* and highly impressed by the way his director handled the film's four-year-old blond child, Cary Guffey. 'You should make a film with kids,' he told Steven, and the movie brat agreed. The first writers on the project, then called *Growing Up*, were the two Bobs, Gale and Zemeckis (now a considerable director in his own right after *Romancing the Stone* and *Back to the Future*), but they failed to pack in enough wonder and were replaced, in due course, by John Sayles. He'd scored with *Piranha* and *The Howling*, material which hardly suggests the unremittingly optimistic view of the universe Spielberg required, and so it turned out to be. *Night Skies*, as *Growing Up* had become, featured eleven angry aliens, later reduced to five by Columbia's cost paring. Sayles was slated to direct, just as Tobe Hooper was making another Spielberg production, *Poltergeist*, at MGM.

By the time Spielberg rejected the hostile invaders and suggested a new approach to Sayles, the writer was involved in his own low budget project, the excellent lesbian film *Lianna*, and bowed out, leaving his ex-employer pacing the boards at Elstree. And there, like a vision before him, stood the lovely Ms Mathison, hanging out with Harrison and with all the time in the world on her hands while he put in fourteen hour days as Indiana Jones. After meeting Ford while working as an assistant on *Apocalypse Now*, she'd stayed with the Coppola stable and written *The Black Stallion* for it, surely one of the most wondrous child-orientated films in a decade.

Why, Spielberg asked himself, was he calling Los Angeles every evening when the answer to his dilemma was right here on the spot? So, one night over dinner, he pitched the simple premise of the single benevolent intruder to Melissa who, shrugging off the prospect of immortality as if it were an unwanted bread roll, replied, 'Thanks, Steven, but I've decided it's time I looked for another line of work. I've just read through some of my recent stuff and I've decided never to write again.'

It was only in Nefta, with Harrison out for the count between bed and bathroom each evening and Spielberg's girlfriend of the time, Kathleen Carey, back in Los Angeles, that the mogul had enough hours alone with Melissa to persuade her to change her mind. She began work on 1 October 1980 and had the first draft ready two months later, having consulted Spielberg once a week at Marina Del Rey where he was editing *Raiders*.

'The story just sort of evolved,' she recalls. 'It came so easily. Naturally I had bad days, but on the whole, it was not hard to write. I quickly became very fond of the character of *E.T.* All I knew about his appearance was that he had to be smaller than the children and as ugly as possible. I found it terribly moving when I was writing it. When I got to the last page, I was in floods of tears. The big question, though, was would anyone else react in the same way?'

The answer is part of history, but history which only peripherally involves Harrison Ford. When *E.T.* swept the board, making $1 million a day through the summer of 1982 and outstripping *Star Wars* as the highest grossing film of all time, his name was not among the credits. Not that he hadn't worked on it. He had, as Elliott's schoolteacher, cast, no doubt, on the professorial aspect of *Indiana Jones*, but he'd ended up on the cutting room floor!

Ben and Willard Ford were in there though, used by Melissa as role models because they'd been around a lot while she was writing her screenplay. Now fifteen and twelve, they were their father's pride and joy. He even suggested to *Ciné-Revue* in March, 1981, that he'd be ready to give up his career to look after them, a state of mind, perhaps, rather than a statement of intent as the decision wouldn't have benefited anyone very much. However, he was certainly happy to be in the same town with lots of time to spend with them.

'My boys come first for me and I like to think I'm a fun dad,' he said, apparently without embarrassment. 'I'm very pleased about the money I'm making because it ensures a good future for them. I don't live high on the hog myself. I prefer hot dogs to caviar, and I've never much liked champagne. I want to keep improving my life, my personality and my work, but I'll never act like a star. My sons would never let me get away with it. Anyway, discos, those symbols of high living, are what I hate most. My idea of hell would be to be confined in one for twenty-four hours a day.'

As the Ford–Mathison family fortunes rocketed during their first prolonged period in their new home, the question of what form that self-improvement should take occupied Harrison a lot. As always, diversification had top priority. Once *Raiders of the Lost Ark* was out, he couldn't set foot in a Hollywood studio without everyone 'searching the dustbins to find a role for me to play' but, Tinsel Town being Tinsel Town and as obsessed with cashing in on the immediate past as ever, those roles were invariably wise-cracking Solo–Indy spin-offs. As he was contracted to interpret each of these characters at least once more, pale shadows were the last things he wanted. But what to do instead? What, for example, about art films, hitherto conspicuously absent from his repertoire?

It is, he admits, a fair question. He does get offers of more rounded characters and he has never had any wish to be a hero per se. 'I'm not typecast heroically,' he says sardonically, 'except by journalists who find it necessary to categorise that simply. I make myself responsible for pointing out that I have played a lot of other characters in between my commercially successful films. I don't play a character as a hero. My behaviour is not in itself heroic except in moments of intense physical confrontation. There's a lot more to my job than pretending heroics.'

This statement suggests a certain amount of inner confusion, not to mention entrenched defensiveness, perhaps natural for a serious man who has had comic-strip greatness thrust upon him. Ford makes the distinction between American cinema as an entertainment medium and the European cinema as an extension, usually unsatisfactory, of literature. It is a naïve analysis, easily explained by his ignorance of cinema history on both sides of the Atlantic, but nevertheless it governs his choices.

'In Europe, I think, films tend to be more like literature, to use the concerns of novels as a basis for character development,' he attempted, rather haltingly, to put over his point of view. 'In America, we have evolved a kind of film that is very different, but I feel there is as much opportunity for expression in a scene without dialogue as in a scene with. Because it's not literature, it doesn't mean it has to be comic-book. That's a fairly general assumption. If it's not full of serious metaphysical concerns, then it must be comic-book, it must be slight.

'There are very complicated ideas in some comic-books, but people imply that the characters are less real than they might be in other circumstances. I don't find this necessarily true. I work hard to avoid making a character too simple. In *Raiders*, the people who created the conception of this character did me a great service by providing me with a strong opening scene in which you think you know everything about the character and then you get a hard cut to the same person under circumstances that you would never have anticipated. In my opinion, this produces anything but a two-dimensional character.'

But surely it does produce a character who plays second fiddle to special effects or stunts or whatever the director is putting up-front to keep his audience enthralled? This is Harrison's least favourite question, because everyone always asks it and it's hard to make the answer stick without facing reality and bowing directly to the mighty dollar.

Nevertheless, he tries. 'There is an idea in Europe that entertainment is less than salutory, that we should look down our noses at it. I think this is very wrong. In America, we've gone through a cycle of films that were full of social commentary and social relevance. What happened in America was that all the socially relevant film did was co-opt the problem. They spoke about a problem and then they presented a solution which was really a movie solution. Not a real solution for the real world. It was imposed by the mechanism, by the necessity to be, to a certain degree, commercially successful.

'You see, film isn't subsidised in America. Our film makers are totally free, except for having to get the money. They can make anything they want. They're free to criticise our government and way of life and so on and so forth. But they have to be commercially viable. That's why Hollywood movies are so exportable, because we're filling a need. We've got something that people want.'

Ah yes, indeed, the naked truth, a truth that led Harrison Ford eventually to *Blade Runner*, a change of image that wasn't really a change of image. The film was as grand in design as any from the fertile minds of George Lucas and Steven Spielberg, only this time the man behind the cameras was known for immortalising sliced bread and soap powder rather than space ships, sharks and biblical artefacts. His name was Ridley Scott. Born in South Shields, his background was strictly visual: art school in West Hartlepool, graphic design at the Royal College of Art in London, then advertising, followed by graphic design for the BBC where he worked on programmes like *Z Cars* and *The Informer*.

The advertising connection meant that he knew David Puttnam, a contact that enabled him to get *The Duellists* (a period first feature starring Keith Carradine and Harvey Keitel), off the ground in 1977. Its extreme elegance and the Jury Prize at the Cannes Film Festival earned it a cult following in California, and Scott had no difficulty in hitching his star to *Alien*, a space horror fantasy which propelled him into the big time with roughly the same force as the entrails erupted from John Hurt's stomach in the film's most dramatic moment. It also gave him a futuristic reputation, hence *Blade Runner*, set circa AD 2020 and based rather loosely on Philip K. Dick's mysteriously entitled novel, *Do Androids Dream of Electric Sheep?*

The transference of this respected work from page to screen took ten difficult years. Martin Scorsese was the first to express an interest in filming it, but the option finally went to Herb Jaffe who turned over the writing of the screenplay to his brother, Robert, in 1973. The result was so bad that when Dick read it he thought it was a rough and enquired if the Jaffes would like him to prepare a shooting script. This insult brought Robert Jaffe to Dick's home in Orange County where the novelist met him at the airport. 'I asked him if he wanted me to beat him up there and then or wait until we got to my apartment,' Dick recalled.

Further unsuccessful attempts were made until, in 1977, the Jaffes called a halt and let their option lapse. It was picked up by Hampton Fancher and his partner, Brian Kelly, who prepared an eight-page outline for Michael Deeley, riding high at the time as producer of *The Deer Hunter*. His initial disinterest turned to enthusiasm when he read it and he commissioned Fancher to write a full script. 'Lord knows,' said Dick, who apparently wasn't easily satisfied, 'I didn't think much of it when they sent it to me.' Deeley, however, loved it and began to hawk it around Hollywood where the response was predictable: how about changing this, how about changing that, how about a happy ending? Four or five drafts later, Ridley Scott came in and Deeley was able to put together a deal for the project, currently called *The Android*, with Filmways.

At the time, Scott was slated to direct another sci fi epic, based on Frank Herbert's classic *Dune* novels, but that, too, was proving intransigent, even in the capable hands of Dino de Laurentis, and it became clear that the British director would have time to put *The Android* on the screen before *Dune* got off the sand. In the event, Scott never returned to a film which finally found its maker in David Lynch. He shot it in Mexico in 1983 and went disastrously over budget from the start. It turned into one of the cinema's most expensive failures as the disillusioned public stayed away in droves when it opened late in 1984.

When Rick Deckard, the hero of *The Android*, first came to Harrison Ford's attention, he turned him down flat, because the film was set to shoot in London. 'They asked me about it when I was making *Empire*, I guess, and I said, "Well, thanks very much gentlemen, but I don't want to work here any more. I want to go home." Five of my last eight films had been made in London. I needed a change.'

Back in Los Angeles, Ford thumbed through stacks of alternatives while Melissa worked away at *E.T.* and *Raiders* went smoothly through post production. It is a task he has always loathed, made more bitter on this occasion by the rash of Solo–Indy clones. Gradually Deckard, now linked to Ridley Scott and Hollywood, became more attractive. At least he didn't crack jokes or whips. Eventually Ford said yes.

Of course he was not the only contender. As *Raiders* hadn't made its impact on the box office yet, he wasn't a certainty as a leading man. In other words, everyone suspected, but no one knew for sure, that he could carry an epic on his own. The first actor to be approached by Ridley Scott was Dustin Hoffman who reacted with astonishment – and his customary bluntness. 'What the hell do you want me to play this macho character for?' he demanded, but he didn't turn him down at once. Indeed he put in some 'wonderful ideas' according to assistant producer Ivor Powell, while he mulled over Deckard.

Once Hoffman was out of the running and the operation re-located in Los Angeles, the way was clear for Ford. Ironically, it was the involvement of Scott, the Englishman, which forced the westerly move across the Atlantic, so securing Harrison's services. Scott wanted Hollywood and, in those heady post-

Alien days, what Scott wanted he got, even if it added $3 million to an already handsome budget.

'I love the Hollywood process,' he said, by way of explanation. 'There's a great sense of optimism about the whole city. Someone once said it was a city forty-five miles wide and one centimetre thick, but I don't find it that way. The conditions of the studios are so good there; us poor British film makers have to set up our equipment in pretty depressing circumstances by comparison.

'I was interested in developing the future environment further after *Alien*,' he continued, elaborating on his acceptance of the project. 'I just didn't want to step off onto ordinary ground again. What I felt was great about the script was that it was dealing with the near future. It had to be a familiar city, which it is. A lot of aspects of that city are familiar right now. In fact, a lot of people who will see the film will experience that kind of future themselves. I also liked the aspect that there was a real character in there, rather than a two-dimensional cardboard character, which happens rather too often with science fiction films. Such films are usually dominated by a monster and the characters have to take second place.'

The initial collaboration between Scott and Ford was rosily optimistic. The actor, faced with that kind of commitment from the director, believed that he'd struck flesh and blood at last, not realising that in Ridley Scott films, actors are outshone by design rather than monsters or stunts. As for the director, he was under the impression that he'd found a leading man who'd play it his way. By the time he knew differently, it was far, far too late. Meanwhile both men endorsed their choices enthusiastically in public.

'Harrison has a very unusual quality that shines through in two pictures, *The Conversation* and *Apocalypse Now*,' said Scott. 'It's a strange, slightly sinister side, very low key and sombre. Almost a different Harrison Ford. Very dangerous. It fitted the nature of both Deckard and the film very well. The only other actor we saw for the part was Dustin Hoffman. He was looking for a different kind of movie but, God knows, I'd like to work with him one day. After things fell through there, we went straight to Harrison. He'd been under consideration from the beginning.'

'I'm preparing to start work on *Blade Runner*,' Ford announced in America. 'I'm sure I was considered as a result of *Star Wars*, just as Ridley proved his capabilities in this genre with *Alien*. I can't complain so far. *Star Wars*, *Empire*, *Raiders* and *Blade Runner* are classy high quality melodramas, not pot-boilers. They all contain currents of intelligence and morality, and are handled with taste. I'm looking forward to *Blade Runner*. I think I can give it an aspect that will set it apart from *Raiders* or *Star Wars* or anything else I've done.'

Plus ça change, plus c'est la même chose. By this time, *The Android* had become *Blade Runner* via another title, *Dangerous Days*. 'With that name it ought to be an ice skating featurette,' wrote Bart Mills in the *Guardian*, but in fact *Blade Runner* was the name of an obscure sci fi paperback by an equally obscure writer called Alan Nourse. It had no connection with twenty-first century replicant hunters, but concerned illegal doctors bringing help to the sick, using surgical instruments supplied to them by blade runners. Logical enough, though the reason why Hampton Fancher used the term as a code name for Deckard in his script remains elusive.

In any event, Ridley Scott liked the sound of *Blade Runner* so that's what the film became, once the rights to Nourse's book, plus the rights to the novelisation with the same name by William Burroughs written from his screenplay based on Nourse's book, had been bought up by the film makers. Complicated indeed, but not so complicated as the scriptwriting process which had entered a new phase with the hiring of David Peoples on 1 November 1980. His brief was to incorporate Ridley Scott's changes into the Fancher *oeuvre*. Fancher, who'd never intended to write the piece but allowed himself to be persuaded so as to have something to show Michael Deeley, realised that he was in a position from which he couldn't see the wood for the trees, and bowed gracefully to the inevitable.

'I was surprised when I read Peoples's script. Those things that Ridley had wanted that I thought couldn't be integrated had been rendered by Peoples in ways that were original, tight and admirable. I really liked it. We never actually collaborated. He came in on very short notice, and he had a lot of work to do, but he did it very fast and very well.'

Peoples also behaved impeccably over material on which the

two men would eventually share the screen credit. 'I felt it was so good when I first read it that I was disappointed. I told them I couldn't make it any better. It was a terrific script. I don't know what Phil Dick didn't like, but the version I saw was absolutely brilliant. And that was the one I worked from to make the changes Ridley wanted.'

His task wasn't made any easier because *Blade Runner* was well into pre-production by the time he finished, and that meant that expensive items were already under construction while he was scrapping them on paper. 'Jesus, you wrote out the ambulance,' Peoples was told. 'So what?' he enquired. 'It's already been built!' came the reply.

This suggests, perfectly accurately, that the film was running into financial minefields even before the cameras turned. Filmways, the company which was supposed to be the distributor and the major source of finance, had serious cash flow problems which were being exacerbated by *Blade Runner*'s escalating budget. Given Scott's obsession with visual perfection, it is hardly surprising that he couldn't find a suitable configuration of American architecture on location, and eventually he abandoned the attempt. That meant that huge elaborate sets had to be built from scratch so that they would reflect his vision precisely. That, in turn, meant they had to be expensive, $12 to $13 million became $21 million. Filmways collapsed.

It was at this stage that Michael Deeley saved *Blade Runner* by turning it over to Tandem Productions and The Ladd Company. Time was short because the Directors' strike was expected later in 1981 and Deeley knew that if he didn't move fast, the film would be grounded, probably for ever. Harrison Ford's dictates aside, it was too late to return to London in an attempt to beat the strike which, ironically, never took place. It was too late to do anything except raise the cash and go for it at Burbank Studios as planned.

So that is what they did. Through the winter of 1980–1, Scott's Metropolis rose on the Warner Bros lot in the North Angelean suburb. The New York street where Cagney and Bogart reigned supreme through the thirties and forties, was transformed into Los Angeles in 2020, a city in which monster garbage trucks never look like dealing with high-rise rubbish and parking meters kill those who tamper with them. Philip Dick, when consulted by the director, proved as critical of the arrangements as ever, as Scott recalls. 'He portrayed the world as an austere, deserted-streeted, curfewed environment which I think is a slightly old fashioned notion of the future. Certainly in western Europe and the western world, I think it's going to be massively crowded and multi-textured and multi-layered.'

Naturally, it suited him to think this way because, in his eyes at least, complex is considerably more photogenic than austere. His twenty-first century city is an architectural nightmare of crumbling baroque streets, towering but tottering under a continuous deluge of acid rain. The neon signs and fast food outlets are predominantly Chinese, suggesting some kind of oriental take over, an impression enforced by streets so chock-a-block with citizens and vehicles that it is impossible to move along them in comfort. Even the skies are full of spinners, flying police cars, inspired by Scott's experience on the Kennedy Airport–New York centre helicopter shuttle.

'I used to fly in at night and sometimes it would be snowing and it was very scary. The copter didn't fly very high above the buildings and at a certain point you have to land so you get very close to the buildings. It felt just like a future metropolis and I had that image in mind for the air traffic when I was doing the effects.'

With so much clutter and decay to compete with, the poor actors didn't have a chance, but mercifully Ridley's view of the future didn't include silver hair and shiny costumes with diagonal zips. In due course, Harrison was kitted out in a drab high-collared coat, checked shirt and tie. And no hat. Scott wanted him to wear a soft felt number like Indy's. Ford refused.

'A lot of futuristic stuff that one sees badly done is fashion,' Scott explained his reasoning. 'Fashion isn't going to change that drastically in forty years. I think a man like Deckard would have a suit that could have been made at any time during the last thirty or forty years. If you'd seen him standing on the street in 1940, he wouldn't have looked out of place and he doesn't look out of place now. That's the reality of the time slot, how time moves and how things move. Things actually move quite slowly.'

The *Blade Runner* story, as evolved for the cinema through its maze of screenplays, takes place in a world from which almost anyone with any clout has long since fled to live in colonies in space. The rich who remain inhabit well-guarded penthouse suites in 400-storey tower blocks erected on top of existing structures in order to avoid the cost of demolition. The replicant industry, originally perfected to fulfil the need for pets in a society which has eliminated real animals, is the only one that thrives. Its latest triumph is Nexus 6, a human lookalike with several times the strength and intelligence of its creators.

Condemned to fight intergalactic wars and work as slave labour in space, the human replicants are banned from earth for fear they might take it over. Why they should want to is hard to imagine but to guard against the possibility, all cities are policed with blade runners, bounty hunters whose job it is to detect and eliminate such invaders. Foremost among them is Rick Deckard, and it is he who is called on to track down four renegade replicants when they hijack a space shuttle and head for earth. He is a reluctant investigator, but blackmail works its sinister magic and, armed with a Voight-Kampff replicant detector, he sets to work.

As replicants are virtually indistinguishable from humans, they can be played by actors and actresses, in this case Rutger Hauer, Brion James, Joanna Cassidy and Darryl Hannah, an attractive and deadly quartet which Deckard must wipe out – if he can. As their only weakness is a four-year life span, pro-grammed into them to reduce the damage they could do if they did take over, his prospects don't look too bright and so it turns out to be. The bulk of the film is routine chase and kill, kill and run, make love and die, complicated only slightly by the fact that the love interest (Sean Young) is an illegal replicant herself. Clearly it is Deckard's duty to kill her but, not for the first time, a hero puts lust before duty and they head for the wide blue yonder, the Utopia of the countryside.

This artificially happy ending, far removed from the sombre tragedy of *Do Androids Dream of Electric Sheep?* was one of the things Philip Dick quarrelled with most virulently, not surprisingly because it quite changed the point of his novel. Harrison Ford wasn't too pleased with it either, nor with a lot of what went on in *Blade Runner* once the honeymoon period with Scott was over.

When *Raiders of the Lost Ark* opened and the name of Harrison Ford was on everyone's lips, the new star told *Films* magazines, '*Blade Runner* is an important step towards more serious roles and I think it will be a very commercial film because of its unique vision. I'm serious about it because of the people involved, and I was happy to find out that Ridley was interested in developing the density of the characters as well. I felt that we could work together to present a character who would be interesting and very different to anything else I've done till now.'

Had he looked more closely at Scott's earlier films, he would have realised that developing the density of characters was a task beyond an essentially visual man who is on record as saying, 'One sketch, one scribble is worth the most articulate two-hour conference.' Accustomed as he'd become to discussing *raison d'être* with Spielberg, Ford was inevitably disappointed when Scott was unable to come up with the goods in this respect. Not that the spirit was unwilling.

'We have a lot of discussions about our scenes,' Ford explained, 'but not about the motivation. I don't ask Ridley what my motivations are and he doesn't ask me what they are. The discussions are usually about practical matters – what we're trying to get out of a scene, what the obligations are on him as master of the story and me as the character. Then we look for common ground to accomplish the story points and the character points at the same time. And sometimes that's done without any discussion at all, and sometimes we discuss the hell out of it!'

Before any of this could happen, set dressing had to take place, painstakingly, detail by detail, the gadgets had to be in working order, as did the smoke and rain machines. The extras, kitted out in Russian and Chinese Army uniforms, Hari Krishna robes, nun's robes, punk and Mexican outfits, anything that would suggest a multi-racial society, had to be assembled and placed in position. 'I work principally as a designer,' Scott enlarged on his own priorities. 'First I create the proscenium, the stage. If you get the environment right, everything tends to fall into place. When I first read the script for this film, it was all interiors. Now it's a real look at the environment of the future.'

Lighting and camera positions came next. Scott's role model

was *Citizen Kane*, with its shafts of light, unusual angles and high contrast black and white photography. *Blade Runner* is in colour but its tones are dark and sombre, reflecting aspects of Orson Welles's masterpiece. As the cameras turned Scott, inspired perhaps by working on the exact location of *The Maltese Falcon*, made *Blade Runner* less of a futuristic thriller and more of a homage to the great *films noir* of the forties. This led to a fundamental disagreement between Scott and Ford as to how Deckard should be played. Scott wanted a Philip Marlowe figure to go with his Chandleresque design and, as Ford had been dubbed 'the Bogart of the eighties', he didn't really see why he couldn't have one. Ford, whose prime concern was to dump that image as thoroughly and as soon as possible, favoured Travis Bickle, the downbeat, crazed character played by Robert de Niro in *Taxi Driver*, the ultimate in depressive reality.

'He's a reluctant detective who dressed like a middle-aged Elvis Costello,' he commented. 'He's a skilled investigator, an expert in his field, but he's a little out of practice when the movie opens. He's lost his motor drive. Exterminating people, even non-human ones, is not something he likes to do, and he's not comfortable with authority. He's very tough, but he's no match for a top-of-the-line replicant.'

Shooting started on *Blade Runner* on 9 March 1981 after a year of pre-production and fourteen weeks of on-site construction. The film was already three months behind at this point, but the schedule was in no way open ended because the Directors' strike against the studio stranglehold was still set to begin on 1 July. *Blade Runner* had to wrap for good on 30 June. Scott had no leeway for error.

His problems were compounded by the fact that the action takes place almost entirely at night, a tampering with the normal sleep cycle which ensured maximum fretfulness for cast and crew. For weeks, the hours-of-darkness schedule meant that they had lunch at midnight and stopped work at six in the morning, leaving neither time nor energy for the socialising which normally binds a unit together. Ford had been here before on *American Graffiti*, but he'd been young and hungry then. By now, he was accustomed to the pampered cocoon of Lucasfilm, where frenzy had long given way to greased wheels.

Nor was he able to compare Ridley Scott favourably with

George Lucas. Where the American had learned to delegate his responsibilities against his natural inclination as soon as he had the money to do so, Scott was obsessed with being involved in every aspect of his film, including operating the camera himself. Lucas had found the British unions hard to handle when he first arrived at Elstree, and Scott soon discovered that their American counterparts were no less obdurate. The local crew worked more slowly and were markedly reluctant to touch the forelock to the director – and they didn't approve of infringements of the regulations.

'It's as if a professional golfer weren't allowed to use his clubs himself,' Scott complained over the camera question. 'His caddy tells him, "Nothing doing, mate. Rules is rules." The golfer has to talk the caddy through it: "Now keep your eye on the ball . . . swing smoothly . . . and hit it! Well, you almost got it, now let's try again."'

Nevertheless Scott had his own way on several occasions, rather to Harrison Ford's disgust. 'He never really got round the problem,' he explained. 'He just learned to accommodate the reality. He was able to shoot a few things he really wanted to. And he's very good, especially with the hand–held camera. I think there's quite a few shots in the film, with Ridley operating his hand–held camera. He likes to watch the performance through the lens. As an actor, I'm glad he wasn't allowed to do that all the time. I think it's better to have his attention on other things. He knows that's the way I feel. I think that when a director is looking through the camera, he's watching the edges to be sure where everything is. I want a director to be helping me with a whole scene, the performance. It's not that this isn't possible, nor that Ridley hasn't done it before.'

Other bones of contention were Ford's appearance and the voice-over, questions on which star and director eventually emerged at 'one all'. Harrison's preoccupation with new ground needed to be satisfied by some fairly drastic alterations in his appearance. If the costume wasn't intrusive in any way, it could hardly be said to change his image. Something more was needed. He would, he decided, cut his hair.

'I had to talk Ridley into the crewcut,' he told Alan Mackenzie. 'He was afraid that it might make me less gorgeous. The haircut couldn't be done unless Ridley was there. It took about four hours to get it. With long pauses for consideration by Ridley. My ambition was always to get it right down. Real short. I wanted to give the impression of a character who has given up on himself, was unconscious of his appearance and lost, to a large degree, that ego that keeps us all doing things like combing our hair, brushing our teeth and all of that. I thought it was important to suggest and change my appearance in some way. I think it's more interesting for an audience, even if they know right away who it is. They don't have the same expectation of you if you don't look the same. It gives you a foot forward.'

Another advantage of the style, as he discovered during the four month shoot, is that it keeps the hairdresser from dashing forward between each take to primp and perfect. 'Some of my best friends are hairdressers, but it does drive me nuts. I'd have short hair on every film if I could.' Perhaps a beard fulfils a similar function by reducing the non-stop attentions of the make-up artist. In any case, Ford decided he'd have one of those too, starting out clean shaven and letting the stubble come. After all, it was quite logical.

'When the events begin to take over my life, it hardly seems a proper time to shave. When things are going the way they are in *Blade Runner*, there doesn't seem time for a bath and a shave. I think that kind of detail goes to make up the character. I try not to lose sight of those little things.'

One who was markedly less than amused by these arrangements was Harrison's love interest, Sean Young, playing Rachel, the glamorous replicant. 'The day we had our first big scene, Harrison had to be unshaven,' she recalls grimly, 'because he's supposed to have come to me after a huge fight. Every time he kissed me, the make-up people had to be all over me to repair the damage. What a beard that guy has. He completely tore my face up. But when I saw it on film, I thought, "Holy Moly, what incredible intensity." The next day my face was all red and broken out.'

As Harrison was living at home during the making of *Blade Runner*, he held himself fairly aloof from the rest of the cast, all of them rather less experienced than he was, and Ms Young, for one, regretted it. 'I think he's probably an all or nothing type of person and he can't relate to other cast members full out, because he feels he might become too wrapped up. By being familiar with the crew, he can avoid that whole mess.'

After the *Raiders* experience, Harrison felt confident of performing his own stunts on *Blade Runner*. One of them is a key scene, the only one he had with the other established actor, Rutger Hauer who, as the replicant leader, Roy Batty, has to haul Deckard twenty feet up onto a roof. 'Harrison didn't want to fall down that twenty foot drop, or whatever it was,' Hauer commented. 'He was hanging there, with a wire for support but it was still kind of tough to get him up. I didn't work that long with him, but he was fine. Our scenes were very clearly written in the script. I didn't feel there was a problem of communication because we didn't have to talk about it. It was just a matter of doing it without getting hurt.'

As the difficult weeks passed, the voice-over became a logical extension, in Ridley Scott's mind, of the Chandler style that was taking over his film. One of the original scripts had included one, and the lack of a world-weary explanation, à la Humphrey 'Marlowe' Bogart, developed from a minor irritation into the thing that would make or break the movie. As the director, he had the power to force his choice on Ford, and so it fell to him to come up with the excuses when the laconic drawl was greeted with scorn and derision by the critics.

'We never addressed the problem early enough,' he summed up. 'I wanted the voice-over from the beginning because it is an essential part of the Marlowe-type character of Deckard and also to a degree helps clarification. One of the most interesting aspects of *Apocalypse Now* was the voice-over. It was incredible. I think Coppola went on for nearly six months trying to get that right. I think, with hindsight, I would have re-done the voice-over, and I think Harrison would as well.'

Wrong. Harrison would have scrapped it altogether, as he has made perfectly plain. 'It was never any ambition of mine to play the character like a forties Bogart figure, but it was always on Ridley's mind. It was always my hope that there wouldn't be a voice-over, that we wouldn't need one. I thought the character needed to be a representation of a certain type of physical environment, the result of that kind of life. The voice-over was always Ridley's idea from the beginning.'

When shooting finally finished on *Blade Runner* two weeks

late in mid July, 1981, tempers were pretty frayed and everyone was glad to go home. Scott had had the foresight to prepare two endings, which was fortunate because the first preview in Denver, Colorado suggested that audiences didn't care for the abrupt departure of Deckard and Rachel in a lift with the doors clanging ominously shut behind them. In due course, this was replaced by the more romantic notion of taking them off in a spinner to the unpolluted north western states, further desecrating Philip Dick's original grim concept. However, the novelist was not around to complain any more because he died tragically on 2 March 1982, a few weeks before *Blade Runner* opened in America.

As has become customary with Ridley Scott films, reactions were divided between those who appreciated the visual exotica and those who wished there was more to back it up. Alexander Walker, writing in the *Evening Standard*, comes in the latter category. 'The physicality of the film is a tour de force. Unfortunately its environmental impressiveness isn't matched by its skill in story-telling or any ability in dealing with the intellectual and moral queries raised by its equivocal admiration of the Fascist elements in the bravura new world Ridley Scott has created.'

Harrison Ford didn't escape unscathed either, but the reviews certainly reflected an added dimension that must have pleased him. The *New Yorker*'s Pauline Kael is never one to mince her words, and she didn't this time. 'All we've got to hang onto is Deckard, and the movie makers seem to have decided that his characterisation was complete when they signed Harrison Ford for the role,' she wrote, a viewpoint endorsed at greater length by Michael Scralow in *Rolling Stone*:

'He can't hide the strain of trying to breathe some spontaneity and wit into this off-white elephant. Screenwriters Hampton Fancher and David Peoples saddle him with a narration full of tough guy clichés that were hoary in 1949, let alone 2019. The performers who play the replicants in this movie have more histrionics than the actors playing humans. But Fancher and Peoples can't even create coherent androids: the replicants' demonic leader, Roy Batty, played by the enjoyably hammy Rutger Hauer, is alternately a futuristic Führer and a pathetic non-person, never sounding both notes at the same time.'

Alan Brien of the *Sunday Times* felt that 'He (Ford) actually shows signs of exhaustion, pain, fear, guilt and doubt, rare among private eyes. The supporting characters are exceptionally well cast and played. But by placing the weight of the narrative on familiar, gun-toting stuff, even under its many laconic and bizarre disguises, Scott rather loses or buries the themes that made Dick's novel such adult and fundamentally serious entertainment.'

So far as American viewers were concerned, the question of whether *Blade Runner* was serious or not was of key importance: were they supposed to laugh or cry? they demanded. Laugh, Scott replied firmly. 'It's all tongue-in-cheek. It's fun, not to be taken seriously. It's just a look at what could actually happen if, let's say, the genetic industry became a large conglomerate, a monopoly. We could have chosen to do a film about genetic engineering, which is a very serious subject. But we decided not to do that kind of movie. We decided to use elements of it and create our own comic strip. This film is not a warning in any sense of the word.'

Except perhaps to Harrison Ford who managed to keep his mouth more or less shut about his differences with his director. He did a lot of publicity for the film around the world, surprisingly for a man who hates it because the schedule reduced the year off he'd promised himself before *Indiana Jones and the Temple of Doom*, to six months. No doubt Melissa's world tour on behalf of *E.T.* during its golden summer of 1982 had something to do with Ford's acceptance of the chore.

'I'm never going to be completely pleased by anything, partly because I am by nature a perfectionist and partly because only part of any film is successful,' he told me during the course of this global trip. 'If you ask me to apply that to *Blade Runner*, I'm afraid we're going to exceed my capacity for frankness very soon because I wouldn't like to specify which bits I think work and which don't. On any film, I get a lot of enjoyment doing the work itself and the rest is pretty much out of my hands, and if it's out of my hands, I may as well put it out of my mouth as well.'

He picked up his coffee, shuddered at the suggestion of *Blade Runner II* and switched the conversation to family matters. Tomorrow, he said happily, he'd be back in Benedict Canyon with his sons.

12   Solo's Last Stand

'IT WOULD take an Act of Congress to get me to work before *Jedi*.'
The speaker is a one-film-a-year actor now, a man who knows
precisely in July, 1981 what 1982 and 1983 will bring him. Han
Solo III and Indiana Jones II may be the lines of least resistance, but
there are obligations, contractual in Indy's case, moral in Solo's,
which must be met. Besides, the decision to make sequels gives
Harrison a breathing space to decide what to do with the rest of
his life. He feels an empathy with the kind of screwball comedies
that put Cary Grant's name in lights above the title, the ones with
the smooth, suave, slightly mocking heroes who make women
swoon. Indeed he is offered one in 1982 opposite the indomitable
Barbra Streisand, but he turns it down.

Perhaps his motive is sheer terror. The little lady with the big
nose is not exactly famous for sharing limelight. More probably,
it is a combination of that and his tendency to idleness. Why
should he not lounge around the house doing nothing much?
He had undoubtedly earned the right to choose.

The five months between *Blade Runner* and *The Return of the
Jedi* allowed Harrison and Melissa to relax in their still relatively
novel domesticity, the first time both had been at leisure together
since they'd moved in two years earlier. The house in the
Canyon was more than habitable and Harrison had hung up his
tools for the time being. He had a workshop planned, but
somehow apathy had overtaken it.

'It's like a writer sitting down and sharpening every pencil in
the house before starting to work. I can't just run down there
at the moment and spend an hour or two. It'd take me a couple
of weeks to get in the right frame of mind. I have a long list of
self-commissions for the house, things I've put off buying for
ages because I could so easily make them myself. Now I find I

don't miss them as much as I did when I first thought I needed them.'

Ben and Willard came over most weekends and family life proceeded smoothly. 'I crafted the dialogue for the kids in *E.T.* by listening to them,' said Melissa, 'but fortunately they quite liked the finished film – more than Harrison did – so we're still friends.' The style is relaxed: although Harrison dresses formally when he's out on business, he has adopted the 'Movie Brat' uniform of plaid shirt, worn jeans and sneakers for home use.

More fundamentally, Harrison began to analyse his acting technique just as he once analysed his approach to carpentry. In the bad old days, his only ambition had been to be continuously employed. Now the ability to keep the periods he set aside as sabbaticals free of pressures so that he could prepare properly for his next part came high on his list of priorities.

'It takes me a long time to come down after a film,' he explained. 'It's not so much that I'm tense because I find so much release in working, but I'm so fully absorbed and engaged in the situation that resetting my life creates inner tension. I have to unwind. Once that's done, I begin to miss the challenge quite quickly. If there's no test for the day, the day tends to slip away.'

One of the challenges built into the Lucas–Spielberg films is competing with special effects, a process that isn't made any easier by the conditions the acting had to be done under. In the *Star Wars* series, the intergalactic marvels are shot in miniature at Industrial Light and Magic in California, then added later as background for the actors who, therefore, have to imagine them when they're building their roles. This requires a very precise approach which Harrison has learned to relish.

'I'm interested in the technical side to the degree that I think of myself as a craftsman. I'm very aware of it. However, the supposed difficulty of working with special effects does not exist. If you're on a set, it's no harder to imagine a dozen star cruisers approaching than, say, the existence of a tennis court or an ocean. If we were on a set, they wouldn't be there either. On the other hand, if we were matting in starships outside the window, I'd be obliged to move past the frame on this side or that side of the window. Filming is a very technical medium so your movement is limited by technical constraints.

'I quite enjoy dealing with those kind of problems. My

method is to create reasons for what I have to do. I make the technical requirements part of my characterisation. My purpose is to weave the bits together to make something as real as possible. On my kind of films, there's not much rehearsal time so you're under the gun to solve the practical problems in as short a time as possible.'

Ford takes pride in his ability to do this because it is in his nature to dissect and define, rather than act by instinct. Despite the long years he has spent in California, he hasn't allowed himself to be touched by the *laissez-faire* approach the good life inspires in many more peripheral inhabitants of Tinsel Town. Just as he doesn't jog or work out or go to Hollywood parties if he can possibly help it, so he doesn't accept the local custom of letting his instincts guide his mind. If this makes him constructive rather than creative, the consummate craftsman rather than the consummate artist, so be it.

It may be knowledge of these limitations, combined with a residual lack of security, a hangover from the long years of under-employment, that made Harrison Ford continue with his sequelisation programme, even after he'd become the best paid actor (as opposed to an actor-producer like Clint Eastwood) in the world..

So it came about that when the future of the carbon-frozen Han Solo in *The Revenge of the Jedi* (as Part III was initially called) was under discussion, George Lucas found his interpreter ready and willing. 'I was committed only to the first *Star Wars*,' said Ford, when he announced his decision. 'As for moral commitment, my greatest one is to myself and my career. But I am very loyal to George. We have a long relationship. If I hadn't made other movies in between, I might have felt differently about coming back, but as it stands I'm delighted. Han, Luke and Princess Leia were created to tell this story, so I'm glad to be in on the third act. In any case, I don't condemn sequels when they're done with the pride that George brings to them.'

Acceptance meant another reunion at Elstree which duly took place on 11 January 1982. Many of the ingredients were familiar, including the small tense figure of Lucas who'd put up all the money this time – and intended to keep a rather closer eye on his investment than he had on *The Empire Strikes Back*. The basic story, of course, was his and once again it had been fleshed out by Lawrence Kasdan, despite initial reluctance when he received his patron's phone call.

'He asked me to do it as a favour,' the writer remembers, 'which was a big surprise because I thought a new team would be used. I told George I hadn't planned on doing any more writing without directing. He said, "Aw, come on. I've done it. Paul Schrader did it for Martin Scorsese. What difference does it make?" So I agreed because I felt I owed George a lot. Besides, I like working with him and there's a certain satisfaction in finishing the trilogy. Additionally, writing *Jedi* will be very rewarding financially.'

Quite so. The debt he owed Lucas was for agreeing to act as unofficial executive producer on the steamy *film noir* thriller, *Body Heat*, the film that launched Kasdan's highly promising career as a writer–director, and therefore a favour well worth repaying. Although the mogul wouldn't endorse the film by putting his name on it (perhaps because he thought the raunchy sex scenes would dent his own image as a golly gosh film maker), his acceptance of a $250,000 fee plus 5 per cent of the profits to make sure it stayed on the rails during production was a key factor in persuading Alan Ladd to back it.

Where *Star Wars* had taken Lucas two years to write, his first draft on *The Revenge of the Jedi* was completed in four weeks. Six years on, the story had its own impetus and logic and the words flowed almost effortlessly onto the page. Of far greater moment was the question of who should direct it and there were times when George Lucas himself was tempted. Then reality struck back. 'I took one look at the amount of work and thought, "Oh my God, my life is complicated enough!"'

Whether Irvin Kershner would have accepted a second bite at the *Star Wars* gold mine is debatable, but it is certain that he never got the chance. By attempting to intellectualise *The Empire Strikes Back*, he'd tampered with Lucas's sacred vision; by going over-budget, he'd committed a capital crime. He was not asked to return. Instead, Lucas looked for a more biddable director and eventually whittled down the hundreds of men who might be willing to bend the knee and touch the forelock to the Force, to two; Richard Marquand, and David Lynch, who'd just made his name with *Eraserhead* and *The Elephant Man*.

In the end, Lynch turned out not to be biddable enough, as Mark

Hamill explained. 'David decided he didn't want to do a George Lucas movie because he felt he couldn't be constantly answering to another producer. George didn't want to restrict somebody that original, so they came to an amiable parting of the ways.'

Lynch's decision, which eventually resulted in his being associated with the catastrophic sci fi failure, *Dune*, instead of one of the highest grossing movies of all time, may not have been career-enhancing, but his loss was undoubtedly Marquand's gain. The Welshman comes from one of Britain's leading political and academic families: he is the son of a university professor who became Minister of Health in 1951, and the brother of David Marquand, the Labour Member of Parliament who went with Roy Jenkins to the European Economic Community headquarters in Brussels. Later, David became disillusioned with politics and took a post teaching modern history at Salford University. With a classical education and a good degree from Cambridge behind him, Richard, too, felt that the intellectual life was open to him.

'I suppose I could have been a university professor somewhere had I wanted,' he told Ray Connolly in the *Evening Standard*. 'And yet here I am in my middle years getting enormous pleasure and self satisfaction out of a very menial job – the sort of job where all I do is go about shouting at people, telling them where to stand and what to do. Yet for me the whole thing is magic.'

The people he was shouting at at the time were the actors and crew of *The Birth of the Beatles*, a two–hour film for American television about the early days of the celebrated songsters from Liverpool. Next, he made the heavily romanticised World War II drama, *The Eye of the Needle*, with Kate Nelligan and Donald Sutherland, a small body of feature work which nonetheless qualified him admirably in Lucas's eyes to take nominal control of *Jedi*.

'It's partly down to that modest track record that I got the job,' says Marquand, with both insight and honesty. 'I don't think George wanted to go the route of using an older and more experienced man. I'd shown that I could get a lot of films made on a tight budget with my TV work, and costs can get away from you so easily on a big budget. In the end we brought *Jedi* in for $32.5 million, which is pretty well what it was budgeted at. It's still an awful lot of money, but I think that your

A time for smiles: Kathleen Kennedy, associate producer of *Raiders of the Lost Ark*, can't hide her admiration for her hot property at the Deauville Film Festival, 1982 (left), and Harrison himself is equally unrestrained in his enjoyment of the company of his girlfriend, Melissa Mathison, now his second wife, at a Hollywood Film Writers' Banquet (below).

Above: Acclaim on the beach at the 1985 Cannes Film Festival for the stars of *Witness*: Kelly McGillis and a crop-headed Harrison Ford.

Right: No hiding place for Harrison Ford, spotted by photographers despite the unaccustomed beard and sunglasses, as he arrives at Los Angeles International Airport off a flight from New York.

Harrison Ford hard at work at home (above) but he finds time to take a break (below).

There's no place like home: Harrison Ford takes his dog-training seriously over coffee in the garden of his house in the Canyons (above), then goes indoors to flip through a book and give the animal, called Taco, a break (below).

ticket-money really gives you a good time at the movies!'

Where Kershner was prepared to stray from what Marquand calls 'the etiquette of the saga,' the prototype laid down by Lucas in the first film, Marquand was properly respectful of the tycoon's audience-winning formula. What was R2-D2 doing painted with black squares instead of the original blue of *The Empire Strikes Back*? Why was Darth Vader allowed to wield a light sabre with one hand? 'Everyone knows that a light sabre is too heavy for one hand,' Marquand complained, and his indignation was for real.

No doubt Lucas was impressed by such subservience to his vision. 'George told me he wanted a director who could work fast, somebody – possibly from television – who would think on his feet, improvise quickly, and work with actors. Finally – and I think this is the most important thing – somebody who could work with him.' Once again Marquand proved that he had no illusions about his mega-production, which was fortunate because George was back on his adrenalin high, obsessed with the purity of his conflict between good and evil.

'My original intention had been to do *Star Wars* and then be a real mercenary and turn the saga over to someone like Fox. I'd sit back and take a big percentage of the gross and I'd go to the movies and see them when they were done. When the time came for me to hand over, I'd fallen in love with *Star Wars*. It's like marriage. You know what they say about women, "You can't live with them and you can't live without them." That's how the *Jedi* is. I want these three films to have a unity because it's one story. I knew I had to be there to keep the look of it consistent, the art direction consistent, the technology consistent. I knew I had to finish this particular film, working with these particular actors for the last time.'

Once Marquand was hired, he found himself locked in conference for a week with Lucas and Kasdan, arguing the toss about how the trilogy should be concluded. Kasdan's brief was familiar: inject pace and humour, and do it fast. Marquand's was to develop the characters, the field in which Lucas was weakest and therefore the one in which a director had the greatest scope for making a significant contribution.

'I had a whole plan of the way I wanted to present each character to make *Jedi* slightly different from the other films. *Empire* ends in a kind of explosion – everyone's going off in different directions. I thought it would be nice if we opened *Jedi* with a tremendous sense of mystery. A "Where is everybody?" sort of feeling. We know that Vader and the Emperor are really on the Rebel's tails after *Empire* which ended on a kind of dark note. I thought it would be nice to pick up on that. All the heroes are scattered to the four corners of the Galaxy and then I could bring in each one in an interesting way. George liked the idea. Larry picked up on it and turned it into something terrific.'

So far, so good, but some things were sacroscant, among them the characters' lives. Marquand, Kasdan and Harrison Ford all claim the idea of killing off one of the principals, most probably Solo, but Lucas was adamant. This was the 1980s. You couldn't go round killing people off. It wasn't nice and it didn't tie in with his liking for happy endings. Han Solo was spared.

All this seems fairly obvious but Lucas, operating out of a suite at Claridges where his dishevelled appearance attracted scornful glances from the uniformed doormen who towered over him, went to great lengths to keep the saga's *dénouement* out of the newspapers. Down at Elstree, the pace was fast and furious as the nine sound stages rang the familiar changes between docking bays and palaces, starships and Yoda's lairs. The Ewoks, cuddly teddy bears who appear for the first time in the final film, had their own village built among the redwood trees in the forested Moon of Endor, the film's most impressive new location.

The British studio was used to keeping Lucas's secrets, but the location work in America called for far sterner security arrangements. After seventy-eight days in North London, cast and crew moved to Arizona where Tatooine, the desert where the *Star Wars* saga began, was re-sited near Yuma, doubling for Tunisia, now out of favour after the trials and tribulations of *Raiders of the Lost Ark*. There an assortment of faces who should have been familiar to the locals were disguised as players in a film called *Blue Harvest*. The daily call sheets asked Mark Hamill as 'Martin', Harrison Ford as 'Harry' and Carrie Fisher as 'Caroline' to be ready for pick up by limousine at 7 a.m. The crew wore T-shirts emblazoned with the message 'Horror Beyond Imagination'. 'Is that what the film's about?' Lucas was asked. 'No, that's the description of the making of the movie,' he quipped by way of reply.

The same procedure was repeated when the unit moved to Crescent City in northern California where the unique redwood groves were used for the further development of the Moon of Endor. As the sole survivors of the forests that once covered the entire West Coast, these splendid trees, 200–300 ft high and up to twenty feet in diameter, needed protection just as much, if not more, than the plot of *The Return of the Jedi*. They were reached by a narrow dirt track turning inland from the coastal highway and leading to a one-lane bridge, the only approach to a steep old logging road which finally opens into a clearing to reveal the majestic virgin redwood stands. The geography was perfect for keeping unwanted spies and fans out and Lucas made full use of this privacy to play his cards as close to his chest as possible.

The false name had the added advantage of protecting the production itself, and those who worked on it, from the all too natural desire of the local traders to profit unfairly from them. Crescent City, for example, has an unemployment rate of 28 per cent out of a population of 2,500, the result of the progressive decline in timber and fishing since the Second World War. *Jedi* personnel spent $2 million in the area on local salaries, food, lodging, transport and materials, a bonanza in a depressed community, but no one doubted that prices would have been raised had the true nature of the venture leaked out.

Richard Marquand repaid Lucas's trust in him by completing the location work in two months, despite sandstorms in Arizona and fog interspersed with bright sunshine in northern California. 'Films are too expensive now to wait for ideal conditions,' he said. 'You've just got to do it. But I have the rare advantage of having the creator of the myth right here to answer all my questions about background detail. It's like having George Bernard Shaw standing behind you while you direct one of his plays.

'My attitude was to interpret the screenplay and put it on the screen as best I could,' he went on. 'Producers always risk hiring murderers as directors. It's significant that I'm the one real change for George. We have the same composer, writer, same actors. What's good about working with George is he understands a director's needs – but recognises that he has to be left alone too – which is something that not many producers can do. He's always available but he stands back.'

In order to give his creativity as free a rein as possible, Marquand's first step was to call Fisher, Hamill, Ford and Williams together to discuss how their characters could be made more weighty. Not surprisingly, he found them ready and willing to co-operate, especially Carrie Fisher who'd suffered quite a lot with Princess Leia, 'A testy space soldier, so single-minded I'm nearly mean' for the best part of six years. She was keen for change, almost any change.

'In *Empire*, the Princess became such a bitch,' Marquand remarked. 'She really was a drag. I was sure there was a lot more depth there we could use, and more comedy too. Turn her into more of a woman. So I worked with Carrie on that. She's a very sexy, attractive lady, and in this film we'll get to find this out.'

And we did. 'I'm so nice and feminine it's almost confusing,' Fisher summed up the scenario in which she dresses as a bounty hunter to rescue Han Solo from his ice box, learns from Luke that they share Darth Vader as a father and falls into Solo's arms, presumably to live happily ever after.

Ford too was happy with his lot, especially as Marquand was prepared to bend his own rules to play it Ford's way. In theory the director believes in rehearsing his actors by showing them the sets, telling them how he sees the action and going through the script very carefully, but without repeating their precise moves. He is on record as saying that he won't allow actors to walk on the set and say they can't deliver lines a producer, director and writer have worked for eight months to perfect, but such artistic integrity crumbled beneath Ford's reputation as a chronic dialogue-switcher.

'If Harrison wants changes, he'll have good reasons for them,' he rationalised, 'and he'll say it a week before shooting. He'll explain why, and you'll either agree, in which case you'll go to the producer and the other actors and express his points, or you'll explain why the line is there. If you can explain it to him, he'll do it because he's a professional.'

Backed by this comforting acquiescence, Ford went through the motions as the man who gets the girl – and walked away from

Han Solo on a happy note. 'I'm well satisfied with what the character has become and the way his usefulness has been completed because this is really the adventures of Luke Skywalker. Solo is a plum role because he's the most contemporary voice in the film, but he defines himself only by his relationship to Luke and Leia. It's no secret that Luke is a kind of alter ego for George Lucas, and that's what's philosophically important in this story.'

For Ford, Fisher and Hamill, *The Return of the Jedi* was an altogether happier experience than *The Empire Strikes Back*. The time they had to spend in London was reduced by Marquand's speed over the boards at Elstree and they then enjoyed the unaccustomed luxury of filming in the United States. Lucas was on hand for 60 per cent of the time for the 1,000 questions a day that only he could answer. The effort cost him a stone and a half in weight that he could ill afford, a number of white hairs in his already greying beard and yet deeper wrinkles round the eyes, but in the final analysis, the collaboration worked for both men.

'*Empire* was excruciating,' he remembers bitterly. 'I couldn't afford to go through that again. A movie company operates to the split second, like a football game. If you are not there when the decision has to be made, you lose the moment, soon those moments add up to hours, days, weeks. I don't have fun on my films. I smile a lot because if I don't everyone gets depressed, but I'd rather be at home in bed watching television.'

Of course there were moments of tension when, for example, Leia, dressed as a man, was told by the director to stand like an English sentry, an order the producer countermanded when he asked her to swashbuckle a bit, but for the most part George kept himself from interfering. However, it wasn't always easy. 'Shit,' he'd think, 'if I could just get in there and clean it up.' But he stifled such unwanted fantasies with more positive statements. 'If I wanted it the way I wanted it, I'd direct it myself, but since I've given that up, I have to accept the way somebody else directs it,' he told himself firmly.

Inevitably, he regained control in the editing room for the most complex post-production yet on a Lucasfilm. *The Return of the Jedi* has 942 special effects, nearly three times as many as *Star Wars*, and they cost over $5 milllion. The bike chases through the redwoods were among the most effective illusions of sheer speed yet seen in the cinema, but the greatest challenge was the climactic imperial battle which has shots made up of sixty-seven layers, each one supplied to fulfil its precise purpose in the scheme of things by ILM's computerised photography.

When it was completed, Lucas emerged from his darkened room a thirty-nine-year-old shadow of his former self, but with all his doubts still intact. 'What if we have finally got to the end of the shaggy-dog story,' he enquired anxiously, 'and everybody says, "That's it?" Technically and logistically this was the hardest of the three films to make – and all I see are the mistakes and the stuff that doesn't work. The sacrifice I've made for *Star Wars* may have been greater than I wanted, and now I'm burned out. I've got to get my life back again . . . before it's too late.'

The answers to his questions came on 25 May 1983 when *The Return of the Jedi* opened in America. The title had been changed less than six months earlier on the grounds that the Jedi were too noble to feel such a base emotion as revenge. The cost ran to several thousand dollars at that late stage, but 'return' reflected Lucas's vision more accurately, so he considered the money well spent.

For the reviewers, harassed by the extraordinary popularity of the saga they habitually knocked, it was time for a reassessment and the wisest took their youngest and dearest along to help them make it by defining the precise nature of the magic. One regular doubter who found that this method had merits was *The Voice*'s Andrew Sarris who paid tribute to his 'young, intelligent, trend-setting godson, Ross,' in coming to these conclusions: 'His critical verdict for which I waited with a pathetic mixture of humility and dependency was clear and lucid: *The Return of the Jedi* was even better than *Star Wars* and *The Empire Strikes Back*. Now that I have thought about it, I tend to agree. Lucas and his collaborators have managed to sustain the psychic tensions in their mythological world through three films over eight years, and by the time the final returns are in from around the world, the gross receipts for *Return of the Jedi* should exceed the national debt of Nigeria.'

Whether or not this figure was reached, the film rocketed up the charts to third position behind *E.T.* and *Star Wars*, relegating *The Empire Strikes Back* to fourth. Sarris had some fairly kind words for the actors too. 'Hamill, Ford and Fisher have not become big enough stars to transcend their roles, but they are more recognisable presences with the ability to modify the characters they play with behavioural accretions acquired from other films. They seem more comfortable with each other, and with their increasingly bizarre environments. For the first time I was aware of three distinctive personalities.'

Other scribes were less happy, and many indeed thought that *The Return of the Jedi* was the weakest film of the trilogy. 'Taken on its own terms,' wrote *Time*, '*Return of the Jedi* is a brilliant imaginative piece of movie making. But it does not diminish the accomplishment of Lucas and his youthful team to say that there are flaws nonetheless. The most obvious, ironically, is an over emphasis on effects and a too proud display of odd-looking creatures. Some otherwise breathtaking scenes, such as the visit to Jabba's lair, the hair-raising chases through the redwoods and the climactic space battle, are extended to the point of satiety. The other flaw is the ending: in all three films, Lucas has almost entirely avoided the rank sentimentality to which the story is vulnerable. In the final minutes of *Jedi*, he succumbs, however, and ends his trilogy with one of the corniest conclusions in recent years.'

There was praise for the acting, though, which *Time* felt was better than in the earlier films. 'Ford was always good as the likeable, daredevil cynic, but Fisher and most particularly Hamill have broadened and matured their talents.' However, it was impossible to please everyone, notably the *Standard*'s Alexander Walker who rather cruelly blamed anno domini for what he saw as a falling off: 'The *Star Wars* stock company are showing their one-dimensional shape very badly now. Older, greyer or simply fatter than when they started the saga, Mark Hamill, Harrison Ford, Carrie Fisher and Billy Dee Williams look battle weary before the fight even begins.'

Win, lose or draw, it was the parting of the ways for the trio who had been through so much together. No plans have been announced as yet for the first and third three-part sections of the saga, though George Lucas has them all mapped out in his inventive mind. The first trilogy, the Clone Wars and the Rise of the Empire, takes place two decades earlier which rules out Solo, Leia and Skywalker in adult form, though there is the likelihood that Luke will appear as a baby in Part III. The final trilogy, the rebuilding of the Galactic Democracy, is set some time in the future, and would not be made until the late 1990s, more than twenty years after *Star Wars*, which at least leaves the possibility of Hamill, Fisher and Ford resuming in their own, and their characters' middle age.

Not that Ford has ever said he would be ready or willing to portray a veteran Solo, nor to my knowledge has anyone ever suggested that he should, but stranger things have happened in Hollywood. Perhaps it was to avoid any such temptation that he wanted the intergalactic cowboy dead. 'I thought it would give the myth some body,' he commented. 'Solo really has no place to go. He's got no papa, he's got no mama, he's got no story. But that was one thing I was unable to convince George of.'

The fate of Carrie Fisher and Mark Hamill since *The Return of the Jedi* underlines Harrison's good fortune in having Indy thrust upon him. Both have sunk without a trace, a danger they had the foresight to put into words shortly after the third film came out. 'Star Wars has typecast me,' Fisher mourned. 'As far as most people are concerned, I'll go to my grave as Princess Leia. In the street, they call out "Hi, Princess," which makes me feel like a poodle. People assume that after *Star Wars*, I must have had lots of offers from other producers, but I haven't.'

Hamill's comments echoed hers only too perceptively. 'Much as I loved the *Star Wars* movies, it was the technicians who made them a triumph. Luke Skywalker was the classic thankless role. I was the straight man – with absolutely no personality or humour.'

Ford, of course, had no cause for such complaints though he sounded defensive when he said, 'People want fairy tales in their lives. I'm lucky enough to provide them. There is no difference between doing this kind of film and playing King Lear. The actor's job is exactly the same: dress up and pretend.'

As he has never played King Lear or any other Shakespearean role since he took up cinema, this can only be an assumption, and a pretty simplistic one at that, but he was in a position to be more sanguine than his fellow actors over the ending of the space age. 'The story that Han Solo was part of, which is the Adventures of Luke Skywalker in my guise of best friend, is over. The story completes itself in this third film. I had a great time on *Jedi*. I'm glad I did it. I'm glad I did all three of them but as well, I'm glad I don't have to do any more.'

13   Elephants Can Be Bastards Too

FOR HARRISON FORD, 1983's task was *Raiders* II, otherwise
known as *Indiana Jones and the Temple of Doom*, but first he had
one or two things to attend to – like getting divorced and
remarried and finding himself a second home. Although he had
been separated from Mary for five years, their split only became
legal in the early months of 1983, leaving him to tie the knot
formally with Melissa Mathison who duly became Mrs Harrison
Ford on 14 March.

The wedding was typically quiet and private, and one of the
couple's first priorities was to choose a retreat outside Los Angeles
where they could live as much like ordinary folk as possible.
Ford's parents had long since moved from Chicago to California,
not, he claims, so much to be near him as because the state is 'very
attractive to mid-westerners'. Like the older Fords, Harrison was
irresistibly urban, but at the age of forty he felt the lure of the wide
blue yonder. 'I haven't really had time to investigate,' he told me
in London a year earlier, 'but I feel I might like the company of
some cows and that kind of life.'

With Ben and Willard growing up fast, the need to live down
the road from their mother was diminishing and contact with
Tinsel Town was no longer necessary as a means to employment. If there was a single spectacular change in Harrison's
post-*Star Wars* fortunes, it was the amount of bulky mail he
received. His agent, his business manager, even the garage
owner who looked after the black Porsche, were bombarded
with scripts, most of them of extremely dubious quality,
accompanied by begging letters urging them to press them into
the maestro's hands immediately. Fan mail poured in as well,
even more of it for Indiana Jones than for Han Solo, a predictable
balance if only because the bullwhipper had the field to himself.

Initially Harrison and Melissa looked at properties in California, but later they spread the net wider and came up with Wyoming, a remote, mountainous state where the man who loathed fashionable West Coast exercise routines at last found a physical release for his inner tensions in a quiet person's rural pursuits: fishing, walking in the woods and, in winter, cross country skiing.

'I like the change of pace and the difference in the weather,' he told Stephen Fay of the *Sunday Times Magazine*. 'The clothes I wear are different and so is the car I drive. I'm a totally different person and I find it very renewing.'

Almost before Ford could adjust himself to his newly married state, 18 April loomed and he was flying out to Macao, where a sufficiently traditional Chinese environment had been found to double for Shanghai in 1935 in the dazzling opening sequences for *Indiana Jones and the Temple of Doom*. Lawrence Kasdan, his debt paid to George Lucas with his *Return of the Jedi* script, had managed to duck more successfully this time because he was making his second feature, *The Big Chill*.

He was replaced at the typewriter by two Lucas old timers, Bill Huyck and Gloria Katz, the husband and wife team who'd realised George's adolescence so spectacularly well in *American Graffiti*. Lucas's ideas for his *Raiders* follow-up were well advanced even before the cameras turned on *Jedi*. He knew the film would be a prequel rather than a sequel and that it would be an altogether darker movie, dabbling with the occult. He first contacted Huyck and Katz in February 1982 and explained the nub of the matter to them at a four-day meeting in his Marin County home.

The preliminary briefing was characteristically succinct and contained all the essential elements in the final film. As Huyck recalls, 'We flew up and, in the first hour, George told us what he had in mind. Essentially the story started in Shanghai and Indy had to get into a situation in which his plane crashes. Then he's asked by villagers to recover a sacred stone. That's the basic outline we were given and we started building from there.'

The rest of the think tank was devoted to developing new characters, but Indy remained sacrosanct. 'if I could be a dream figure, I'd be Indy,' Lucas told *Rolling Stone*. 'It's not just that

I'm interested in archaeology and anthropology; alot of that got into *Star Wars* too. It's just that Indy can do anything. He's alot of thirties heroes put together. He's this renegade archaeologist and adventurer, but he's also a college professor, and he's got this Cary Grant side too. In some stories, we'll see him in top hat and tails. We don't want to make him Superman – he's just open to all possibilities.'

Also present at the meetings was Steven Spielberg who'd been enthusiastic about the second project from the start. 'I'd hate to let it slip through my fingers into someone else's hands. I won't be involved in the third or fourth ones, but I really want to do the follow-up because the story is even more spectacular than *Raiders*. These movies are fun, but they're technical exercises beside the stuff that comes from inside me – like *Close Encounters* and *E.T. Indiana Jones* isn't a personal movie for me. I like making films about relationships. In unashamed adventure stories, there just aren't any.'

Yet, he explained, there were advantages. 'Point one: I love good adventure films. As a moviegoer, I'm starved of them. No one makes them any more. I tired of having to look for them on TV at two or three in the morning. Point two: adventure is part of everyone's imagination. As a kid, I was always rescuing the lovely fifth grader as she dangled from the monkey bars. Weren't you? Course you were. Everyone has those fantasies. It's my good luck that I can make them into movies.'

Harrison had never been in doubt either. 'Of course I'm doing the second *Raiders* film. With great pleasure. And for the first time, I think, in the history of sequels and good directors, Steven Spielberg is going to direct it. So this is very exciting for me. It was one of the best working relationship experiences of my life, working with Steven.'

Like James Bond, the secret agent with whom he does not wish to be compared, Indiana Jones has a new woman for each film, and the Huyck/Katz team's orders were to make her as different as possible from Marion Ravenwood. Indy's *Raiders* helpmate had been dark and intrepid and outspoken; so his *Temple of Doom* companion would be dizzy and blonde and silly, a hindrance rather than a help. After much discussion, it was decided to call her Willie, after Spielberg's dog, just as Indiana had been named after Marcia's. The Huycks got in on the canine act too, with their own pet, Short Round, called after a Korean child in Sam Fuller's 1951 movie, *The Steel Helmet*.

Lucas gets the credit for wanting a child around Indy, but it was Huyck and Katz who developed Short's role into the intrepid, resourceful boy hero who at times takes over the plot. Lucas had favoured a girl child but the writers didn't fancy that, and Spielberg, no doubt with visions of his diminutive alter ego saving that fifth grader in his mind's eye, backed them up: a boy would be best. Well, said Lucas, who genuinely does go out of his way to suggest that there are commendable people in the world other than White Anglo-Saxon Protestant Males, if you won't give way on sex, you can give way on nationality. Short Round became Korean, making the Fuller connection especially relevant.

Once the writers were released from bondage, they were fired with a burning enthusiasm to out-zing both *Raiders of the Lost Ark* and Lawrence Kasdan. Their first and second drafts took six weeks each, their third a lightning-fast month, and their material reflects this speed off the keyboard. In between they had to answer to Spielberg and Lucas, who was always in there suggesting changes. It was a tough brief, not least because part of the pressure was of their own devising. Their first project with Katz as producer and Huyck as director, *French Postcards*, had been modestly praised and their second, *Best Defence*, awaited them. Unfortunately the Dudley Moore vehicle with what has been rather elliptically called 'a strategic guest appearance' by Eddie Murphy, is catastrophically bad, but no doubt the fee for *Temple of Doom* was a handsome consolation prize.

After the 'what', it was time for the 'where' and, as with *Raiders*, it fell to the reliable 'line' producer, Robert Watts, to make the initial world tour in pursuit of suitable locations. Spielberg, unlike Lucas and Ford, had taken to Elstree and was happy to shoot 80 per cent of the picture in the controlled environment of the studio. 'The older I get,' he confessed, 'the more I'm getting the homing instinct to build it and shoot it indoors. I don't like to wait. When it rains on me, I want sun, or when it's sunny, I want it to be overcast; I feel better when I can create the environment.'

However, even a B movie needs a degree of verisimilitude, and

Indiana Jones and the Temple of Doom was supposed to take place in exotic Indian spots. A grand panorama of Maharajah's palaces, elaborate temples and elephants trampling through jungles was required. Elstree it was not. Nor, in the event, was it India, a sub-continent rich in all these factors but poor in the ways and means of covering the huge distances between them and in its addiction to bureaucracy, inspired by the British Raj and perfected by local usage into red tape that can bind a project up like a mummy.

Having discovered that Hong Kong's skyscraper canyons were manifestly too modern for 1935, Watts had little difficulty in selecting nearby Macao instead. Next he proceeded dutifully to Bombay and set up a production office as a base from which to tour the country. In due course he found everything he needed before moving on to Sri Lanka, much more compact, with superior communications and a government that will do any-thing to acquire much-needed foreign exchange. In and around the beautiful hill town of Kandy, a tourist attraction that has the added advantage of the kind of modern hotels, with fridges in the bedrooms, beloved of film crews, the logistics fell much more readily into place than on the mainland. All that was missing was a suitable Maharajah's palace.

Watts settled for Sri Lanka without more ado, leaving three days for shooting the palace he'd found in the spectacular Pink City of Jaipur, the capital of Rajastan. However, even that was not to be, for the Indian authorities demanded script changes that were unacceptable to Lucas, and Watts had no alternative but to drop the country altogether. Instead, the palace rose on the back lot at Elstree, but at least the elephants were real.

One of the key factors in keeping a film on schedule and on budget is a 'line' producer who can bring the nuts and bolts together in the most effective way, and Spielberg gave Watts due credit for his achievement when he said, 'Every director, in order to be responsible to the people who have hired him to make a good movie, has to be a good producer, as good a producer as he is a director. If he doesn't actually function as a producer at least he needs to rely on people who are good producers and whom he trusts. On *Indiana Jones*, I had a great belief in Robert Watts, and I trusted him with everything from scheduling and set construction to set striking to location hunting. Watts was on top of everything.'

Watts also had his part to play in casting, his principal task being to comb the Chinese quarters of New York, Vancouver, London and Los Angeles for oriental boys who could speak English well enough to make themselves understood without sounding as if they were native-born Americans. The child Watts chose, Ke Huy Quan, was a Vietnamese refugee rather than a Chinese, a resident of Los Angeles with no previous acting experience, and he was duly signed.

It was the merest chance that brought Kate Capshaw onto the scene as Willie Scott. She'd been taken to see *Raiders of the Lost Ark* under duress when it opened in 1981, as she freely admits. 'I went, very petulant and sulky, and stayed that way for about two minutes. When I came out, I would have been a great advertisement for going to see that movie.'

The Texan-born ex-history teacher, a relatively unknown newcomer to California after a career in commercials in New York, was fortunate that her agent went jogging with one of the *Indiana Jones* talent scouts. As they panted through the streets, the blonde's name came up and Kate eventually landed the part. Not that it was a sinecure, because Huyck and Katz had been so determined to fulfil their brief to make Willie as far removed from Marion Ravenwood as possible that they'd created one of the cinema's more irritating little women.

Whenever things go wrong, as they do every time a Lucas cliffhanger is injected into the scenario, she flaps and squalks and panics, driving this viewer – at least – completely nuts. Where Marion was rude and gutsy and decisive, Willie depends on feminine wiles to get by, as if the ability to flutter eyelashes was all that was needed for survival. A feminist personality for the eighties she assuredly is not.

The characterisation follows fairly predictably from her profession as a nightclub singer, a dramatic device which means that she first appears under the best possible circumstances giving a stirring rendering of 'Anything Goes' in the pre-credit sequence in the Obi-Wan Night club in 'Shanghai'. This is her world and her song and dance routine leads into a completely new image of Indy – and indeed Harrison Ford – as a suave white-tie-and-tails man searching among spilt ice cubes for a missing diamond and the antidote to the deadly drug the wily Chinese villain has slipped into his champagne.

So far, so good, but deterioration is rapid once Short Round has rescued the ill-assorted couple and the trio have to float out of the Himalayan sky on an inflatable raft, doubling for a parachute, a scene originally scripted for *Raiders* which came in useful here instead. Whether she's riding an elephant or being asked to eat chilled monkey brains and eyeball soup at the child Maharajah's banquet, Willie's natural reaction is to complain. Nor does she come through for Indy when the feasting is over, probably because Lucas still has no room for lust in his movies. Soon it is only too clear that she is a lousy travelling companion.

Perhaps some of her deficiencies come from the fact that even her creators have slightly differing perceptions of her. For Bill Huyck, she's a bit of a bore. 'I never really cared for the character, but we felt she was reacting realistically to the kind of things Indiana Jones goes through, the kind of situations where, since she's not so tough – as few people would be in those situations – she'd scream.'

Gloria Katz held her in greater esteem. 'People have mixed feelings about Willie,' she admits. 'I'm a little offended by the idea of a macho woman. I don't think that's a woman that necessarily exists. When you're covered in insects, your instinct is to scream. So I think Willie represents the audience's realistic viewpoint, what they'd be like if they were thrown out into the jungle. She's not brave and strong, but she's a different kind of woman and, I think, a more realistic one.'

'Willie leads a pampered life,' Kate Capshaw summed up her own attitude to this dubious alter ego, 'and she feels that's what's due to her – to be cared for and looked after. She meets Indiana Jones, a person unlike anyone she has ever been involved with, and ends up going off with him. In the course of their adventures, all of her earlier life is stripped away from her and Willie must fall back on her own resources. She discovers she's a strong woman and a very gutsy lady.'

Up to a point perhaps, but there is a fair amount of evidence to suggest that Ms Capshaw was at least as volatile as Willie at times. One of the scenes scripted for her was a fight with a boa constrictor, and a fine, strapping non-poisonous snake had been meticulously trained for the role. At the last minute, however, the actress refused to do it. She had, she claims, been trying to psyche herself up for it for weeks but when she touched the reptile, it 'undulated' as snakes will, and she thought she was going to die. When it was draped over her shoulders, she sweated profusely and had hysterics.

'Steven went sort of ashen and said, "That's alright,"' Bill Huyck recalls. 'They didn't do it. Kate just couldn't do it. That's when Steven said, "Okay, if you're not going to do this, there's no way you're not going to do the bug scene."'

It is not too hard to imagine how much Spielberg must have longed for Karen Allen, the actress who'd overcome her terror of snakes enough to stand up to her knees in them for five days. As for the bugs, the director remained true to his word and Ms Capshaw duly delivered. However, Spielberg proved his own flexibility by adjusting his cherished plans for the scene when he saw what the score was, as he explained:

'I'd drawn several renderings of insects crawling over Kate in the Spike Chamber. But I had all sorts of shots planned showing the migration of bugs up and around the actress, and I was going to do a study of that. But once I got on the set and saw how she was reacting to being around the bugs, I felt the best thing to do was throw the storyboards out and take one camera and hold Kate wide, and a second camera panning from the bugs up to her face. I shot most of her footage that way, with two cameras operating at the same time, reacting as she would react. We were being as spontaneous as she was. The situation for her was very real, as it would have been for anybody having a thousand creepy insects crawling all over their body.'

Harrison Ford, meanwhile, was displaying his new liking for high intensity action with a whole range of stunts, but this time one of the near misses became a painful hit. His career as an elephant rider began in Sri Lanka where the first intimations of the worries in store made themselves felt. 'We had a bunch of elephants and I had to fight a battle on their backs. Those brutes are harder to ride than camels, and I've had experience of both. They sway all over the place and if they shift one way and you're going the other – that's it, brother. You're in the dust. In any case, when you ride an elephant, your legs are hyper-extended in both directions to accommodate the girth of the animal. It's as if they're being pulled apart. The pain started with twinges in my back which gradually got worse.'

After three weeks on the idyllically beautiful island in the Indian Ocean, cast and crew returned to Elstree to face another long wet British summer. However, the damned elephants were still in evidence on the set, and further very typical sequences like falling off a moving train and somersaulting across a bed didn't help Harrison's problem. By mid July, he was in such evident distress that Spielberg had no alternative but to send him back to California for treatment.

The Centimela Hospital, which specialises in sports injuries, had no hesitation in diagnosing a ruptured disc, a condition normally treated by a painful operation known as a laminectomy. Well aware that time was money, the doctors experimented with a new technique, injecting an enzyme taken from papaya fruit to 'eat' the affected disc, rather as acid dissolves metal. Much to everyone's relief, it worked. 'Most people are fascinated by the idea,' Ford laughs off his ordeal. 'I've found just about everyone has a bad-back story to tell.'

Six weeks later he was back at the studios with the insurers of *Indiana Jones* roughly $1.5 million the poorer. Spielberg had tried to shoot round his star's absence but such was Indy's importance that there were inevitable delays. The elephants had gone back to the zoo by the time Harrison returned, but there were several action sequences still to come, notably the climactic fight on the rope bridge over the gorge. Much of the strain fell on the broad shoulders of Harrison's double, a stuntman called Vic Armstrong, who looks so like the actor that he'd stood in for him on *Blade Runner* and *Return of the Jedi* when things got tough.

'Guys like Vic never get any credit,' says Harrison in tribute. 'They are invisible.' The stuntman agreed, but without bitterness. 'Yes, we have to be invisible if people are going to believe in the film. Harrison is a natural athlete and he wants to do it all. I say to him "We can't afford to get you smashed up in this scene because we've got a crew that needs to make a living." And he said, "Yeah, you're right," and does the scene anyway! He could have made a great stuntman himself.'

No Armstrong is undervaluing his own contribution, but the crew were unanimous in their admiration for Ford's true trouper's grit, as he forced himself to go on in circumstances in which others would have been quick to beat a retreat. He may have been dispirited by the dysentery on *Raiders*, but there was no trace of self-pity this time and, as a result, *Temple of Doom* wrapped up on 8 September 1983 five days under schedule.

'We had a budget of $28 million,' Spielberg remembers, with justifiable if understated pride, 'and we delivered Paramount a $28 million movie. I went over budget in some sequences and came in under budget in others. I went over schedule with certain scenes, and came way under in others.'

The 'Movie Brat' ascribes this proven ability to juggle with time and place to his precise storyboarding, no less than 4,000 individual frames for *Indiana Jones*. These were drawn up in strip cartoon form by artists from Spielberg's own thumb-nail sketches, and stuck into loose-leaf albums. This gave him a frame of reference from which he worked out his master shots, ten in all, which he then used to pick his angles. At this point, members of his team converted the two dimensional into the three dimensional by building all the sets in miniature, complete with half-inch figures for the actors. Spielberg then got to work with his Nikon, photographing all the angles until he was aware of the full potential of the material.

Next came the cutting down, and with it the knowledge of what would be vital to the finished product, what would help it if there was enough time to shoot it and what was superfluous, a scale of priorities he applied relentlessly to each day's schedule. The actors, too, were drawn into the process, each according to his ability.

'*Indiana Jones* is not a "personal film,"' Spielberg explained. 'It's an audience entertainment. It's fun for everybody, and all the actors learned to act in a different way. They learned to paint their emotions by numbers. Kate Capshaw, Harrison Ford, even the young boy, Ke Huy Quan, who had never acted before, fell into step with the storyboards. They were able to give credible performances when the light was hitting them at a certain time or when they hit the mark which put them into exact alignment with the blue screen. *Indiana Jones* is a very technical movie and the actors had to be technical without losing their own believability as characters in order to pull it off.'

After such impressively detailed groundwork, Spielberg found he was able to work to a ratio of three or four weeks to one usable shot, an economical rate for such a complicated and fast-moving production. The vital factor was lighting each scene correctly first time, so that the master shot went smoothly into the can. 'It may take two hours to set up but if you can get it on take three, you can get several other shots before lunch. If you get it on take twenty, all you're going to do is that master before lunch, maybe even after lunch. The actors are more comfortable and more spontaneous getting it all out in takes one, two or three. I've been lucky to have actors who like to do it fast and move onto something else.'

Spielberg was showing how well he'd learned his Lucas lessons, and Harrison was equally satisfied with the second manifestation of *Indiana Jones*, despite its physical demands. 'It was the most strenuous film I've ever been involved in,' he said, a comment that was becoming familiar. When had the last project not been the hardest? As he often jokingly admits: 'Boy, does a guy get bruised. But it's okay. That's what I'm here for. That's why people like him so much. He gets hurt, see? Everyone can identify with him. But he's also determined, which is why I like him. He just won't give up, whatever they throw at him.'

Among the things that Spielberg and Lucas threw at Indy were poison, drugs, crushing by spikes, frustration at Willie's refusal to go to bed with him, attacks by Thuggee, the notorious Indian assassins who strangle their enemies with silk scarves, and the celebrated roller-coaster train ride down the mine shaft which leads, via a threat of drowning by flooding, to the cutting of the rope bridge over the crocodile-infested river. It's hard to imagine what the unused dramas for *Raiders III* could be, but Lucas, Spielberg and Ford can see limitless potential in their creation. Even before *Indiana Jones and the Temple of Doom* came out, they publicly announced their solidarity on a third picture. 'Playing Indy is a fun thing to do,' said Harrison, 'and I certainly couldn't hope for better company than Lucas and Spielberg. I'll be back, but it's one at a time for me. If they're talking five, they must be talking to Roger Moore.' And Spielberg, despite being on record as saying he wouldn't make any sequels to *Temple of Doom*, endorsed his star's opinion. He, too, will be back.

Meanwhile the second film had to be launched on an expectant public over the Memorial Day weekend, by now the traditional date for the annual Lucas–Spielberg blockbusters, in late May 1984. As with *Raiders*, Spielberg had final cut, but when he showed his one hour, fifty-five minute rough to George Lucas, the two moguls were unanimous in their astonishment: it actually moved 'too fast'. Was it possible? A rip-roaring adventure that ripped too quickly? Yes, it was. The audience had no time to catch its collective breath. Deceleration was the name of the game, and Spielberg showed his metal by achieving it not by lengthening the film, as most directors would have done, but by clipping the action in favour of atmosphere.

The question of cutting of a different kind was raised as soon as the film opened. The Americans gave it a PG rating, and thirteen million people went to see it in less than a week, even more than had attended *The Return of the Jedi* in the same period the year before. Criticism, however, wasn't far behind. What was this film, showing an Indian villain ripping a pulsating heart out of a sacrificial victim, doing with a certificate that merely suggested parental guidance?

Parents and journalists rose in their wrath, as *Variety* reported. '*Indiana Jones*, which recounts its hero's adventures amid an Indian cult that eats monkey brains and live eels and likes to tear the hearts out of living victims before burying them in molten lava, has already caused a considerable furore among those who feel that the movie is too violent for its PG rating. A Los Angeles television critic, Gary Franklin, gave the movie a zero for children on his scale of one to ten, with an angry statement that the film's violence deserved an X rating. Paramount has put a small cautionary box in its ads calling its movie "too intense for younger children".'

As a general rule, children have a rather higher tolerance of lurid violence than the adults who wish to shield them from it, probably because it is less real to those who haven't been exposed to it nightly when the war and famine footage comes up on the television news. However, the British Board of Film Censors were quick to take up the fight on the other side of the Atlantic. Evidently agreeing with Gary Franklin, they refused even a fifteen certificate unless the slow burning victim was taken out. An eighteen certificate was useless to Paramount who knew full well that the film was not quintessentially adult fare, and they hastened to remove this and other offensive sequences, including the beating heart, from the British release print.

The scribes may have had less violence to carp about, but they found other causes for complaint. 'Spielberg's *Indiana Jones* is all funny, fast-springing traps, full of belief-defying feats that should ideally, be a constant zingy delight,' wrote Armond White in *Films in Review*. 'The problem is that in making the most extravagant, seamless, best-directed adventure movie in Hollywood history, Spielberg has not really brought it up to date. The picture's sophistication is all external. He has revved-up the adventure genre without renewing it or altering its ideas or possibilities.

'There are two major unfortunate results: first, that Spielberg's intrepid Great White Hero's exploits in the third world still have the xenophobic racist and macho sexist pieties of the least enlightened Hollywood films of fifty years ago: Indy drags with him an oriental orphan and a screeching hysterical woman. *Indiana Jones* takes place in a make-believe world of no politics, the world of generic lies and conveniences that most people have been fighting to resist, to expunge from the recesses of their minds since Watergate and Vietnam when the political and sexual promises and assumptions of popular culture were exposed as impossible and false.

'Second, by ignoring modern sensibility, Spielberg's movie making regresses to the old-fashioned, thrill-a-minute sort that contemptuously condescended to the public, controlling an audience's reactions and responses, leaving no room to breathe. Not since *Jaws* has Spielberg practised such all-out shameless manipulation of motor responses and left our minds alone starved.'

Alas, poor Lucas. In certain circles, he was never going to get his liberal image set to rights though, in this instance, it may have been some consolation to find the ball placed so firmly in the wrong court!

Critics in more widely read journals raked through their stores of clichés for such phrases as 'technical wizardry', 'the golden glow of instant success', 'irresistible helter-skelter ride of spectacular stunts and outrageous last minute escapes' and 'must be a monster hit', and the public showed they believed them by voting with their feet: they walked in and stayed to cheer.

Indiana Jones and the Temple of Doom was just shaded out of the top spot by *Ghostbusters* in the 1984 blockbuster's charts, but that was just fine by Harrison Ford. 'This is a completely moral tale,' he told the anti-violence brigade firmly, 'and in order to have moral resolve, evil must be seen to inflict pain. The end of the movie is proof of the viability of goodness.'

14 The Growing Pains of a Regular Actor

MANY AMERICANS whose business brings them regularly to Britain become honorary Englishmen, but Harrison Ford is not one of them. Perhaps he'd have felt more at home in Europe if the coin he flipped twenty-two years ago on that snow-bound September day in Chicago had sent him east instead of west, to New York rather than Los Angeles. As that was not to be, he has had to struggle with London's seedy traditional charms for the past decade, despite an appreciation for its museums, art galleries and, on occasion, its theatre.

However, there is one area of local culture for which his enthusiasm is unfeigned and that is its beer, especially served on draught in pint glasses in country pubs. If that is the cause of his small, but perfectly formed paunch, so be it because this is territory in which he moves with a freedom that has become precious over the years as his face becomes ever more famous. The British are not much of a nation of cinema-goers nowadays and no one would expect a tall, quietly-spoken man nursing a pint at the next oak gate-legged table to be Indiana Jones. Nor is star-spotting a national sport in rural England, so the man with the sardonic twist to his scarred lip can afford to smile confidently. He really would have to crack a bullwhip for anyone to recognise him here.

It is easy to imagine him sitting in just such a secluded corner during one of his brief respites from *Indiana Jones and the Temple of Doom* in the summer of 1983. He is bruised and slightly battered from an excess of stunts, a forty-one-year-old matinée idol with a high-action profile and a vital choice to make: what should he do next? Indy will be back, but not for at least two years, so as to give his public the chance to miss him. The gap could be filled by idleness, as indeed could the rest of his life:

his financial position is so strong that he need never work again, but Ford knows that's not the right way.

However, at this point, which he sees as a crossroads, he is particularly keen not to go the wrong way. 'Unlike some actors, I can't be good in a bad picture,' he admits without embarrassment. Failures are inevitable, of course, but in film they live for ever and they're forty feet wide and twenty feet high. Ford has no intention of letting the Indy clones who compete for his mail box take on those horrific dimensions, or anyway not with his face filling the frame. He sends them back unread.

'To be honest, I'm not particularly brave myself,' he comments, 'but since I've got into this mould, I've been inundated with these action scripts. Hollywood follows a successful trail of footprints, doesn't it? But there comes a point where you become independently bankable, where they want you for things that aren't just one type of slam bang role – and I'm glad to say, I seem to have reached that point at last. People know that I want to do other things.'

One man who was aware of the current state of Ford's ambition was producer Edward Feldman who dispatched a script by TV writers Earl W. Wallace and William Kelley to Britain. Its title was *Called Home*, and Harrison was quick to spot its potential, both artistically and in a business sense. Later rechristened *Witness*, it told of John Book, a Philadelphia cop who is obliged to take charge of an Amish widow and her eight-year-old son when the boy sees a murder committed in a railway station cloakroom. The Amish are a German-speaking sect who came to the United States in the late eighteenth century and contrived to live there untouched by the nation's characteristically all-embracing materialism for the next 200 years.

In today's terms, that means they have no television, no cinema, no cars, no telephones, no zips, no manufactured clothing, no sex outside marriage and, of course, no violence and no guns. It was this element of contrast between all our yesterdays and the Amish's todays that turned a routine thriller about police corruption combined with an inter-denominational romance into something rather more interesting, in Ford's eyes anyway.

'I don't want to bemoan any films of the past, but I think this is the most complicated role I've played in quite a while! And this time it's one with more adult appeal. The moral context is one of the important things about the film. That's what makes it work. Without the Amish serving as a kind of parameter of violence, this would have been the usual indulgence. This is what attracted me to the project. I think the film has something to say.'

Having decided he liked what he'd read, it is not beyond the bounds of possibility that Ford ordered another pint and turned to practicalities. 'The film was about ninety per cent there, I thought, which is a much higher grade than I give most screenplays when I first get them. But I felt that if we didn't have a really good director, it wouldn't gain anything – in fact it would most likely lose something in the translation.'

Did he then list the directors he'd like to work with on the back of the menu? Maybe. In any case, he made his choices and despite his much vaunted ignorance of the cinema, past and present, they were wide-ranging and international. Among them was Peter Weir, a fourth generation Australian who'd headed up the Antipodean New Wave with *The Cars That Ate Paris* and *Picnic at Hanging Rock*, before moving into glossier areas with *Gallipoli* and *The Year of Living Dangerously*.

It is easy to see why Harrison chose him, because Weir's work combines artistry with a certain necessary accessibility. The actor knew, as several who'd come before him had not, that the jump from mass market to rarefied independence was too great to make in one. His two appearances for Francis Coppola in *The Conversation* and *Apocalypse Now* may have held his own self-belief as a serious artist together through the light relief of Solo and Indy, but realistically the parts were too little and far too long ago to open similar avenues in 1983. If he wanted to do a small film, it had better be only slightly distanced from Hollywood, and Ford knew it.

Peter Weir, as a resident of Sydney and a film maker of fifteen years standing, was looking for opportunities to cut loose from what he has described as 'the back stabbing and bitchery' of his local industry. Accordingly he had his eye on Tinsel Town, as did his compatriots, Gillian Armstrong, Bruce Beresford and Fred Schepisi. His number one project was very dear to his heart: *Mosquito Coast*, an adaptation of Paul Theroux's splendidly idiosyncratic novel set in Central America.

'We were ready to begin pre-production, with office staff standing by in Los Angeles, all our locations picked and knowing

we had to start shooting by a certain date because of the weather,'
Weir recalls with some puzzlement. 'There we were, sitting
around waiting, but the final element didn't fall into place. So,
very sadly, we all said goodbye and packed up. I'd never had
that happen with a film before.'

It was a short sharp introduction to Hollywood for which
Weir, the product of an industry which enjoys the safety net of
national and state support for its films, was totally unprepared.
Looking around him gloomily in 1984, he knew he had only
three options: pack up and go home with his tail between his
legs; stay hungry in Los Angeles while he tried to re-finance
Mosquito Coast; or take a film that had already been developed
by someone else, something he'd never done before.

Facing the choice that was no choice, he bit the bullet and
rang his agent. 'I said, "You know all those scripts in their
brown paper envelopes you've been sending me for years and
I've kept turning down? If you can send me any now which are
go projects, I promise you if one is half-way decent, I'll take it."
He sent me three, and *Witness* was half-way decent so I took it.
As I'd insisted, it was a package almost as good as ready. Of
course, Harrison Ford wasn't actually signed up – he was only
"interested", depending on who was going to direct – but the
script was in a very advanced state with a very sound structure.
It meant I could get straight into casting.'

On the face of it, the collaboration between Weir and Ford
could have been a recipe for disaster. Ford was looking for a
basis for the rest of his life while Weir, on his own admission,
wanted to take the money and run. The sociological elements
relating to the Amish interested him but what, he demanded,
was all this melodrama doing mucking up the purity of his
vision? 'On my first rewrite, I dismissed the melodrama, removed it even, and the producer brought me back to earth and
back to realities. He spoke as a great American showman and
therefore, for me, connected with the 1940s and the golden age
of Hollywood. He kept saying "audience" and "Remember it's
a thriller, and if you keep that in mind you'll construct a kind
of hybrid between your style and the genre."'

To Weir's credit, he was flexible enough to recognise the
hard-nosed truth in this statement and, eventually, to find some
merit in it. 'I came to realise that if the Fords and the Capras

had had total control, they might have had shorter careers – and made less good films. Here on *Witness*, I was facing a genre film, something that one was very familiar with – go in quickly, do it with style and grace, collect your cheque and leave. It was a great experiment and I think I'd like to do a couple of them now and again and put them among the projects which are much loved and much more difficult to mount.'

Weir first contacted Ford by phone and they agreed to meet. Time was short because *Witness* really was on the green light: Paramount had put up the $12 million budget and the cameras were set to roll in eight weeks time. Nevertheless the film gave Harrison welcome scope for research, a rather superfluous activity for a man engaged in laser sabre fights and snake-baiting, but one which he rather hankered after, having seen the verisimilitude – and indeed the kudos – it brought to the work of distinguished contemporaries like Robert de Niro.

Philadelphia was the first stop, and Weir and Ford visited the exhibition of Flemish school paintings at the City's museum together. Although of German origin, the Amish are known as the Pennsylvania Dutch (from 'Deutsch') in America, and the splendid oils gave Weir the feeling for muted colour which he used so successfully for their simple homely interiors in the film.

Ford's local research became rather more testing when he decided to hang out with the homicide squad from the Philadelphia Police department for two weeks to see what really went on behind the scenes, even to the extent of going on a raid with them to catch a killer. 'I was a bit frightened beforehand, but I think they were more nervous having me along,' he quipped. 'In the end, the raid was so quickly over, there was no time to be scared.'

Meanwhile Kelly McGillis, a young actress who'd recently made her mark as the bright contemporary student opposite Tom Conti in the comedy *Reuben, Reuben*, had been chosen as the repressed Rachel, the Amish widow who is awakened – to a degree – by John Book's manly charms.

The feeling of old-fashioned doomed romance in *Witness* appealed to Ford, McGillis and especially Peter Weir who, as the archetypal emotionally strangled Anglo-Saxon, realised that the passion between Rachel and Book was a challenge he needed to face up to. 'Americans are more open and direct than Europeans,' he said. 'If you've waged, as I have, an inner war with your education and upbringing to give some status to your emotions, America is a good place to be.'

Although Rachel takes Book into her home after he is wounded in a gun fight and nurses him tenderly back to health, then protects him by dressing him up as her dead husband when his own side come looking for him, the couple never openly make love. Indeed Weir and Ford decided, after lengthy discussions during the eight week location shoot, to leave the question whether they had sex when the cameras turned away to the audience's imagination. Nevertheless Ford and McGillis generate a smouldering physical longing for one another, all the more intense for being possibly unfulfilled, without going through the motions.

'I don't think that watching how the plumbing works is what people want,' Ford comments dryly. 'The relationship between two people and the tension is far more interesting.' But it was McGillis's boyfriend who had the last word on the film's only moment of nudity when Book catches Rachel bathing. 'Everyone in the audience could do with a cold shower at that point,' he said succinctly.

In another key sequence in *Witness*, Harrison reverted to his old carpenter's skills when he helped the Amish folk to build a barn, a scene that shows the community feeling which binds the sect together, even when intrusive factors like Book and Rachel's forbidden love threaten to burst it apart. In the original script, the barn-building is a contest between Book and the other, and as far as the locals are concerned the only acceptable, candidate for Rachel's hand: an Amish farmer played by the Russian expatriate dancer, Alexander Godunov. Initially the farmer was the better woodworker, but Harrison's arrival tipped the scales in his favour as the barn went up, exactly as we see it on the screen, but in spruce rather than oak for economy's sake.

'We took advantage of my past experience,' Harrison explained. 'I've often said there's not much difference between acting and carpentry. There's a real simple-minded analogy: you have to have a logical plan. You have to perceive it from the ground up. You have to lay a firm foundation. Then every step becomes part of a logical process.'

Witness was made on location in Pennsylvania in the early

summer of 1984 over an eight week period that stretched only modestly to eight and a half. The Amish neighbours carried on a love-hate relationship with the film makers, intensely curious about the picture their religion would prevent them seeing, yet hostile about the invasion of their territory. Paramount representatives offered up to $700 a day to one family for the use of their dairy farm. 'We first thought it was kind of tempting,' the owner's wife admitted. 'After all, we are only human. But it didn't take long to decide this isn't what we want. Money is nothing compared with our way of life.'

Another wife, who insisted on anonymity so as not to commit the sin of pride, said that she'd read about *Witness* in the paper. 'The kids cut out Harrison Ford's picture,' she conceded, 'but it doesn't really matter that much to them. Somebody told us he was in *Star Wars*, but that doesn't mean anything to us.'

Faced with such other-worldly attitudes, the scouts moved on to non-Amish households like that of Emma and Paul Krantz who were glad to take the money and allow the unit to invade their territory, though they took the precaution of asking around first. 'We tested Amish opinions before we agreed,' Mrs Krantz remembers. 'They said it wouldn't bother them, then they started asking for souvenirs. At first they ignored it, but then they'd lie in the grass and look down on the set through binoculars.' Obviously Amish opinions are divided on what goes and what doesn't when it comes to twentieth-century technology!

The studio hired John King, a lapsed Amish lumber salesman, as the guardian of the film's authenticity and Kelly McGillis was introduced to an Amish widow who agreed, despite protests from her neighbours, to take the actress into her home for a few days. 'Living with them, even for a short time, did change my outlook,' Kelly commented. 'Seeing how happy they are with so few material possessions made me appreciate the beauty of simplicity.'

Harrison Ford, as the intruder into the rigidly traditional community, had no need for such encounters, but he did find himself in closer contact with a cow than he'd thought likely when he set up his retreat in Wyoming. Not that his inexperience mattered because John Book, tough city cop, was equally ill at ease in the milking parlour.

From the start, Ford's association with Peter Weir developed along mutually satisfactory lines. The Australian director likes to go on a set and ask, 'How are we going to shoot this scene?' a technique that Americans, accustomed to a big boss telling them what to do, can find disconcerting. Not so Harrison, with his history of input, and he paid generous tribute to the man who had become his friend when the fifty-two-day shoot finished on 30 June 1984.

'Peter and I were veterans of a campaign. We'd been in the same place and seen the same things. Our visions of the film were mostly consistent and when they were not we were able to influence each other without destroying our enthusiasm. My relationship with Peter worked more than it ever had with a director before. Would that it were always the same.'

Even taking into account Harrison's facility for paying lip service to his most recent experience, these words have the ring of truth, and Weir was quick to repay in kind. 'The films he has been involved in have been mainly comic book action adventures, but I feel Harrison always managed to establish quite a credible character. I felt quite clearly that he'd not been able to display what was there. And any remaining doubts I might have had were cleared up during our conversations before shooting actually began. He had a sharp mind, a very clear idea about his role, and some damn good ideas about the film itself. It became quite a partnership.'

So a collaboration that could have been stormy ended on a high note of mutual admiration. Weir knew that he'd made 'a good little film' which he thought would find its own audience and make a dollar or so, but as the opening date in early February, 1985 approached, he began to feel pretty edgy. Would viewers, expecting Indiana Jones Rides Again, stay away in droves from an honest policeman with stars in his eyes? A questionnaire circulated among the first recruited audience confirmed that everyone had come to see Harrison Ford playing a hard-hitting cop, and Weir recalls his terror when he arrived at 6 p.m. for the 7.30 p.m. screening.

'There to my horror stretched a line of people several hundred yards long, all of them chattering and laughing. The anticipation for a *Raiders* Mark III was terrifying. I struggled up to the cutting rooms because I wanted to make a few last minute changes and the editor and I just looked at each other. I was in a cold sweat.

When it was 7.30 I told myself that within two hours I'd have their verdict. At first, I could sense they were puzzled because they were expecting more action; but by the middle of the film, they were loving the humour. Whether that became some sort of substitute for the expected shootings, I don't know, but they got lost in the story and were obviously entertained.'

His sigh of relief turned to amazement when reviewers and the general public responded to *Witness* with a quite unexpected enthusiasm. Fifty-two days after its American opening, its takings stood at $46.5 million, not in the *Star Wars* class, but handsome indeed for an adult thriller with no sex scenes. And this time there was no way that the critics could diminish the part played by Harrison Ford.

'Peter Weir's *Witness* is a remarkable film – both an exciting thriller and a beautifully directed meditation on violence,' the reliable David Denby picked up the mood of the moment in *New York* magazine. 'One of the nicest things about it is that it gives Ford a role in which he can be unaffectedly serious without straining against his own temperament. Since he's a highly stylised actor, with a big wide mouth – almost a clown's mouth – genre films may be the best place for him. I don't see him creating characters realistically from the ground up, like Dustin Hoffman and Robert de Niro. In *Witness*, he has a solid tough-guy role and he gets to show off his physical prowess and his talent for bravura underplaying.

'The movie's central situation is comic: the specialist in urban corruption has to live among the spotless Amish people in Lancaster County, Pennsylvania. This time Ford's curling smile has a double edge: he is amused at the Amish who are narrow, harsh and exhaustingly virtuous, and also amused at himself for liking their ways so much. In *Witness*, Harrison Ford has become a real movie star in the old-fashioned sense – he's interesting no matter what he's doing.'

This penetrating analysis was echoed around the world as *Witness* proved it travelled well too. The *Financial Times*'s Nigel Andrews, one of London's more intelligent film critics, said: 'Weir's great talent is for the weird: the wondrous-weird of *Picnic at Hanging Rock*; the sweltering weird of *The Year of Living Dangerously*. And *Witness* thrives best, like an exotic weed, in the surreal crack in cultural cohesion between Ford's big city round-neck and the prim and pristine community in which he tries, for most of the film, to camouflage himself. The elegiac otherness of this world is magically caught: both in John Feale's photography – perhaps the most beautiful I have seen in a Hollywood film this decade, light-rinsed images of exquisite warmth and texture – and in Harrison Ford's masterclass repertory of comic-rueful asides and "takes". Watch his expression, like a lightly flabbergasted frog, when Miss McGillis insists on saying grace before a hot dog snack in a Philadelphia nosherie.'

For Harrison Ford, it was time to say thanks for noticing – at last. Characteristically he did so, a little plaintively, but in the nicest possible way as he put his all into a gruelling publicity tour for *Witness*. He'd been doing his best for nearly twenty years, he told any journalist who'd listen – and this time they all did. 'I've never been reviewed as an actor,' he concluded. 'I've always been reviewed as some phenomenology of one kind or another. But I've never thought, "Well, this is some two dimensional comic book character so I'll not have to work on it." I've always suffered greatly worrying about what I was doing, and doing my best. The *Witness* reviews are my first as an actor, but doing this movie didn't feel different to any other movie. The process was the same. It was regular acting.'

When the Oscars for 1986 came around, the Academicians delivered too with a handsome total of eight nominations for *Witness*, including the three most prestigious ones: Best Film, Best Director, for Peter Weir, and Best Actor, for Harrison Ford.

In the event, these glittering prizes went to *Out of Africa* and its director, Sydney Pollack, with William Hurt justly adjudged Best Actor for his astonishing portrayal of the transvestite prisoner in *The Kiss of The Spiderwoman*. Ford, perhaps having seen the writing on that particular wall, didn't fly back from Central America for the protracted ceremonies, and *Witness* had to be content with recognition for Thom Noble's editing. Harrison's consolation prize is the fact that the nomination has reduced the number of Hollywood luminaries who think of him as a perfectly formed cardboard cut-out to a rapidly diminishing handful, and even they now know that, given the right part, he will be back.

15   The Once and Future Star

ALL THE best stories have a tranquil beginning, a turbulent middle and a happy ending, and this one is no exception. In early February, 1986 the cameras turned on a Peter Weir film in Belize in Central America. Its name was *Mosquito Coast*, its budget was $17 million – and the mad New Englander who drags his family into the jungle to satisfy his own alienation from contemporary America was played by Harrison Ford. By lending his name to Weir's pet project, Ford more than repaid the director's faith in him on *Witness*, and found himself a truly adult part at last.

Mosquito Coast is Paul Theroux's best novel to date, a strong mixture of distorted vision, steamy tropical atmosphere and black humour that makes you laugh aloud at times. It is also totally dominated by Allie Fox, a tyrant who is prepared to sacrifice everything and everyone on the altar of his own impossible dreams. The man who came to mind for this role originally was Jack Nicholson, an automatic choice in the late eighties when there is massive mania on the daily call sheet. However, the size of the egos he can portray is more than matched by the size of the fee and the percentage he demands for doing so, and it was his enthusiasm for the mighty dollar that stranded the film in the first place.

It will be interesting to see how Harrison Ford copes with such a total departure from the mild-mannered, jokey screen persona we have come to know and love. Fourteen weeks in Belize City, and its water-logged environs, make the Tunisian desert, even combined with Elstree, look like a picnic. The small, recently independent, Central American state, a rump of the British Empire that is still guarded from neighbouring Guatemala's expansionist policies by Her Majesty's troops, is short of almost all life's pleasures except good off-shore island beaches which have no place in Theroux's swampy travels through a dangerous and uncharted land.

Ironically, Nicholson once took over a part that had been offered to Harrison Ford – and won an Oscar for Best Supporting Actor for it. The film was *Terms of Endearment* which waved the magic wand for almost everyone involved with it at the Academy Award ceremonies of 1984, but Ford felt he wasn't right for the astronaut and sexual athlete who lived next door to Shirley Maclaine. At least, that's what he said in public. More probably he could see the essential tawdriness in a screenplay that struggles to wring the viewer's emotions dry. Success could not have come to a nicer man than James Brooks, the writer–director of *Terms of Endearment*, but there are no prizes for recognising the briefness of its moments of glory or the transitory nature of the vogue that inspired them.

Typically, Harrison has no regrets. 'I don't choose parts for their award potential,' he says scornfully. 'Of course if I won one, I'd say thank you and feel flattered but when I choose a film, I choose it on its own merit.'

To date, Ford's leading men have been loners. Even John Book was unencumbered by anything so mundane as family ties. This omission will be amended in *Mosquito Coast* which calls for a *pater familias*, albeit one who puts his responsibilities to bizarre use. A loner bounding out of the wide blue yonder cracking a whip has a certain leeway when it comes to rounded emotions that is denied to a brilliant egomaniac endangering his nearest and dearest for purposes of self-aggrandisement, and it is fair to say that Ford will face a considerable day of judgement when *Mosquito Coast* comes out.

The level of his portrayal may well decide his artistic future. Will he follow in the footsteps of golden oldies like Cary Grant and Gary Cooper who were instantly recognisable in everything they did, their own good looks and personalities swamping the men they played? Will he attempt what many believe is the impossible for him by submerging himself into his characters, like Robert de Niro and his fellow 'method' men? Or will he be hailed as the next Nicholson, an unmistakable, mesmeric middle-aged oddball?

Steven Spielberg and Peter Weir are currently in the best

position to assess Ford's true potential, but their comments suggest that even they can't be sure just yet. 'What is so attractive about Harrison is that you wouldn't recognise him on the street,' said Spielberg. 'You wouldn't know him in a crowd, you might not even know him at a small cocktail party of a dozen people. He really is a chameleon. When he's acting, he becomes the character he's playing and afterwards he reverts to being Harrison Ford, wood-cutter and furniture-maker. His magic is that he's a very accessible, common guy.'

But surely a chameleon should be able to sink his personality into the characters he plays to create someone not in his own image, something Ford has consistently been accused of not being able to do. Weir, though he must believe that Ford will be an acceptable substitute for Nicholson in *Mosquito Coast*, likened him rather to Sean Connery.

'He has that brooding quality. He's someone who radiates strength without the need for dialogue and regardless of content. With the exception of Connery, perhaps, it is something which seems to be unique to the American experience, and to the movies. People talk about stage presence, the way some actors can walk onto and dominate the stage, holding your attention with the simplest gestures or actions. But his quality is something different, something which has a lot to do with the power of the close up.

'Harrison is enormously likeable,' he continued, 'and I was impressed with his lack of interest in show business and power and status. He is for me in the great tradition of Hollywood heroes – the strong silent type. I feel that we have yet to see his best work.'

It is a point of view that Ford himself certainly shares. The once indolent Chicagoan is now as dedicated a workaholic as any high-achieving Californian. When he's making a film, he finds it impossible to relax over a good book between takes. Instead he paces around 'bumping into my trailer' or sits and stares at the walls, ruminating over what his character would do, what he'd wear, how he'd live, what kind of music he'd like, what colour socks he'd buy, every tiny detail that goes to build a convincing portrait.

'I'm a technical actor,' he said, with a craftsman's pride. 'There is no magic involved, only work and circumstance. If you ask me what gives me most of a kick now, I'd have to say it's the work. I'd like to tell you it's family and friends and of course they're important to me. But if this doesn't sound silly, I honestly find myself dedicated to the work that I do and I want to do even better things in the future. I'm happiest when I'm in the thick of it. The running, jumping, and falling down – that's fun. So is the fantasy of being someone else, living out of a dream world. But the best thing about it all is that at the end of the day I can hang up my whip and my hat and become normal again. The day I can't do that is the day I quit.'

Ford will make one more Indiana Jones film under Spielberg's direction in 1987, but has said that he wouldn't do a fourth for 'all the tea in China'. For 'an ordinary creaky bag of bones' in his mid forties, with no liking for working out, less hyperactivity would be welcome in the not too distant future. On another level, there is the moral question which occupies him frequently as he looks at more serious options. 'I get a lot of scripts that I find morally reprehensible. So much of what entertains us is not good for us. Demonstrably bad for the organism, like driving a car down the street at 120 miles an hour. You're going to hurt someone. There's no reason to do it.'

Many an actor in his position has set up his own production company, a move which can maximise profits, as it has in Clint Eastwood's case. More usually it provides a commercial framework in which to develop projects along lines that are acceptable to the people who set the company up. Harrison Ford would have no trouble using his name to hone his moral and artistic integrity in this way, as *Mosquito Coast* bears witness, but he says he won't be tempted. It's too much like hard work. 'One of the things that attracted me to being an actor was that you work for two or three months, then you're off on something new.'

Another familiar movie industry device he's not too keen on is having films made in his own image – or the image the money men see him in. 'If something's developed for you, the temptation to play to supposed strengths can be a disadvantage. I like to see something have a life of its own, or have its own reason for being. Then I'll come along and try to add something to that.'

Nor does he plan to go into any kind of business partnership with Melissa. That is not what their marriage is about. She pursues her career on one level, Harrison on another. 'We have good communication about the things we're doing. We're helpful to one another, but we have no intention of working together.'

The projects on which Harrison is a self starter are still more of the wood-working kind, notably a house in the Santa Monica mountains to replace the Benedict Canyon home as the Fords' Los Angeles base. Now that he's down to one film a year, he divides the majority of his time between California and Wyoming, the hideaway he heads for immediately the cameras stop turning. He has set up a carpentry shop there too and has plans to build the ultimate symbol of American backwoodsmanship: his own log cabin.

Unfortunately he has now been integrated into the local tourist circuit, as he notes ruefully. 'One of the attractions of Wyoming is the possibility of running into me. People stop me and say, "We heard you were here. Would you just stand here for a minute while I get my camera?"'

As for the locals, they look on their new neighbours with the wide-eyed wonder their children reserve for *Star Wars*. Is he playing cowboy, this tall quiet man in a plaid shirt driving a red pick-up just like theirs, collecting wood from the hardware store and having a beer in the village bar? Often he thinks they'd prefer it if he did behave like a star, but he has no intention of obliging. They'll have to learn to accept him for what he is.

And what is that? A very rich man? 'Yes, I am very, very rich. That's what you want to hear, isn't it? Usually I demur when people ask me that. They also ask exactly how rich I am, but it's none of their goddam business.' He has acquired a reputation for being tight with his fortune, perhaps because he spends so modestly on himself and has so little liking for the glitterati and the satellites who circle them. Yet he unstintingly paid the exorbitant American hospital bills for a dying friend, then typically tried to prevent word of it leaking out.

If he has an obsession, it's guarding his privacy, and friends who want to remain friends with the once hesitant youth who has grown into a forceful middle-aged man know full well they must keep their mouths shut.

More peripherally, many actors will tell you how much

they've enjoyed talking to you, even if they sound slightly surprised by such an admission. Harrison never does. Indeed he often goes out of his way to tell interviewers how much he hates interviews. Yet when we met as strangers, then as acquaintances, I was first welcomed, then remembered, which suggests he can act pretty well after all. By my book, Peter Weir is right: we have yet to see the best of Harrison Ford.

Filmography

1966

Dead Heat on a Merry-go-round
Cast   Eli Kotch: James Coburn; Inger Knudson: Camilla Sparv; Eddie Hart: Aldo Ray; Frieda Schmid: Nina Wayne; Milo Stewart: Robert Webber; Margaret Kirby: Rose Marie; Alfred Morgan: Todd Armstrong; Dr Marion Hague: Marian Moses; Paul Feng: Michael Strong; Miles Fisher: Severn Darden; Jack Balter: James Westerfield; George Logan: Philip E. Pine; William Anderson: Simon Scott; General Mailenkoff: Ben Astar; Officer Howard: Lawrence Mann; Captain William Yates: Michael St Angel; Translator: Alex Rodine; Willie Manus: Albert Nalbandian; Lyman Mann: Tyler McVey; Sergeant Elmer K. Coxe: Roy Glenn; Bellboy: Harrison Ford.

A DeHaven–Girard production for Columbia Pictures. Producer: Carter DeHaven; Director and Writer: Bernard Girard; Cinematographer: Lionel Linden; Art Director: Walter M. Simonds; Music: Stu Phillips. Running time: 107 minutes.

1967

Luv
Cast   Harry Berlin: Jack Lemmon; Milt Manville: Peter Falk; Ellen: Elaine May; Linda: Nina Wayne; Attorney Goodhart: Eddie Mayehoff; Doyle: Paul Martman; Vandergrist: Severn Darden; with Harrison Ford.

A Jalem production. Producer: Martin Manulis; Director: Clive Donner; Screenplay: Elliott Baker, based on a play by Murray Shisgal; Cinematographer: Ernest Laszlo. Running time: 96 minutes.

The Long Ride Home (British title: *A Time For Killing*)
Cast   Major Walcott: Glenn Ford; Captain Bentley: George Hamilton;

Emily Biddle: Inger Stevens; Blue Lake: Paul Petersen; Sergeant Luther Liskell: Max Baer; Lt. Prudessing: Todd Armstrong; Billy Cat: Timothy Carey; Sergeant Cleehan: Kenneth Toby; Corporal Paddy Darling: Richard X. Slattery; Lt. Frist: Duke Hobbie; Sergeant Dan Way: Dean Stanton; Little Mo: James Davidson; Lt. Shaffer: Harrison J. Ford; Sergeant Kettlinger: Charlie Briggs; Owelson: Kay E. Kuter; Zollic Officer: Dick Miller; Bagnef: Craig Curtis; Colonel Harries: Emile Miller; Stedner: Marshall Reed; Lovingwood: Jay Ripley; Bruce: Dean Goodhill.

A Columbia/Sage Western Pictures Production. Producer: Harry Joe Brown; Director: Phil Carlson; Screenplay: Halsted Welles, based on *Southern Blade*, a novel by Nelson and Shirley Wolford; Cinematographer: Kenneth Peach; Editor: Roy Livingston; Music: Mundell Lowe. Running time: 83 minutes.

Journey to Shiloh
Cast Buck Burnett: James Caan; Miller Nalls: Michael Sarrazin; Gabrielle Du Prey: Brenda Scott; Todo McLean: Don Stroud; J. C. Sutton: Paul Petersen; Eubie Bell: Michael Burns; Little Bit Buck: Michael Vincent; Willie Bill Beardon: Harrison Ford; General Braxton Bragg: John Doucette.

A Universal Pictures production. Producer: Howard Christie; Director: William Hale; Screenplay: Gene Coon, based on *Fields of Honour*, a novel by Will Henry; Cinematographer: Enzo A. Martinelli. Running time: 81 minutes.

1970

Getting Straight
Cast Harry Bailey: Elliott Gould; Jan: Candice Bergen; Nick: Robert F. Lyons; Dr Wilhunt: Jeff Corey; Ellis: Max Julien; Dr Kaspar: Cecil Kellaway; Vandenburg: John Lormer; Lysander: Leonard Stone; Wade Linden: William Bramley; Judy Kramer: Jeannie Berlin; Herbert: John Rubenstein; Dr Greengrass: Richard Anders; Luan: Brenda Sykes; Sheila: Jenny Sullivan; Garcia: Gregory Sierra; Landlady: Billie Bird; Jake: Harrison Ford; Alice Linden: Elizabeth Lane; Cynthia: Hilarie Thompson; Mrs Stebbins: Irene Tedrow; Room-mate: Joanna Serpe; Airline Representative: Scott Perry.

An Organisation production. Producer and Director: Richard Rush; Screenplay: Robert Kaufman, based on a novel by Ken Kolb; Cinematographer: Laszlo Kovacs; Editor: Maury Winetrobe. Running time: 125 minutes.

1973

American Graffiti

Cast Curt: Richard Dreyfuss; Steve: Ron Howard; John Milner: Paul Le Mat; Terry the Toad: Charles Martin Smith; Laurie: Cindy Williams; Debbie: Candy Clark; Carol: Mackenzie Phillips; Disc Jockey: Wolfman Jack; Bob Falfa: Harrison Ford; Joe: Bo Hopkins; Carlos: Manuel Padilla; Ants: Beau Gentry; Peg: Kathleen Quinlan; Blonde in Thunderbird: Suzanne Somers; Falfa's Girl: Debralee Scott; Budda: Jana Bellan; Mr Wolfe: Terry McGovern.

A Lucasfilm/Coppola Company production for Universal Pictures. Producer: Francis Coppola; Co-producer: Gary Kurtz; Director: George Lucas; Screenplay: George Lucas, Willard Huyck and Gloria Katz; Cinematography: Haskell Wexler, Ron Eveslage and Jan D'Alquen; Editors: Verna Fields and Marcia Lucas; Sound and Recording: Walter Murch; Casting: Fred Roos and Mike Fenton. Running time: 110 minutes (original release); 112 minutes (re-release).

1974

The Conversation

Cast Harry Caul: Gene Hackman; Stan: John Cazale; Bernie Moran: Allen Garfield; Mark: Frederic Forrest; Ann: Cindy Williams; Paul: Michael Higgins; Meredith: Elizabeth MacRae; Amy: Terri Garr; Martin Stett: Harrison Ford; Receptionist: Mark Wheeler; Mime: Robert Shields; Lurleen: Phoebe Alexander; The Director: Robert Duvall.

A Coppola Company production for Paramount Pictures. Producers: Francis Coppola and Fred Roos; Director and Screenplay: Francis Coppola; Cinematographer: Bill Butler; Editors: Walter Murch and Richard Chew; Music: David Shire. Running time: 113 minutes.

1976

Dynasty (TV Movie)

Cast Jennifer Blackwood: Sarah Miles; Matt Blackwood: Stacey Keach; John Blackwood: Harris Yulin; Mark Blackwood: Harrison Ford; Harry Blackwood: Tony Schwartz; Amanda Blackwood: Amy Irving; Sam Adams: Charles Weldon; Lucinda: Stephanie Faulkner; Elvira: Karmin Murcello; Benjamin McCullum: John Carter; Margaret McCullum: Sari Price; Carver Blackwood: Gerrit Graham; Mark (aged 12): Dennis Larson; Mark (aged 6): Gary Lee Cooper.

A David Paradine TV productions/Marjay production for NBC's

Saturday Night At The Movies. Producer: Buck Houghton; Director: Lee Philips; Teleplay: Sydney Carroll, based on the novel by James Michener. Running time: 99 minutes.

1977

Star Wars
Cast Luke Skywalker: Mark Hamill; Han Solo: Harrison Ford; Princess Leia Organa: Carrie Fisher; Grand Moff Tarkin: Peter Cushing; Ben 'Obi-Wan' Kenobi: Sir Alec Guinness; C-3PO: Anthony Daniels; R2-D2: Kenny Baker; Chewbacca: Peter Mayhew; Lord Darth Vader: David Prowse; Uncle Owen Lars: Phil Brown; Aunt Beru Lars: Shelagh Fraser; Chief Jawa: Jack Purvis; General Dodonna: Alex McCrindle; General Willard: Eddie Byrne; Red Leader: Drewe Henley; Red Two (Wedge): Dennis Lawson; Red Three (Biggs): Garrick Hagon; Red Four (John D.): Jack Klaff; Red Six (Porkins): William Hootkins; Gold Leader: Angus McInnis; Gold Two: Jeremy Sinden; Gold Five: Graham Ashley; General Taggi: Don Henderson; General Motti: Richard Le Parmentier; Commander 1: Leslie Schofield.

A Lucasfilm production for Twentieth-Century Fox. Producer: Gary Kurtz; Director and Screenplay: George Lucas; Cinematographer: Gilbert Taylor; Editors: Paul Hirsch, Richard Chew and Marcia Lucas; Production Designer: John Barry; Music: John Williams; Special Photographic Effects Supervisor: John Dykstra; Production Supervisor: Robert Watts; Production Illustration: Ralph McQuarrie; Costume Designer: John Mollo; Casting: Irene Lamb, Diane Crittenden and Vic Ramos. Running time: 121 minutes.

Heroes
Cast Jack Dunne: Henry Winkler; Carol: Sally Field; Kenny Boyd: Harrison Ford; Bus Driver: Val Avery; Jan Adcox: Olivia Cole; Dr Elias: Hector Elias; Gus: Dennis Burkley; Chef: Tony Burton; Peanuts: Michael Cavanaugh; Bus Depot Manager: Helen Craig; Mr Munro: John P. Finnegan; Mrs Munro: Betty McGuire; Ticket Clerk: John O'Leary; Second Patrolman: Tom Rosqui; Nathan: Fred Struthman; Frank: Caskey Swain; Leo Sturges: Earle Towne; Waitress: Verna Bloom; Charles: Kenneth Augustine; Andy: Rick Blanchard; Stokes: Louis Carillo; Robert: Robert Kretschman; Patient: Lee Cohn; Artie: Dick Ziker.

A Turman-Foster Company production for Universal Pictures. Producers: David Foster and Lawrence Turman; Director: Jeremy Paul Kagan; Screenplay: James Carabatsos; Cinematographer: Frank

Stanley; Editor: Patrick Kennedy; Music: Jack Nitzsche. Running time: 107 minutes.

1978

Force 10 From Navarone
Cast Mallory: Robert Shaw; Miller: Edward Fox; Colonel Barnsby: Harrison Ford; American Sergeant: Carl Weathers; Traitor: Franco Nero; Yugoslavian Partisan: Barbara Bach.

A Navarone production for Columbia Pictures. Executive Producer: Carl Foreman; Producer: Oliver Unger; Director: Guy Hamilton; Screenplay: Carl Foreman and Robin Chapman, from a novel by Alistair Maclean. Running time: 118 minutes.

1979

Apocalypse Now
Cast Colonel Kurtz: Marlon Brando; Lt. Colonel Kilgore: Robert Duvall; Captain Willard: Martin Sheen; Chef: Frederic Forrest; Chief: Albert Hall; Lance: Sam Bottoms; Clean: Larry Fishburne; Photo Journalist: Dennis Hopper; General: G. D. Spradin; Col. G. Lucas: Harrison Ford; Civilian: Jerry Zesmer; Coby: Scott Glen.

An Omni Zoetrope Ltd. production. Producer/Director: Francis Coppola; Co-producers: Fred Roos, Gray Frederickson, Tom Sternberg; Associate Producer: Mona Skager; Screenplay: John Milius, Francis Coppola; Narration written by Michael Herr; Cinematographer: Vittorio Storaro; Supervising Editor: Richard Marks; Editors: Walter Murch, Gerald B. Greenberg and Lisa Fruchtman; Music: Carmine Coppola, Francis Coppola; Production Designer: Dean Tavoularis; Sound Montage and Design: Walter Murch; Executive Assistants: Melissa Mathison and Jack Fritz. Running time: 148 minutes.

Hanover Street
Cast David Halloran: Harrison Ford; Margaret Sellinger: Lesley-Anne Down; Paul Sellinger: Christopher Plummer; Major Trumbo: Alec McGowen; 2nd Lt. Jerry Cimino: Richard Maur; 2nd Lt. Martin Hyer: Michael Sacks; Sarah Sellinger: Patsy Kensit; Harry Pike: Max Wall; Colonel Ronald Bart: Shane Rimmer; Lt. Wells: Keith Buckley; Phyllis: Sherrie Hewson; Paula: Cindy O'Callaghan; Elizabeth: Di Trevis; French Girl: Suzanne Bertish; Soldier in Barn: Keith Alexander; Corporal Daniel Giler: Jay Benedict; Sergeant John Lucas: John Ratzenberger; Farrell: Eric Stine; Captain Harold Lester: Hugh Frazer; Beef: William Hootkins.

A Hanover Street production. Producer: Paul N. Lazarus III; Executive Producer: Gordon G. T. Scott; Director and Screenplay: Peter Hyams; Cinematographer: David Watkin; Editor: James Mitchell; Music: John Barry; Associate Producers: Michael Rachmil and Harry Benn. Running time: 108 minutes.

The Frisco Kid
Cast Avram Belinski: Gene Wilder; Tommy Lillard: Harrison Ford; Mr Jones: Rammon Bieri; Chief Gray Cloud: Val Bisloglio; Darryl Riggs: George Ralph DiCenzo; Chief Rabbi: Leo Fuchs; Rosalie: Penny Peyser; Matt Diggs: William Smith; Samuel Bender: Jack Somack; Sarah Mindl: Beege Barkett; O'Leary: Shay Duffin; Old Amish Man: Walter Janowitz; Monterano: Joe Kapp; Mr Ping: Clyde Kusatsu; Mr Daniels: Cliff Pellow; Mr Bialik: Allan Rich; First Farmer (Amish Man): Henry Rowland; Brother Bruno: Vincent Schiavelli; Booking Agent: John Steadman; Father Joseph: Ian Wolfe; Herschell Rosensheine: Steffen Zacharias: Mrs Bender: Eda Reiss Merin; Julius Rosensheine: David Bradley; Second Farmer (Amish Man): Richard Dunham.

A Mace Neufeld production for Warner Bros. Executive Producer: Howard W. Koch Jr; Producer: Mace Neufeld; Director: Robert Aldrich; Screenplay: Michael Elias, Frank Shaw; Cinematographer: Robert B. Hauser; Editors: Maury Winetrobe, Irving Rosenblum, Jack Horger; Music: Frank DeVol; Associate Producer: Melvin Dellar. Running time: 119 minutes.

1980

The Empire Strikes Back
Cast Luke Skywalker: Mark Hamill; Han Solo: Harrison Ford; Princess Leia Organa: Carrie Fisher; Lando Calrissian: Billy Dee Williams; C-3PO: Anthony Daniels; R2-D2: Kenny Baker; Chewbacca: Peter Mayhew; Lord Darth Vader: David Prowse; Yoda: Frank Oz; Ben 'Obi-Wan' Kenobi: Sir Alec Guinness; Boba Fett: Jeremy Bulloch; Lando's Aide: John Hollis; Chief Ugnaught: Jack Purvis; Snow creature: Des Webb; Performing Assistant for Yoda: Kathryn Mullen; Voice of Emperor: Clive Revill; Admiral Piett: Kenneth Colley; General Veers: Julian Glover; Admiral Ozzel: Michael Sheard; Captain Needa: Michael Culver; General Rieekan: Bruce Boa; Zev (Rogue 2): Christopher Malcom; Wedge (Rogue 3): Dennis Lawson; Hobbie (Rogue 4): Richard Oldfield; Dak (Luke's Gunner): John Morton; Janson (Wedge's Gunner): Ian Liston; Major Derlin: John Ratzenberger.

A Lucasfilm production for Twentieth-Century Fox. Executive Producer: George Lucas; Producer: Gary Kurtz; Director: Irwin Kershner; Screenplay: Leigh Brackett and Lawrence Kasdan, from a story by George Lucas; Cinematography: Peter Suschitsky; Production Designer: Norman Reynolds; Music: John Williams; Editor: Paul Hirsch; Special Visual Effects: Brian Johnson and Richard Edlund; Design Consultant and Conceptual Artist: Ralph McQuarrie; Associate Producers: Robert Watts and James Bloom. Running time: 124 minutes.

1981

Raiders of the Lost Ark
Cast   Dr Indiana Jones: Harrison Ford; Marion Ravenwood: Karen Allen; Belloq: Paul Freeman; Toht: Ronald Lacey; Sallah: John Rhys-Davies; Brody: Denholm Elliot; Dietrich: Wolf Kahler; Gobler: Anthony Higgins; Satipo: Alfred Molina; Barranca: Vic Tablian; Colonel Musgrove: Don Fellows; Major Eaton: William Hootkins.

A Lucasfilm production for Paramount Pictures. Executive Producers: George Lucas and Howard Kazanjian; Producer: Frank Marshall; Director: Steven Spielberg; Screenplay: Lawrence Kasdan, from a story by George Lucas and Philip Kaufman; Cinematographer: Douglas Slocombe; Production Designer: Norman Reynolds; Music: John Williams; Editor: Michael Kahn; Visual Effects Supervisor: Richard Edlund; Mechanical Effects Supervisor: Kit West; Casting: Jane Feinberg, Mike Fenton and Mary Selway; Associate Producer: Robert Watts; Second Unit Director: Michael Moore; Stunt Co-ordinator: Glenn Randall; Costume Design: Deborah Nadoolman. Running time: 115 minutes.

1982

Blade Runner
Cast   Rick Deckard: Harrison Ford; Roy Batty: Rutger Hauer; Rachel: Sean Young; Gaff: Edward James Olmos; Bryant: M. Emmet Walsh; Pris: Daryl Hannah; Sebastian: William Sanderson; Leon: Brion James; Tyrell: Joe Turkel; Zhora: Joanna Cassidy; Chew: James Hong; Holden: Morgan Paull; Cambodian Lady: Kimiro Hiroshige; Sales lady: Carolyn DeMirjian; Sushi Master: Robert Ozkazaki; Taffy Lewis: Hy Pyke; Bear: Kevin Thompson; Kaiser: John Edward Allen.

A Blade Runner partnership production. Executive Producers: Brian Kelly and Hampton Fancher; Producer: Michael Deeley; Director:

Ridley Scott; Screenplay: Hampton Fancher and David Peoples, based on *Do Androids Dream of Electric Sheep?*, a novel by Philip K. Dick; Cinematographer: Jordan Cronenweth; Production Designer: Lawrence G. Paul; Music: Vangelis; Supervising Editor: Terry Rawlings; Special Effects Supervisors: Douglas Trumbull, Richard Yuricich and David Dryer; Visual Futurist: Syd Mead; Associate Producer: Ivor Powell. Running time: 114 minutes.

1983

The Return of the Jedi
Cast Luke Skywalker: Mark Hamill; Han Solo: Harrison Ford; Princess Leia Organa: Carrie Fisher; Lando Calrissian: Billy Dee Williams; C-3PO: Anthony Daniels; R2-D2: Kenny Baker; Lord Darth Vader: David Prowse; Chewbacca: Peter Mayhew; Ben 'Obi-Wan' Kenobi: Sir Alec Guinness; Anakin Skywalker: Sebastian Shaw; The Emperor: Ian McDiarmid; Yoda: Frank Oz; Voice of Darth Vader: James Earl Jones; Boba Fett: Jeremy Bulloch.

A Lucasfilm production for Twentieth-Century Fox. Executive Producer: George Lucas; Producer: Howard Kazanjian; Director: Richard Marquand; Screenplay: Lawrence Kasdan, from a story by George Lucas; Cinematographer: Alan Hume; Production Designer: Norman Reynolds; Music: John Williams; Editors: Sean Barton, Marcia Lucas and Duwayne Dunham; Special Visual Effects: Dennis Muren, Ken Ralston and Richard Edlund; Mechanical Effects: Kit West; Costume Designers: Aggie Guerard Rodgers and Nilo Rodis-Jamero; Make-up and Creature Designers: Phil Tippett and Stuart Freeborn; Co-Producers: Robert Watts and Jim Bloom. Running time: 123 minutes.

1984

Indiana Jones and the Temple of Doom
Cast Dr Indiana Jones: Harrison Ford; Willie Scott: Kate Capshaw; Short Round: Ke Huy Quan; Mola Ram: Amish Puri; Chattar Lal: Roshan Seth; Captain Blumburtt: Philip Stone; Lao Che: Roy Chiao; Wu Han: David Yip; Kao Kan: Ric Young; Little Maharajah: Raj Singh; Shaman: D. R. Nanayakkarah; Chieftain: Dharmadasa Kuruppu; Sajnu: Stany de Silva; Chief Guard: Pat Roach.

A Lucasfilm production for Paramount Pictures. Executive Producers: George Lucas and Frank Marshall; Producer: Robert Watts; Director: Steven Spielberg; Screenplay: Willard Huyck and Gloria Katz, from a story by George Lucas; Cinematographer: Douglas Slocombe; Supervising Editor: Michael Kahn; Production Designer:

Elliott Scott; Special Effects Supervisor: Denis Muren: Mechanical Effects Supervisor: Donald Gibbs; Stunt Arrangers: Glenn Randall and Vic Armstrong; Music: John Williams; Associate Producer: Kathleen Kennedy. Running time: 117 minutes.

1985

Witness

Cast   John Book: Harrison Ford; Rachel: Kelly McGillis; Schaeffer: Josef Sommer; Samuel: Lukas Haas; Eli Lapp: Jan Rubes; Daniel Hochleitner: Alexander Godunov; McFee: Danny Glover; Carter: Brent Jennings; Elaine: Patti LuPone; Fergie: Angus MacInnes; Stoltzfus: Frederick Rolf; Moses Hochleitner: Viggo Mortensen; Bishop Tchantz: John Garson; Mrs Yoder: Beverly May; Sheriff: Ed Crowley; Zenovich: Timothy Carhart; Tourist Lady: Sylvia Kranders; Mrs Schaeffer: Marian Swan; Schaeffer's Daughter: Maria Bradley; Angel Food: Rozwill Young.

An Edward S. Feldman production for Paramount Pictures. Producer: Edward S. Feldman; Director: Peter Weir; Screenplay: Earl W. Wallace and William Kelley, from a story by William Kelley, Pamela and Earl W. Wallace; Director of Photography: John Seale; Production Designer: Stan Jolley; Editor: Thom Noble; Casting: Diane Crittenden; Music: Maurice Jarre; Co-producer: David Bombyk. Running time: 112 minutes.

Bibliography

Amis, Martin. Interview with Steven Spielberg, *Observer*, 21 November 1982

Arnold, Alan. *Once Upon a Galaxy: A Journal of the Making of The Empire Strikes Back*. Sphere, London, 1980

Bachman, Gideon. Location Report on *Star Wars*. *Guardian*, 1 March 1977

Bilbow, Marjorie. Interview with Peter Weir, *Screen International*, 22 June 1985

Bock, Audie. 'Secrecy Shrouds a *Star Wars* Sequel', *New York Times*, 11 July 1982

Bonner, Hilary. 'Superstar Who Shuns the Limelight', *Sun*, 28 July 1981

Borie, Bertrand and Delcourt, Guy and Valerie. 'Entretien', *L'Ecran Fantastique*, No 22, 1982

Brodie, Ian. Interview with Harrison Ford, *Sunday Telegraph Magazine*, 20 May 1984

Broeske, Pat H. 'With the Indiana Joneses', *Cinema Papers*, May 1985

Bygrave, Mike. 'A Ford With Unlimited Mileage', *You Magazine*, 14 November 1982

'Sydney Goes to Hollywood', *Guardian*, 14 March 1985

'Down Under in L.A.', Interview with Peter Weir, *Stills Magazine*, May 1985

Clarke, Gerald. Interview with George Lucas, *Time*, 23 May 1983

'Stardom Time for a Bag of Bones', *Time*, 25 February 1985

Corliss, Richard. 'I Dream for a Living', Profile of Steven Spielberg, *Time*, 15 July 1985

Cotton, J. V. Interview with Harrison Ford, *Ciné-Revue*, 3 December 1981

Crawley, Tony. *The Steven Spielberg Story*, Zomba Books, London, 1983

'Harrison Ford', Interview in *Starburst*, No 43, 1981

'Harrison Ford: A Superstar for the Eighties', *Cinema UK*, 1981

Interview with Harrison Ford, *Cinema UK*, 1982

Davis, Ivor. Location report on *Blade Runner*, *Daily Express*, 4 August 1982

'Sensational Sight', *The Times*, 23 August 1982

Davis, Victor. 'Ford's Ace role Is Being Nobody', *Daily Express*, 24 December 1984

Duncan, Andrew. 'In and Out Of Oz', Interview with Peter Weir, *Observer*, 19 May 1985

Fay, Stephen. 'Harrison Ford Delivers The Groceries', *Sunday Times Magazine*, 26 May 1985

Floyd, Nigel. 'Culture Shocker', Interview with Peter Weir, *New Musical Express*, 8 June 1985

Goodman, Joan, 'Back to the Old School of Hollywood Heroes', *The Times*, 15 July 1981

Interview with Harrison Ford, *The Times* 18 May 1985

Goodman, Joan and Bygrave, Mike. 'Portrait of a Crazy War', *Observer Magazine*, 2 December 1979

Hall, William. Interview with Harrison Ford, *Sunday Magazine*, 3 June 1984

Harvey, Alex. Interview with Harrison Ford, *Sunday Magazine*, 29 November 1981

Hirschorn, Clive. 'Harrison Ford's Life', *Sunday Express*, 26 September 1981

Hodenfield, Chris. 'The Sky Is Full of Questions', Interview with Steven Spielberg, *Rolling Stone*, 26 January 1978

Holden, Anthony. 'The Childhood Dream Machine', Interview with Stephen Spielberg, *Sunday Express Magazine*, 27 May 1984

Lewin, David. Interview with Francis Coppola, *Daily Mail*, 28 December 1974

'It's Sky-high Success for the Princess and the Robots', *Daily Mail*, 1 August 1977

Interview with Harrison Ford, *Daily Mail*, 29 July 1981

McKenzie, Alan. *The Harrison Ford Story*, Zomba Books, London, 1984

McTrevor, Joan. Interview with Harrison Ford. *Ciné-Revue*, 27 October 1983

'Harrison Ford; Je Déteste Faire Parler De Moi', Interview with Harrison Ford, *Ciné-Revue*, 2 May 1985

Mills, Bart. 'Marlowe Meets Alien', *Guardian*, 5 May 1981

Noble, Peter. 'Harrison Ford Climbs The Ladder To Success', *Screen International*, 18 September 1982

Pollock, Dale. *Skywalking: The Life and Films of George Lucas*, Elm Tree Books, London, 1983

Pratt, Tony. 'The All-action Raider who Just Wants to get Lost', *Daily Mirror*, 31 July 1981

Pye, Michael and Myles, Linda. *The Movie Brats*, Holt, Rinehart and Winston, New York, 1979

Radin, Victoria. Report on *Force 10 From Navarone*. *Observer*, 29 January 1978

Bibliography

Rees, Jenny. 'The Galactic Cowboy Comes Down To Earth', *Daily Mail*, 13 December 1977

Russell, Sue. 'The Indiana Man', *Sunday Magazine*, 12 May 1985

Scobie, William. 'Spielberg, Lucas and "Escapism"', *Observer*, 10 June 1984

Spielberg, Steven. Talking about *Indiana Jones and the Temple of Doom*, *American Cinematographer*, July 1984

Sragow, Michael. Interview with Harrison Ford, *Rolling Stone*, 25 June 1981

Interview with Steven Spielberg, *Rolling Stone*, 22 July 1982

Taylor, Derek. *The Making of Raiders Of The Lost Ark*, Ballantine, New York, 1981

Thompson, Douglas. 'The Unknown Face of Harrison Ford', *Daily Mail*, 24 December 1984

Vallely, Jean. Interview with George Lucas, *Rolling Stone*, 12 June 1980

Walker, Alexander. 'Steven Spielberg: A Million A Day', *Sunday Express Magazine*, 3 October 1982

Wells, Colin. Article on the making of *Raiders of the Lost Ark*, *Sunday Mirror*, 26 July 1981

White, Timothy. 'The *Star Wars* Kids Talk Back', *Rolling Stone*, 24 July 1980

Index

The abbreviation 'HF' is used for
Harrison Ford in all sub-headings in
this index.